PENGUIN BOOKS

Mediterranean Seafood

Alan Davidson, who counts himself a
Scotsman, was born in 1924. He won a
scholarship from Leeds Grammar School to
The Queen's College, Oxford, and took a
double first there in Classical Greats. His
studies sandwiched several years' wartime
service in the RNVR, including a spell in the
Mediterranean.

He joined the Diplomatic Service in 1948,
and has served in Washington, The Hague,
Cairo, Tunis and Brussels as well as in the
Foreign Office.

From 1971–2 he enjoyed a sabbatical year
at Sussex University, writing on East/West
relations. In 1973 he was appointed British
Ambassador in Vientiane, Laos.

His other publications include a study of
snakes and scorpions in Tunisia, and on fish
and fish dishes of Laos. Apart from writing, he
finds recreation in doing paintings of little-
known saints, drawing his inspiration from
the Sienese masters. He is married and has
three daughters.

A tunny-merchant of the fourth century B.C.,
from a vase in the Museum at Cefalù in
Sicily.

ALAN DAVIDSON

Mediterranean Seafood

A handbook giving
the names in seven
languages of 150 species
of fish, with 50
crustaceans, molluscs
and other marine
creatures, and an essay
on fish cookery followed
by 200 Mediterranean
recipes

PENGUIN BOOKS

Penguin Books Ltd, Harmondsworth,
Middlesex, England
Penguin Books Inc., 7110 Ambassador Road,
Baltimore, Maryland 21207, U.S.A.
Penguin Books Australia Ltd, Ringwood,
Victoria, Australia
Penguin Books Canada Ltd, 41 Steelcase Road West,
Markham, Ontario, Canada
Penguin Books (N.Z.) Ltd, 182–190 Wairau Road,
Auckland 10, New Zealand

First published 1972
Reprinted 1976

Copyright © Alan Davidson, 1972

Made and printed in Great Britain by
Richard Clay (The Chaucer Press) Ltd
Bungay, Suffolk
Set in Monotype Times

I dedicate this book to my wife Jane, whose casual request on a spring day in Carthage for a list of Tunisian fish and their English names was the seed from which the book grew, and who has tolerated and even encouraged the consequent invasion of her household by fish experts, fish documents and fish cookery experiments.

Mindful of other ladies in my life to whom I should like to make a tribute both literary and culinary, I adorn this dedication with honorific mention of my mother Constance; my sister Rosemary; and my daughters Caroline, Pamela and Jennifer, whose readiness to reflect and thereby intensify my own enthusiasms has been a great help.

Contents

The drawing by Peter Stebbing is of the rascasse rouge, archetype of Mediterranean fish (see catalogue entry on page 160)

Acknowledgements

In the first place I must thank the General Fisheries Council for the Mediterranean (of the Food and Agriculture Organization of the United Nations) for allowing me to make full use of the written material and drawings in their comprehensive *Catalogue of the Names of Mediterranean Fish, Molluscs and Crustaceans*, published by them jointly with Vito Bianco Editore of Milan. In particular I thank the editor of their Catalogue, Professor Giorgio Bini, who has given me without stint the benefit of his profound knowledge of the subjects with which this book deals.

My own national authorities have been equally generous. Mr Alwyne Wheeler at the Natural History Section of the British Museum has combined patience in helping me to correct mistakes with enthusiasm in supplying additional information. To him and to his colleagues, and to Mr Arthur Lee and Dr Richard Shelton of the fishery laboratories at Lowestoft and Burnham-on-Crouch, I owe a great deal.

For advice about the chapter on the Mediterranean Sea I thank Professor J.-M. Perès, Director of the Station Marine d'Endoume, and Professor François Varlet of the Musée Océanographique at Monaco; and for advice on Mediterranean fish in classical times, Dr John Richmond of University College, Dublin.

In Tunisia I had much willing help from M. Mahmoud El Ghoul, Président de l'Office National des Pêches, and from his staff at Tabarka, Bizerte, La Goulette, Kelibia, Mahdia, Sfax and Houmt Souk as well as in the Central Fish Market of Tunis and at sea. I thank too my friends in the Institut Océanographique de Salammbô; M. Othman Kark and his staff at the Bibliothèque Nationale in the Medina of Tunis; M. Zakaria Ben Mostafa of the University of Tunis; and M. and Mme M'hamed Essaafi.

Mr Hugh Whittall of Istanbul distilled his great knowledge of Turkish fish into a monograph written to meet my needs. Signor Vito Fodera, resident expert of the FAO in Cyprus, presented to me the results of his researches there. Dr Radosna Mužinić, of the Oceanographic Institute at Split, advised me about fish in Yugoslav waters.

Mr Anthony Bonner carried out for me a special study of Catalan fish names.

On the cookery side an acknowledgement *hors catégorie*, both for inspiration and for help, is due to Elizabeth David. And I place blue sashes on the shoulders of Pamela Coate, for research on the Spanish Mediterranean coast; Dr Alfred Kühn and again Mr Anthony Bonner for inquiries in Mallorca; Mme Jean Ricard and Mme Totte Feissel for practical help in Provence; Signora Jeanne Caròla for advice on Neapolitan and other Italian recipes; Signor Mario Forcellini of Venice; Mrs Delia Lennie of Bari; Mrs Ilse Maijcen and Mrs Marjanović-Radica of Split; Mrs Dimítri Gófas of Athens; Mrs Selma Göksel in Turkey; Mrs Helen Essely in Beirut; and my editor, Jillian Norman, for helpful culinary research in Menorca and in her own kitchen.

Many of my colleagues, in posts around the Mediterranean, and their wives, have put me in touch with local experts or obtained information for me. I am particularly grateful to Alan Banks, Paco Dalby, Timothy Daunt, Julie Dodson, John and Armine Edmonds, George Evans, Romildo Farrugia, Giles FitzHerbert, Esa Hazou, Mary Henderson, Robin and Diana Jasper, Ronald Juchau, John and Christine Little, Bill Lyall, Yvonne Newman, Laurence O'Keeffe, Sir Hugh Parry, Desmond and Miranda Pemberton-Pigott, Bruce Scott, Thomas Tuite, Edgar Vedova, Brigadier Paul Ward and Michael Warr.

I likewise thank my colleagues in NATO. The southern flank of the North Atlantic alliance includes four important Mediterranean countries, important not only to military strategists, but also to students of fish cookery. Such a student, installed as I have recently been in the headquarters of the alliance, will find that many of his colleagues take pleasure in gastronomic discussions. I thank especially Alexander and Maria Coundouriotis, Franco and Graziella Ferretti, Luigi Grasso, and Şermin and Haluk Ozgul.

Preparing the typescript of a book like this demands not only typing skill but also organizing ability and an interest in fish and cookery. Beryl Richards, who has all these characteristics, kindly volunteered to do the job and gave me much useful advice during its execution.

I am indebted to Sally Bicknell for her meticulous compilation of the index.

To all those named above, to all the contributors identified in the recipes and for all the help implied in the bibliography, I express my sincere gratitude.

Introduction

The main purpose of this book is to help readers who visit or live in the Mediterranean region to enjoy fully the seafood there available. Two things are needed for this: the ability to identify the various sea creatures, and the knowledge how best to prepare each for eating. So half the book consists of catalogues for identification, and the rest is largely taken up by Mediterranean recipes. The catalogues are intended to be useful also to underwater fishermen; and the cookery part has been designed to interest cooks in Britain and North America as well as in the Mediterranean.

Mediterranean fish names are very confusing. I would never have tried to map the labyrinth if I had not lived in Tunisia, where every circumstance encouraged me. From our house on a cliff near Carthage we daily viewed the blue, green or wine-dark waters of the Mediterranean, and saw the fishing boats sailing homewards with their catch; and down the road, by a dark inlet which was once the port from which Hannibal sailed to conquer Rome, stood the great Oceanographic Institute of Salammbô. Above all we were encouraged by the friendly interest of Tunisians. Since then I have extended my studies considerably. But the forerunner of this book, published in Tunis with a Mediterranean-blue cover and a picture of a rascasse upon it, remains the kernel of the present work.

Although I have had much expert help this book is, evidently, the compilation of an amateur. I disavow any but a superficial knowledge of natural history, linguistics and cuisine. Claiming only a proper degree of enthusiasm for my subject, I wish my readers as much pleasure in using the book as I have had in writing it; and I invite them all to send me whatever suggestions they may have for correcting or improving the contents.

ALAN DAVIDSON

Amilcar by Carthage
The World's End
Ukkel/Uccle
1962–70

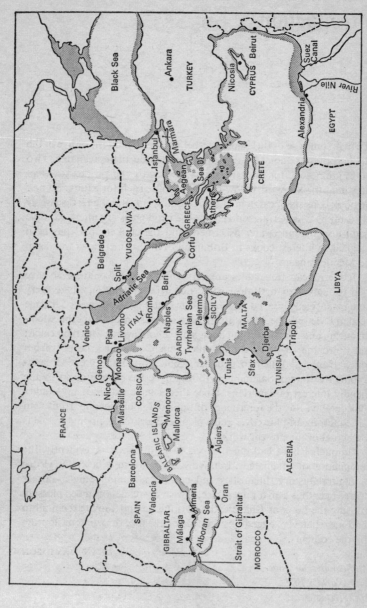

The shaded areas represent the 'Continental shelf', where the depth of water is less than 100 fathoms/200 metres/600 feet.

The Mediterranean Sea

Our study of the edible creatures living in the Mediterranean Sea will be more interesting and comprehensible if we take a look first at the characteristics of that sea itself.

In oceanic terms the Mediterranean as it exists today is quite small and not particularly deep. By area it accounts for roughly 1/140th of the sea water on our globe, by volume only 1/355th. Its mean depth is just about 1500 metres, compared with figures close to 4000 metres for the Atlantic, Pacific and Indian Oceans. But it would be wrong to describe the Mediterranean as shallow; it is still of a respectable depth and has a comparatively small area of continental shelf (i.e. the shallow areas adjacent to the land, which provide good fishing grounds). The map shows this, and that the Adriatic is a fortunate exception. I should explain here that the general narrowness of the continental shelf in the Mediterranean is a highly unfavourable factor for the fish population. The shelf is in effect the nursery on which the baby fish must settle in order to grow up. But when the shelf is narrow and there are currents flowing away from the coast this system does not work properly. What happens in many parts of the Mediterranean is that vast numbers of tiny fish find themselves when the time comes poised over deep water instead of over the shelf, and perish accordingly.

As a result of the warm climate, the Mediterranean loses a lot of its water by evaporation. And it is not fed generously by rivers, of which there are hardly any of importance along most of the North African coast, for example. Indeed the loss by evaporation is greater than the gain from rainfall and the influx of rivers. Yet the level of the Mediterranean remains constant, and so does its salinity level, although the latter varies from one part of the sea to another.

What keeps the Mediterranean going is the Atlantic. About one million cubic metres of Atlantic water flow into the Mediterranean past Gibraltar every second. At the same time Mediterranean water flows out into the Atlantic, in slightly less volume. These two flows take place at different levels. The inflow of Atlantic water, which has a low density, takes place at surface level. The outflow of the saltier

Mediterranean water, which is denser, takes place along the seabed. The net effect of the exchange is to keep the Mediterranean stable in level and salinity.

This happy situation originated in the Pliocene Age, when convulsions of the earth opened the Strait of Gibraltar. In the preceding period the Mediterranean, almost deprived of any connection with the oceans, had been deteriorating into a series of brackish and shrinking lakes in which the marine fauna seemed doomed to disappear. The opening of the Strait of Gibraltar literally saved the life of the Mediterranean and the Strait has remained its life-line ever since.

The existence and dimensions of the Strait have other important effects as well. Besides being narrow (seven miles) it is also shallow (350 metres and less). It thus forms a raised sill between the Mediterranean and the Atlantic, leaving the Mediterranean almost sealed off in both dimensions. This is why there are practically no tides in the Mediterranean, which in turn accounts for many of the characteristics of the Mediterranean coastline. But the existence of the sill produces another important phenomenon, which bears on the deep waters. Wherever you have such a sill separating an enclosed basin such as the Mediterranean from the open ocean the temperature of the deep water in the basin, right down to the bottom, will tend to be the same as the temperature at the lowest point of the sill. As a result all the Mediterranean fauna which live at depths below 300 metres or so live in a constant temperature of 13° C. This is in striking contrast to the Atlantic temperature which has already fallen to 5° C at a depth of 1000 metres. It is therefore easy to see how difficult it would be for Atlantic deep-water species to settle in the Mediterranean – and the Mediterranean is certainly poor in deep-water species. There is a further point to be mentioned here. The deep waters of the Atlantic are not only colder, but also much richer in nutrients. This difference is another factor which (quite apart from new phenomena such as pollution, to which the smaller sea is particularly vulnerable) has restricted the fertility of the Mediterranean.

But the Mediterranean is not only connected with the Atlantic. It is also joined to the Black Sea by the Bosphorus and the Dardanelles. Here too there is an exchange of waters, but on a less important scale. Here too more flows into the Mediterranean than out. The Black Sea water, which is low in salt, can be traced as it fans out through the Aegean.

And there is the Suez Canal. This constitutes a lock-free link with the Gulf of Suez and the Red Sea, through which water and fish can pass without hindrance. The volume of water which passes is negligible, but the fish traffic is important and has become more so in recent years because of a change in the salinity of the Bitter Lakes in the Suez Canal. Previously they were too salty for certain species of fish which would otherwise have passed through the Canal from the Red Sea into the Mediterranean. But the diluting effect of the Canal, now 100 years old, has gradually lowered the salinity of the Lakes until it has fallen below the threshold which these fish are willing to cross. One example is *Siganus rivulatus* (Forskal), the rabbit fish, which appears to be establishing itself in increasingly large numbers in the eastern Mediterranean; and quite a few others are now thriving there, including the Indo-Pacific relations of the red mullet, *Upeneus moluccensis* (Bleeker) and *Upeneus tragula* Richardson. Further changes may be expected. It is a comforting thought, when surveying the currently (1970) intractable problem of reopening the Suez Canal to ships and people and goods, that the fish at least are using it more and more.

This is not the only example of a major change brought about by the works of man. Another is the result of the completion of the Aswan Dam, in 1964, in Upper Egypt. This has almost halted the annual release of the Nile flood water into the Mediterranean. This water, which was rich in phosphates and nitrates, had a remarkable fertilizing effect on the waters of the eastern Mediterranean, most noticeable near the mouths of the Nile but extending as far north as Cyprus. Now of course the flood waters are being stored and used to fertilize land instead. But the loss is felt by the fishermen. Where up to 20,000 tons of sardine were formerly taken in a year the catch has dropped to below 1,000 tons.

The distribution of species in the Mediterranean is however mainly influenced by natural phenomena such as variations in depth, in maximum and minimum temperatures, and in the availability of plankton. I should say here that a very large number of species are found throughout the Mediterranean, and in the Black Sea too for that matter, although the Black Sea and Mediterranean lists are by no means indentical. But it is also true that there are quite a few species which are found in the eastern basin only, not only Indo-Pacific immigrants but also survivors of an era when the whole Mediterranean was warmer than it is now; and equally there are plenty of Atlantic species which come some way into the western basin, encouraged no doubt by the streams of Atlantic water which flow in past Gibraltar, but are unwilling to venture past the Sicilian Channel.

There is little to choose between the western and eastern basins as regards depth. It is to be noted that in both basins the continental shelf and the continental slope have been over-exploited, and that these are poorer in the eastern basin than in the western one. The variation in salinity between the two basins is not significant in terms of the distribution of species.

Temperature is a more important factor. I have already explained that in the deeper waters the temperatures remain remarkably constant. However there is a variation of perhaps $\frac{1}{2}°$ c from the western to the eastern basin, which is quite enough to confine some of the species to the eastern basin and to deter others from entering it. Variations in surface temperature are naturally much more noticeable. The effect of the north winds which blow down on certain parts of the Mediterranean (the mistral of Provence, the bora of the Adriatic and the meltem of the Aegean) is important here in chilling the surface waters and also in producing a vertical movement of the waters which is favourable to the supply of plankton.

Plankton is the basic food of fish in the larval state, and of pelagic and some other fish in the adult state. Where it is lacking the whole fish population is affected, because even those fish which do not feed directly on plankton will feel its loss at one or two removes. The Black Sea, well fed by great rivers such as the Danube, is comparatively rich in plankton. The Mediterranean itself is poor. The famous blueness of the Mediterranean and the clarity of its waters betray this poverty, and while they attract human beings they signal a marine desert to fish. The relative poverty of the Mediterranean, most severe in the eastern basin, accounts for the limited population of pelagic fish. The net effect of the exchange of waters with the Atlantic is not helpful in this respect.

Looking ahead to the future, scientists are wondering whether some artificial means can be found of creating a greater vertical movement of waters in the Mediterranean, since there are nutrients at depths where they cannot be utilized. Meanwhile it is unhappily true that the broad trend is for fish supplies in the Mediterranean to diminish, although much valuable work is being done, often with stimuli and help from the FAO, to offset the disadvantageous factors, for instance by improving the cultivation of fish in the numerous brackish lagoons around the Mediterranean coast.

(*Right*) A coin of Acragas, showing a crab and a fish which might be either a mérou or a rascasse.

Catalogues and Notes

1. Explanation of the Catalogues

The catalogues which follow have been constructed on the principle of including all the species of fish and other seafood which occur in the Mediterranean and which are likely to be met in Mediterranean fish markets or restaurants. Although willing to stretch the principle in order to accommodate something of special interest, I have generally left out rarities and creatures which are hardly worth eating. The list is therefore much shorter than that given in the comprehensive and official Catalogue* edited by Professor Bini for the FAO. My list is also arranged somewhat differently; but I have given to every species the number which it bears in the FAO Catalogue in order to make cross-reference easy and to make due acknowledgement of the major work as the standard by which lesser or partial studies should be aligned.

A LITTLE SCIENCE

In the catalogues the name of each species is given first in a Latinized form. This is the scientific name. It usually consists of two words, the first indicating the genus and the second the species within the genus. Some species are shown with more than one Latin name. The explanation is that different naturalists have given them different names and that more than one is in current use.

The first scientific name given is the preferred name and is followed by the name of the naturalist who bestowed it on the species in question. Sometimes the naturalist appears in brackets, sometimes not. The brackets are used to show that the specific name bestowed by the naturalist has been retained, but that the generic name has been changed since the species is now assigned to a different genus. (This business with the brackets is the correct and long-established way of conveying information on this point, but one could wish that a method had been chosen less apt to give the layman an impression of erratic punctuation or haphazard type-setting.) The reader who would,

*See Bibliography p. 395. Even fuller information, for the specialist, has since been provided in the FAO Species Identification Sheets for the Mediterranean and Black Sea, issued in 1973.

very properly, like to know something about these naturalists, whose work in the eighteenth and nineteenth centuries provided the basis for modern ichthyology, but who normally figure in modern books only as bracketed or unbracketed appendages to Latin names, will find what he seeks on page 248.

Where a generic name is followed by the useful abbreviation 'sp.', this means that reference is being made to a number of species in the genus together. This device is employed when it would be tedious and unrewarding to list the species separately.

A species belongs to a genus, which belongs to a family, which belongs to an order, which belongs to a class. The narrative passages with which the catalogue entries are threaded together will enable the reader to keep track of the broader categories if he wishes to do so.

THE LANGUAGES

The names of the species are also listed in French, Greek, Italian, Spanish, the Tunisian version of Arabic, and Turkish. Many Catalan names and the most common Serbo-Croat and Maltese ones are also given, as explained below. I thus cover the Mediterranean languages most important for my purpose, while reluctantly omitting a few (such as certain other versions of Arabic, and Hebrew) which would require treatment in a comprehensive survey.

The Mediterranean languages vary considerably in the extent to which they have names for fish. Italian is the richest – to each species not only one generally accepted name but up to fifty or more regional alternative variations! French has a high standard of differentiation, and so have Spanish and Catalan. Greek is less liberally furnished with specific names. (Greek fishermen at any rate do not always have a word for it.) The Turkish language, although borrowing from Greek some names in this field, seems to be a shade richer. Serbo-Croat is a battle-field in which foreign and indigenous names contend for acceptance. Arabic is not rich in fish names, partly because Arabs are not great fishermen.

It is remarkable that many fish names, like other nautical terms, have spread across the language barriers. Familiarity with Italian names will be of help in Yugoslavia, Malta, Tunisia and Libya, while other names are shared by Greece, Turkey and Cyprus, and yet others show little variation from the south of France through the Spanish coast to the Arab countries of the Maghreb.

I usually give only one name for each fish in each language in the main list. But where two names, or two variants of one name, are in more or less equally common use I give them both. And I have also included under the heading 'Other Names' not only the important Catalan names (in use along much of the Spanish Mediterranean coast and in the Balearic Islands) and the principal Maltese and Serbo-Croat names but also a number of local names and variants from Provence, Sicily, etc. These other names have been selected because they are widely used or seem to me to be interesting; but the selection is of course a very limited one in relation to the scores of names which could be listed for most species.

The principal names which I give coincide for the most part with those recommended by the FAO. But I differ from them in some instances. Paradoxically, I show fewer English names than they do. This is because I prefer not to cite English names which exist only in text-books. If a popular English name is lacking – as it surely will be when we are dealing with a fish which is neither caught in British waters nor sold in British shops, nor so remarkable as to have aroused the attention of the British people in other ways – it seems better to use the scientific name or the popular name from another language which possesses one.

The transliteration of Arabic names is a problem. Tunisian Arabic names are usually transliterated according to French practice. I have generally done the same, but with some modifications intended to help the English-speaking reader.

The reader is also asked to note that there is not an absolutely standard method of transliterating modern Greek; and that the Greek names in this book are not all spelled in accordance with Greek pronunciation. Thus the Greek letter *gamma* is usually represented by 'g', but 'gh' or 'y' would often be better as a guide to pronunciation. Note too that the Greek letter *kai* may be represented by 'c' or 'k', so that carcharías on p. 27 might appear in another book or list as karcharías (or karkharías or karkarías!).

Finally, I mention that Turkish spelling is variable; and that the undotted 'i' which appears in many Turkish names is meant to be undotted.*

THE DRAWINGS

These are mostly taken from the FAO catalogue. They were prepared under the direction of Professor Bini with the purpose, which they

*It is also worth noting that the basic Turkish word for fish is balık. Combined with another noun, the word is written balığı. Thus kalkan balığı for turbot – kalkan meaning shield. The inclusion of balığı is optional in many Turkish fish names. Turbot is commonly referred to as kalkan without any addition.

admirably fulfil, of making identification easy. The reader must of course remember two things in using them. First, they are not to a uniform scale. Second, a fish out of water will not have its fins erect as they are shown in the drawings.

Twenty-four of the catalogue drawings have been prepared for this book by Peter Stebbing. They are those on p. 64, 156, 173, 203, 207, 208, 210, 212, 215, 216, 217, 219, 220, 221, 226, 227, 232, 236, 237, 238, 239 and 240. He also did the decorative drawings throughout the book.

REMARKS

For each species I have shown the maximum normal length of the adult fish. The swords of the swordfish and the tails of the rays are included in the measurements. For the purposes of identification it is important to refer constantly to information about the size of the fish (remembering, however, that many fish are caught before they are fully grown). Information about colour is also to be kept in mind – but the colours of many fish vary according to where they live and may change when they are taken out of the water. Surer clues to identification are provided by such things as the general shape of the fish, the number and position of the fins and the course of the lateral line (the line running along each side).

USING THE CATALOGUES

In each catalogue entry the reader will find, under the heading 'Cuisine', a summary indication of how the fish or other sea creature can best be cooked (and sometimes the outline of a recipe which could not be included in the recipe section of the book). In most catalogue entries a further heading 'Recipes' covers signposts to full recipes, in the recipe section, which are specifically suitable.

The design of the catalogue entries – one to a page and in almost every instance some space left over – ensures that readers who use the book in the Mediterranean area will be able to jot down in the right place notes on other names or recipes which they come across. Not all books are suitable for annotation; but this one is designed so as to invite it.

ABBREVIATIONS

Besides conventional abbreviations which need no explanation I have used the following: Alg., Algeria; Bal., Balearic Islands; Cat., Catalan; Eng., English; Fr., French; Gr., Greek; It., Italian; S.C., Serbo-Croat; Sp., Spanish; Tun., Tunisia.

2. Catalogue of Fish

The Family Petromyzonidae

The first family in the catalogue is, appropriately, the most ancient. It belongs to the class *Marsipobranchii*, which includes both lampreys and hagfish, and which is introduced by Wheeler as follows: 'This small group of slimy-skinned eel-like creatures are the most primitive of all living vertebrates. They are not, strictly speaking, fish, but as they are fish-like in appearance and edible, they are thought of as fishes. . . .

'In fact, they are structurally totally dissimilar to fish. They have no bones and instead of a bony vertebral column there is an elastic noto-chord studded with separate pieces of cartilage. The remainder of the skeleton is cartilaginous, including the feeble supports for the "fins". They have no true jaws.'

Although they have no true jaws lampreys have heads which are equipped in an interesting way with a single nostril on top of the head, seven pairs of gill slits along the side, and a rounded sucking disc, armed with horny teeth, below. The first five years of their lives are restfully spent as blind and toothless larvae snugly settled in the muddy bottom of a suitable river, where the creatures feed on organic matter, giving no hint of the vampire-like activities which are to ensue. But in the sixth year their horny teeth are ready and the lampreys descend to the sea in search of their prey – which may be anything from shad to shark or sturgeon. Once it has located a victim and attached itself thereto the lamprey rasps with its toothed tongue at the victim's skin, while the oval disc provides a powerful sucking apparatus which enables it to drain most of the victim's blood from its tissues. 'In addition,' (so Wheeler tells his increasingly horrified readers) 'glands in the lamprey's mouth secrete a substance which both inhibits clotting of the blood and breaks down the muscle tissue of the victim's body. The effects of attacks on smaller fishes are invariably fatal.'

The sea lamprey returns to a river to spawn, and may then sometimes be seen clinging to a stone by its suctorial teeth to avoid being carried away down to the sea again by the current.

The single Mediterranean species listed below occurs also in British waters, and on the American Atlantic coast as far south as Florida.

It is matched on the other side of North America by the Pacific and Arctic lampreys. But it is not easy to find sea lampreys for sale in Britain or North America, or the Mediterranean. The flesh is fine, but the taste for sea lampreys seems almost to have disappeared. It seems to me that, although modern opinion may be right in its lower estimation of the merits of the lamprey's flesh, there is none the less a certain special sensation which its consumption affords to the imaginative diner who is aware of its habits and antiquity.

Sea lamprey

Petromyzon marinus (Linnaeus)
FAO 0

REMARKS. Maximum length about 90 cm. Greenish-grey or olive-brown on the back, with black marbling, and greyish-white below. Behind each eye is a row of seven small orifices. A primitive creature with a round mouth, no jaw and no paired fins.

French: Lamproie
Greek: Lámbrena
Italian: Lampreda marina
Spanish: Lamprea de mar
Other names: Llampresa de mar (Cat.); Xuclador (Bal.); Sept yeux, Sept trous (Fr.); Stone-sucker

CUISINE. Lampreys are bought and prepared like the eels which they resemble. But they have finer flesh. Although only one specific Mediterranean recipe for the lamprey is listed below, I believe that Lamproie à la Mode de Bordeaux used also to be made on the French Mediterranean coast. This is a sort of matelote of lamprey, for which summary directions are as follows. Clean and skin lampreys (keeping the blood) and cut them into three-inch sections. Lay these, with a bouquet garni and garlic, on a bed of thinly sliced onion and carrot, all in a buttered oven dish. Add red wine to cover and cook vigorously for 10 minutes. Remove the fish. Strain the cooking liquid and make it into a sauce with a roux. Cook this for 12 minutes and strain it again. Replace the fish in the dish with matching sections of lightly sauté leeks, pour the sauce over all and cook gently, uncovered, for 15 minutes. Lastly, blend the reserved lamprey blood with the sauce.

RECIPE.
Pasticcio di Lampreda, p. 337.

Sharks

We pass to the order *Squaliformes*, which comprises the creatures usually called sharks and dogfish. Most of them are disagreeable in appearance and only some are worth eating. The seven listed below include the best ones, but there are others which are perfectly edible.*

There are patches of confusion in the vulgar nomenclature of this order, perhaps because people so rarely see these fish in recognizable condition. Thus the French name chien de mer and the Italian pesce cane and the Tunisian kalb bahr are used loosely of a number of species. Such names are met more often than the correct, specific names given below. Moreover, as some of the entries indicate, these are creatures on which fishmongers often bestow euphemistic names on the pattern of the British 'rock salmon'.

This is perhaps the place to say, for the benefit of those who may wonder, that there are very few sharks in the Mediterranean which present any danger to human beings. The only really dangerous one – *Carcharodon carcharias* (Linnaeus), the white shark, not listed below – is uncommon and for practical purposes such as bathing in the sea may be disregarded.

The order is well represented in both British and North American waters. All the species listed are to be found in British waters, except for the hammerhead shark which is a rare visitor. The hammerhead is however well known on the North American Atlantic coast. North Americans also have a good selection of dogfish and smoothhounds, the porbeagle shark, and both the Pacific and Atlantic angel shark to match the excellent angel shark of the Mediterranean.

*I have not listed, for example, *Galeorhinus galeus* (Linnaeus), the tope, French milandre or ha, Spanish cazón, Italian canesca; nor *Prionace glauca* (Linnaeus), the blue shark, French peau bleue, Spanish tintorera, Italian verdesca, which has reddish flesh which is sometimes passed off for tunny.

Porbeagle shark

Lamna nasus (Bonnaterre)
Lamna cornubica
FAO 5

REMARKS. Maximum length 400 cm. Not common, and probably not found at all east of the Adriatic.

CUISINE. Provides good steaks, something like swordfish (No. 199). A porbeagle shark was displayed at the Brompton Road branch of MacFisheries in 1968. It attracted general public attention: but it was the *cognoscenti* from the near-by British Museum (Natural History) who were quick to buy and bear off pieces of it.

French: Taupe
Greek: Carcharías
Italian: Smeriglio
Spanish: Cailón
Turkish: Dikburun karkarias
Other names: Pixxi plamtu (Malta); Marraix (Cat.)

Dogfish, Lesser-spotted dogfish, Rough hound

Scyliorhinus caniculus (Linnaeus)
FAO 10

REMARKS. Maximum length 75 cm. Very common in British waters. The colour is normally a light or medium shade of brown, with small darker brown spots. A third but inferior member of the family, *Galeus melastomus* Rafinesque, is identifiable by the bold pattern of blotches on its sides and by its having a mouth which is black inside (hence the Italian name, boccanegra: in French the species is chien espagnol).

French: Petite roussette
Greek: Skyláki
Italian: Gattuccio
Spanish: Pintarroja
Tunisian: Kalb bahr
Turkish: Kedi balığı
Other names: Huss, Flake
  (in English fish shops);
  Gatoulin, Cata, etc.
  (Midi); Gat (Cat.);
  Mačka (S.C.)

CUISINE. As No. 11, but better. The fish dealers of Izmir, having heard no doubt of the popularity of rock salmon in England, have bestowed on the dogfish the subtle and attractive name of Chios bass.

Nurse hound, Large-spotted dogfish, Huss

Scyliorhinus stellaris (Linnaeus)
FAO 11

REMARKS. Maximum length 120 cm. This, the larger of the two dogfish listed, is normally of a sandy or grey colour and marked by fairly large darker spots. Common off the southern shores of England.

CUISINE. To be cooked very fresh with strong added flavours. This and No. 10 are similar, but inferior, to the émissole (Nos. 13, 14). This is perhaps the place for introducing what Mr Hugh Whittall of Istanbul calls his Recipe for Coarse or Tasteless Fish. Chop up some tomatoes and onions finely and place them in a frying pan. Add just enough water to cover, bring to the boil and cook until a fairly thick sauce is formed. Remove from the fire, add salt, bay leaves and a few thin slices of lemon, and pour a moderate amount of olive oil over all. Lay the inferior fish or fish steaks on this bed, with another thin slice of lemon and plenty of chopped parsley on top. Then cook, covered, until the fish is ready. You may also add pepper and – if you wish to introduce what will be, from the Mediterranean point of view, an exotic touch – a little Worcestershire sauce.

French: Grande roussette
Greek: Gátos
Italian: Gattopardo
Spanish: Alitán
Tunisian: Qattous
Turkish: Kedi balığı
Other names : Flake (in English fish shops); Gatvaire (Cat.); Gató (Bal.); Pesciu gattu (Corsica); Gat, Cata (Midi); Mačka (S.C.)

RECIPES.
Pesce alla pizzaiola, p. 324.   Borthéto, p. 354.

Smooth hound

Mustelus sp.
FAO 13, 14

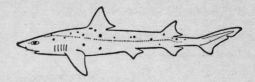

REMARKS. Maximum length 160 cm. These are rather sluggish sharks, which feed upon crabs, lobsters, etc., their smooth pavement-like teeth being adapted for crushing shells rather than for seizing and holding active fish. The two species, which have often been confused, are *Mustelus asterius* Cloquet and *Mustelus mustelus* (Linnaeus). The former (which is, incidentally, the more common of the two in British waters) has lots of small white spots on its back and sides. The latter (No. 14) is the one illustrated above.

French: Émissole
Greek: Galéos
Italian: Palombo
Spanish: Musola
Tunisian: Ktat
Turkish: Köpek balığı
Other names: One English authority has apparently named this fish the Unprickly hound. The ironic fishermen of Devon call it Sweet William, the Irish, contrarily and straightforwardly, Stinkard.

CUISINE. In Venice the fishmongers refer to the flesh of this and some related species as vitello di mare (veal of the sea), a device seemingly too transparent to deceive their astute fellow-citizens. But palombo is often presented under its own name in the popular Italian combination of Palombo con Piselli (i.e. with peas, which may be cooked either with the fish or separately).

Some Sicilian cooks prepare slices of palombo for frying by dipping them in vinegar before flouring them. But Signora la Bruna in Evans keeps to the better-known treatment with beaten egg and fine breadcrumbs for her Costolette di Palombo. Having first fried the slices of fish a good golden-brown, she then leaves them to imbibe flavour (for 5 minutes or so, on a very low flame) in a sauce made as follows. Set half an onion, finely chopped, to cook in olive oil, add almost at once ¼ kilo of mushrooms, and once all this has taken colour 400 grammes of tinned tomatoes. Cook gently for 30 minutes, then add chopped parsley and half a clove of garlic, also chopped, and the sauce is ready to receive the fish. An adaptable recipe.

RECIPES.
Musola con Pasas y Piñones, p. 274.   Zuppa di Pesce alla Barese, p. 318.

Hammerhead

Sphyrna zygaena (Linnaeus)
Zygaena malleus
FAO 18

REMARKS. Maximum length 400 cm. Quite common in smaller sizes. The head, viewed from above, looks like the head of a hammer.

CUISINE. To cook a hammerhead is less of a feat than one might think, since baby ones are often taken in some areas. The only one which I have cooked was just small enough to fit the poissonière in which I poached it. The flesh was excellent. The fifteen ladies who had watched the preparation of the sinister young creature tasted it with hesitation but quickly went on to eat it all up.

French: Requin marteau
Greek: Paterítsa
Italian: Pesce martello
Spanish: Pez martillo
Tunisian: Ain fi garnou
Turkish: Çekiç
Other names: Guardia civil (Sp.); Llunada (Cat.); Cornuda (Bal.)

Spur dog

Squalus acanthias Linnaeus
FAO 20

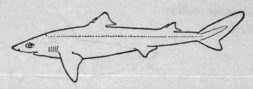

REMARKS. Maximum length 115 cm. Grey-brown on top. The spur dog is often found in shoals. The slightly smaller *Squalus fernandinus* Molina is also aiguillat in French.

CUISINE. See Nos. 13, 14. Venetians count this the best shark for eating. Faber (*Fisheries of the Adriatic*, 1883) also puts this species at the top of his list, which he introduces however with the deprecatory explanation: 'The smaller ground sharks ... constantly furnish the markets with food for the lower classes.'

French: Aiguillat tacheté
Greek: Skýlos acanthías
Italian: Spinarolo
Spanish: Mielga
Turkish: Mahmuzlu camgöz
Other names: Agulia (Provence); Agullat (Cat.); Cassó, Quissona (Bal.); Pas* kostelj (S.C.)

* Pas is a general name for shark in Yugoslavia.

Angel shark, Angel fish, Monkfish

Squatina squatina (Linnaeus)
Squatina angelus
FAO 26

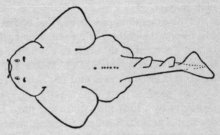

REMARKS. Maximum length 200 cm. A strange fish which, viewed from below, looks something like a Thurber angel. This is one of the sharks whose dried skin can be used for polishing by cabinet-makers.

CUISINE. You will find the body and tail only in the market. This fish deserves more attention than it customarily receives, for it is delicious and convenient to serve (no small bones). Its merit is attested by a report from Istanbul that restaurants have been known to introduce pieces of it into dishes of lobster or other highly-priced fish served under a mask of mayonnaise. The Turks most commonly cut steaks and fry them (in batter or breadcrumbs). But there are many ways of serving angel shark.

French: Ange de mer
Greek: Ánghelos
Italian: Squadro
Spanish: Angelote
Tunisian: Sfinn (but Wagess is also used)
Turkish: Keler
Other names: Escat (Cat.); Xkatlu (Malta); Squeru (Corsica)

RECIPE. Ange de Mer au Four, p. 376.

Rays

The order *Rajiformes*, like the previous order, includes a fairly large number of species – all the various rays and skates – but is dull gastronomically.

All these creatures have broad, flat bodies, either round or rhomboid, and live on the bottom of the sea, whence they are often brought up in trawls. Trawlermen take care to cut off the tails of the big ones quickly before they can do damage or cause injuries. And they watch out for the dangerous sting rays and the electric rays (not listed here as they are not good to eat). The electric rays are capable of discharging electricity by which they stun their prey. Large specimens have been rated at 220 volts/8 amps. Classical writers noted that a dangerous shock could pass along a spear to the hands of a fisherman; and Plato described Socrates as being like an electric ray in administering the shock of doubt to his hearers.

The list begins with the guitar fish, which belongs to the family *Rhinobatidae*. The other species listed are from the family *Rajidae*. As Wheeler writes: 'A good deal of confusion arises over the use of the names skate and ray. The two names are more or less synonymous, although it is usual to refer to the larger species, particularly the long-snouted ones, as skates, and the smaller species as rays. In so far as common names are of value this seems to be a useful distinction. . . . There is, however, no biological reason for this division into two groups.' This is the position in Britain. In North America the general rule is that the edible members of the family *Rajidae* are all called skate, while the term ray is reserved for the electric and sting rays etc., which are not normally eaten there.

The few rays which I list have been chosen for edibility and availability. Identification of the various species is comparatively difficult, as characteristics change during growth. But it is worth noting that the thornback ray (No. 31) is considered the best of the Mediterranean rays, and is also the most common ray in British inshore waters. There are plenty of species available in North American waters.

Guitar fish

Rhinobatus rhinobatus (Linnaeus)
FAO 27

REMARKS. Maximum length 100 cm. Shape as you would expect from the name. Not found in northern Italian waters (nor in the Black Sea), but abundant around Sicily and common in the southern parts of the Mediterranean.

CUISINE. Not as good as the angel shark (No. 26), but equal in merit to the best rays.

French: Guitare, Violon
Greek: Seláchi rinóvatos
Italian: Pesce violino
Spanish: Guitarra
Tunisian: Mohrat
Other names: Pisci chitarra
(Sicily)

Thornback ray

Raja clavata Linnaeus
FAO 31

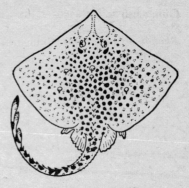

REMARKS. Maximum length 110 cm. Grey on top, white below, with 'bucklers' on its back. This is the ray known as roker (a name of Viking origin) in East Anglia.

CUISINE. The best ray, and best eaten au beurre noir, according to the first recipe listed below. Only the 'wings' (and liver) of a ray are edible, and it is usual to buy these ready dressed from the fishmonger. Unlike most fish, rays are not at their best if eaten very fresh. On the other hand, if they are kept too long (more than say a couple of days) their characteristic ammoniac smell becomes unpleasantly strong. The au beurre noir technique and deep fat frying are both cooking methods which counter this tendency. Non-smelly ray can be poached in water to which vinegar or lemon juice has been added and then masked with a cheese sauce and finished off au gratin.

French: Raie bouclée
Greek: Seláchi
Italian: Razza chiodata
Spanish: Raya de clavos
Tunisian: Gardesh
Turkish: Vatoz
Other names: Clavelado (Provence); Clavell, Clavellada (Cat.); Raža (S.C.)

RECIPES.
Raie au Beurre Noir, p. 302.
Pasta e Broccoli col Brodo d'Arzilla, p. 327.

Scapece alla Vastese, p. 341.
Raya a la Malagueña, p. 277.

Raja miraletus Linnaeus
Raja quadrimaculata
FAO 33

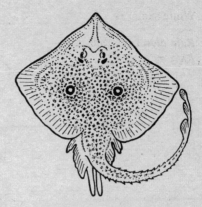

REMARKS. Maximum length 60 cm.

CUISINE. As No. 31, but less good.

French: Raie miroir
Greek: Seláchi
Italian: Razza quattrocchi
Spanish: Raya de espejos
Tunisian: *
Turkish: Vatoz
Other names: Rajada de
   taques (Cat.)

*Hassira and sajedda (both meaning rug or mat), hammema (pigeon) and raya are all names applied in Tunisia to the general run of rays. The last two appear also in Malta as hamiema and rajja.

White skate

Raja alba Lacépède
Raja marginata
FAO 36

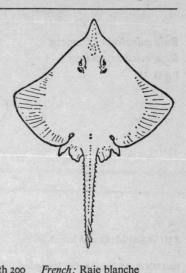

REMARKS. A big one. Maximum length 200 cm.

CUISINE. As No. 31, but less good.

French: Raie blanche
Greek: Seláchi
Italian: Razza bianca
Spanish: Raya blanca,
Raya bramante
Tunisian: (see footnote to
No. 33)
Turkish: Vatoz*
Other names: Cardaire (Cat.)

*The Turkish names tırpana and rina are probably used to indicate the related species *Raja batis.*

Sturgeon

Passing now into the realm of fish with bones, we come first to the order *Acipenseriformes* and the family *Acipenseridae.* This is the family of the sturgeon, huge partly armoured fish which present a somewhat prehistoric appearance. This fish is in fact a survivor from the very remote past. Moreover it is equipped inside with a skeleton which is only partly bone, and partly cartilaginous, and not many fish can boast such an unusual arrangement.

But it is neither the antiquity nor the bones of the fish which excite general interest. The sturgeon is famous as the source of caviare, which consists of the eggs carried by the female (as many as two million per fish). The sturgeon lives at sea, but when the time for reproduction comes (in the spring) it goes up the rivers, for example the Po, for this purpose. The number of sturgeon in the Mediterranean seems unhappily to be diminishing. (The elder Pliny said that it was scarce, which encourages one to think that the diminution may be asymptotic.)

There are several species present in the Mediterranean, but I do not treat them separately. Most readers will be lucky if they see one at all. The family is also represented in British and North American waters, but the same applies there too.

There is in the Bonnefantenmuseum at Maastricht a curious painting by P. Gysels which depicts a classical interior of colossal dimensions in which appear a fruit market and a fish market. The latter consists mainly of several magnificent sturgeon laid side by side on the marble floor. A fishwife holds up some smaller fish. But the customer, an elegant and haughty lady, wearing a halo-shaped headgear and a flowing tangerine-coloured robe, accompanied by her small and naked daughter, indicates one of the sturgeon. 'Absurd creature,' she seems to be saying to the fishwife, 'do you think to tempt me with mullet? I will have a sturgeon as usual.' Some day I hope to be in a position to do the same, even if the architectural surroundings and the garb of those present are very different.

Sturgeon

Acipenser sp.
FAO 47, etc.

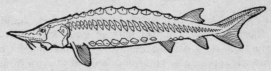

REMARKS. Maximum length 600 cm. The best known species (and the one illustrated) is *Acipenser sturio* Linnaeus. The Greek name means 'sharp-nose', and was used in classical times. But the same name was applied also to a Nile fish, sacred to Osiris,

French: Esturgeon
Greek: Oxýrhynchos
Italian: Storione
Spanish: Esturión
Turkish: Mersin balığı

which also had a pointed snout and which evidently gave its name to the famous Egyptian town of Oxyrhynchos.

CUISINE. The flesh of the sturgeon is rich and meaty. It is often compared with veal, and many of the recipes for preparing it are expressed in terms usually reserved for meat. Thus a large piece of sturgeon, after spending 24 hours in a white-wine marinade, may be cut into slices which are cooked like escalopes de veau. Cavanna (the Italian author who wrote at the beginning of the century when sturgeon seems to have been more plentiful) says that you can cook a piece of sturgeon in the oven as you would cook 'rosbif', using a mixture of olive oil and butter and serving the dish with an anchovy or mushroom sauce. And a piece of sturgeon which has been cooked by steaming may be sliced thinly, marinaded in olive oil and served cold as an antipasto.

Cavanna also gives instructions for spit-roasting a large piece of sturgeon (brushed with olive oil and seasoned) or small sturgeon taken from the river, as I have had them in Belgrade. 'Small sturgeon are cooked whole on the spit, after having been cleaned and scaled and kept for several hours in a marinade of olive oil, salt, parsley, rosemary and lemon juice. Up to the halfway point of cooking the sturgeon is encased, as it turns on the spit, in cooking paper smeared with butter, but thereafter it is uncovered so that it will take on a fine golden colour, while you continue of course to baste it with the marinade. The sturgeon should be brought to the table hot, with an anchovy or piquant sauce.'

In Turkey the only sturgeon to be eaten fresh is the small species *Acipenser ruthenus* (Linnaeus) (English sterlet). The large sturgeon is treated thus: steaks are cut, washed well and thoroughly salted, and kept in wood for ten days; then soaked in fresh water for two days to clear the salt; then hung in the sun for a few days to dry; and finally hung in airy shade for five weeks. The result (oddly, as my informant, Mr Whittall, points out) is known as 'smoked sturgeon'. Turkish expertise reflects the fact that sturgeon are still taken in fair numbers in the Black Sea area.

The Clupeid Fish

In the order *Clupeiformes* we examine the important family *Clupeidae*. This is the family of the herring, sprat, shad, pilchard and sardine. The herring, so familiar in Britain and North America, is not a Mediterranean fish (although there are species such as the Azov herring in the Black Sea), but all the others are. So is the anchovy, which some authorities place in the same family, while others assign it to a separate family, *Engraulidae*. Finally there is the argentine, of the family *Argentinidae*.

The clupeid fish constitute one of the most important groups, from the economic point of view, in the world. They are numerous and heavily fished. They are all pelagic fish, and typically move around in great shoals. They are delicate fish, and their flesh has a relatively high fat content.

The name sardine is a confusing one for British readers. English-speaking people think in terms of tinned sardines. But what they buy in tins as sardines are normally young pilchards (the same fish which, when adult, are taken in large numbers off the Cornish coast – and also of course sold tinned, but as pilchards, which creates the false impression that sardines and pilchards are two different species). What are called sardines in North America (other than tinned ones imported from Europe) are of related but not the same species.

In the Mediterranean area fresh sardines are common in the fish markets, and worth identifying since they can be delicious. The same applies to fresh anchovies. From the gastronomic point of view the anchovy is of exceptional importance, since it has a unique flavour which is important in many recipes and not only Mediterranean ones. The Turks are the greatest Mediterranean connoisseurs of the anchovy, which is taken in great abundance on the Black Sea coast. The Turkish word for anchovy – *hamsi* – is a nickname for Turks of this region.

Cockney readers may be glad to hear that the presence of anchovies in the lower reaches of the Thames has recently been established, following the great efforts made to lessen the degree of pollution in London's river. Large catches are made from time to time in British waters, although the anchovy is not fished systematically. Several varieties of anchovy are present in North American waters.

Sprat

Sprattus sprattus (Linnaeus)
FAO 53

REMARKS. Maximum length 14 cm. The sprat migrates inshore in winter.

CUISINE. Small ones are fried. The sprat is far inferior to the anchovy (No. 61), but the two may be confused either from ignorance or by design.

British readers will be familiar with the sprat under other names too. Whitebait are very small sprats and herrings in the first years of their lives. Brisling is the Norwegian name for sprat.

French: Sprat
Greek: Papalína
Italian: Papalina
Spanish: Espadín
Tunisian: *
Turkish: Çaça
Other names: Amploia (Cat.); Papalína (S.C.)

*For a severe rebuttal of the idea that the sprat is found in Tunisian waters see Note No. 32 of the *Station Océanographique de Salammbô*, by Mme Heldt, 'Sur la Prétendue Existence du Sprat dans les Mers Tunisiennes'.

Twaite shad

Alosa fallax nilotica (Geoffroy Saint-Hilaire)
Clupea finta
FAO 55

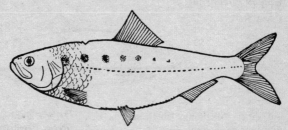

REMARKS. Maximum length 54 cm. Has half a dozen or so spots along the side. *Fallax* means false. The allis shad or true alose (*Alosa alosa* (Linnaeus) or *Alosa vulgaris*) lacks the spots and is not so common in the Mediterranean. Both enter rivers in the spring to spawn and the twaite shad may even live permanently in fresh water. Both are present, but not plentiful, in British waters.

French: Alose feinte
Greek: Fríssa
Italian: Cheppia
Spanish: Saboga
Tunisian: Shbouka
Turkish: Tirsi *
Other names: Alosa (It.); Sábalo (Sp.)

CUISINE. Grill, braise in a bed of sorrel. Not a very good fish, but specimens taken in rivers when their ovaries are ripe make better eating than those caught in the sea. Wherever you catch them, they are bony.

RECIPES.
Alose à l'Oseille, p. 294.
Shad Cooked with Stuffed Dates, p. 382.

*In full: dişli tirsi, i.e. toothy shad, in distinction from karagöz tirsi, i.e. black-eyed shad (*Alosa alosa*). The alternative spelling is tersi.

Pilchard (adult), Sardine (small)

Sardina pilchardus (Walbaum)
Clupea pilchardus
FAO 56

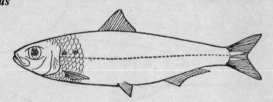

REMARKS. Maximum length 20 cm. Has two spots on each side near the head. Larval sardines and anchovies (No. 61) are known as poutine or poutina in the south of France, and bianchetti or gianchetti in parts of Italy.

CUISINE. The smaller ones are better. Sardines are excellent fresh as well as tinned. They may be grilled, baked or fried. For deep-frying first cover the cleaned fish with a mixture of chopped parsley and fennel, salt and pepper, and lemon juice; then, when this mixture has sunk in, dip the fish in batter, fry, drain, and serve with a tomato sauce.

French: Sardine
Greek: Sardélla
Italian: Sardina
Spanish: Sardina
Tunisian: Sardina
Turkish: Sardalya
Other names: Assili (Alg.); Sarda (It.); Parrocha (Sp., small ones); Srdjela (S.C.)

RECIPES.
Beignets de Sardines, p. 307.
Pasta con le Sarde, p. 328.
Sarde a Beccaficcu, p. 342.

Sarde alla Napoletana, p. 342.
and also the two Italian recipes for fresh anchovies on p. 331.

Sardinella aurita Valenciennes
FAO 57

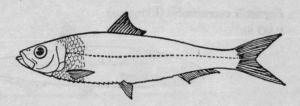

REMARKS. Maximum length 30 cm. Not found in the northern parts of the Mediterranean, where the waters are too cold for it. The same applies to the slightly larger species *Sardinella maderensis* (Lowe), which is found along the southern shores and especially in the south-east. Its body is deeper as well as being a little longer. It is the French grande allache, and Italian alaccia africana.

CUISINE. As for No. 56.

French: Allache
Greek: Fríssa tríchios
Italian: Alaccia
Spanish: Alacha
Tunisian: Lacha
Turkish: Sardalya
Other names: Ouzef (Tun. for the fry of this and related species); Alatxa (Cat.)

Anchovy

Engraulis encrasicolus (Linnaeus)
FAO 61

REMARKS. Maximum length 20 cm. Note that the lower jaw projects markedly less than the upper one. Blue-black and silver sides. See under No. 56 for names applied to larval sardines and anchovies. The Catalan name aladroc applies both to larval anchovies and to larger specimens.

CUISINE. The anchovy is usually bought filleted and preserved in tins or jars, but it is also very good fresh and fried, or indeed cooked in other ways.

French: Anchois
Greek: Gávros
Italian: Acciuḡa, Alice
Spanish: Boquerón, Anchoa
Tunisian: Anshouwa
Turkish: Hamsi
Other Names: Anxova, Aladroc (Cat.); Amplovo, Anchoïo (Provence); Brgljun (S.C.)

RECIPES.

Boquerones a la Malagueña, p. 273.
Acciughe Tartufate, p. 330.
Alici Ammollicate, p. 331.
Alici Ripiene, p. 331.
Anchovies as an Antipasto, p. 332.
l'Anchoïade, p. 294.

Four Turkish Ways with Anchovy, p. 364.
Also French and Italian recipes for the sardine, beginning on pp. 307 and 342.

Argentine

Argentina sphyraena Linnaeus
FAO 62

REMARKS. Maximum length 20 cm. Not very common. This is a slim silver-coloured fish, with a pale green back, found in relatively deep water. It is occasionally marketed in Britain. There is a species on both east and west coasts of North America.

French: Argentine
Greek: Gourlomátis
Italian: Argentina
Spanish: Pez plata
Other names: Polido
(Balearics)

CUISINE. Fry.

The Lizard Fish and the Eels

The lizard fish, which belongs to the family *Synodidae* in the order *Myctophiformes*, is a fairly small deep-water fish. It is unknown in British waters (and unlikely ever to be imported), but related species are to be found on both the Atlantic and Pacific coasts of North America.

Anguilla is the Latin name for eel, and eels belong to the order *Anguilliformes*. The three edible eels listed belong to the families *Anguillidae*, *Muraenidae* and *Congridae*. Two of them, the common eel and the conger, are found in British waters. In North American waters the American eel is closely akin to the common eel, and there are nine species each of conger and moray.

The conger and moray are purely marine creatures. But the common eel has a complicated life cycle which keeps it in fresh water for much of its life. Its spawning ground is the Sargasso Sea in the western Atlantic. There the eel eggs hatch into larvae, which turn up two to three years later in European coastal waters as leptocephali, tiny transparent creatures which are recognizable as baby eels. In the next stage they ascend rivers of their choice, develop pigment cells in the skin and turn into real young eels or elvers. Their growth to maturity is accomplished in fresh water, but after eight to fifteen years of river life they will set off back again for the open sea. The fishermen who lie in wait for the eel on this last journey downstream refer to it now by names such as silver eel or anguille argentée, since its sides and belly have turned metallic silver in colour. The eels which make it back to the salt water head for the Sargasso Sea, where they arrive in a sorry state (enlarged eyes, atrophied gut, weakened jaws and swollen gonads) just in time to spawn before death overtakes them.

The Romans esteemed the moray, and kept them as pets in special pools. It is popularly believed that they fed live slaves to them. The basis for this belief seems to be an anecdote about a certain Vedius Pollio, who had Augustus dining with him. A careless slave of Pollio broke a piece of his glass. Pollio had him thrown into a pool full of '*muraenae*'; and Pliny remarks that the point of this procedure was that no other living creatures could afford Pollio the spectacle of a man being torn entirely to pieces in one moment. But this is beyond the capability of morays, and the story is equally implausible if we suppose, with d'Arcy Thompson, that the fish in the pool were lampreys. Noting also that according to some versions of the story the slave was reprieved by Augustus, I conclude that the affair amounted to a non-event, and that our attitude to the moray should not be affected by a tale grossly exaggerated to further the purposes of Roman moralizers.

The moray also had a reputation for unusual sexual activities. If the description given by Oppian reproduced below in Mair's translation were true this would, I believe, be the only instance of a creature from one of the three elements (water, earth, air) mating with a creature from another. But I am advised that what Oppian wrote must have been based more on imagination, of a powerful and poetical kind, than on observation.

Touching the Muraena there is a not obscure report that a Serpent mates with her, and that the Muraena herself comes forth from the sea willingly, eager mate to eager mate. The bitter Serpent, whetted by the fiery passion within him, is frenzied for mating and drags himself nigh the shore; and anon he espies a hollow rock and therein vomits forth his baneful venom, the fierce bile of his teeth, a deadly store, that he may be mild and serene to meet his bride. Standing on the shore he utters his hissing note, his mating call; and the dusky Muraena quickly hears his cry and speeds swifter than an arrow. She stretches her from the sea, he from the land treads the grey surf, and, eager to mate with one another, the two embrace, and the panting bride receives with open mouth the Serpent's head.

Lizard fish

Synodus saurus (Linnaeus)
Saurus griseus
FAO 63

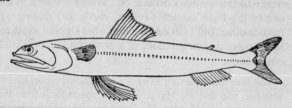

REMARKS. Maximum length 35 cm. Brought up from deep-water trawling. Has a head rather like that of a lizard. The species *Aulopus filamentosus* (Bloch) is very similar, but a little larger. Another deep water fish from the same order is the smaller *Chlorophthalmus agassizi* (Bonaparte) to be distinguished at once by the big green eyes set on top of its head, but not often met in the markets (it is ojiverde in Spanish, gourlomátis in Greek and occhi verdi, or in some places occhione, in Italian).

French: Lézard
Greek: Scarmós
Italian: Pesce lucertola
Spanish: Pez de San Francisco
Tunisian: Zerzoumia
Turkish: Zurna
Other names: Dragó (Cat.)

CUISINE. Fry in batter.

Eel, Common eel

Anguilla anguilla (Linnaeus)

FAO 66

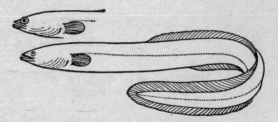

REMARKS. Maximum length 150 cm. The life story of this species is related above. The colour of adults is variable. Some grow especially big and fat, rather like capons and perhaps because they do not mature sexually in the normal way. The Italian name capitone fits such an eel, although it is also used of any large specimen. Tiny eels are civelles or piballes in France; angulas in Spain; cedioli, cirioli, cieche, capillari and sementare in various parts of Italy.

French: Anguille
Greek: Chéli
Italian: Anguilla
Spanish: Anguila
Tunisian: Hansha
Turkish: Yılan balığı
Other names: Bisato (Venice), Ancidda, Anguidda, etc. (Sardinia and Sicily); Jegulja (S.C.)

CUISINE. Buy alive, bleed, skin, bone, cut into pieces and then fry or grill; or cook gently in white wine with onions, mushrooms, etc. Or make an eel pie. The eel has more fat than most fish and makes a heavy dish. The tiny ones (civelles) can be deep-fried whole.

Catigot d'Anguilles is a traditional eel recipe of Provence. Just as eels are slippery, so is this recipe difficult to grasp, there being many variations. Escudier ascribes to the gardiens of the Camargue this simple version. Into an earthenware casserole put ½ wineglassful olive oil, 12 (yes, 12) crushed cloves of garlic, a bay leaf, a sprig of thyme, a piece of orange peel and a tiny scrap of a hot red pepper. Cut the prepared and skinned eels into pieces, salt them, add them to the casserole with a wineglassful of red wine and water to cover; then cook, uncovered, for about 25 minutes.

RECIPES.
Terrine d'Anguille à la Martégale, p. 295.
Anguilla Arrosto, p. 332.
Angulas, p. 271.

Bisato in Tecia and Bisato sull'Ara, p. 333.
Ce'e alla Salvia, p. 334.
All i Pebre, p. 271.

Moray eel

Muraena helena (Linnaeus)
FAO 67

REMARKS. Maximum length 150 cm. Of varying colours, but always distinctively mottled (e.g. off-white on dark brown). They have a dangerous bite and are both cunning and greedy. According to Euzière some fishermen believe that the moray likes to live near an octopus, of which when other food fails he will eat a tentacle, knowing that it will grow again. The skin of the moray can be cured and used, e.g. for bookbinding, although this is not done commercially.

French: Murène
Greek: Smérna
Italian: Murena
Spanish: Morena
Tunisian: Mrina, or Lefâa (viper)

CUISINE. Opinions vary. Professor Bini, in correspondence, has told me that in his view the flesh of the moray is perhaps the finest of all Mediterranean fish. Others would expect to use it only in bouillabaisse. The Romans seem to have grilled the moray or boiled it, and Apicius gives sauces for both dishes. Avoid the bony tail-end.

Conger eel

Conger conger (Linnaeus)
FAO 68

REMARKS. Maximum length 200 cm. Colour variable. The upper jaw projects slightly beyond the lower one. The conger hides by day and comes out to feed at night.

CUISINE. Good to eat, especially the dark-coloured specimens. Some may find the conger rather smelly and flat-tasting, but it is esteemed in Turkey for example. A length of the eel (not from the bony tail-end) may be skinned, cooked lightly in butter and then in a casserole with white wine, small onions and seasoning. Or take a piece the size of a *filet de bœuf*, lard it, surround with small onions and 'roast', basting with butter. The conger is often used in bouillabaisse.

French: Congre
Greek: Mougrí
Italian: Grongo
Spanish: Cóngrio
Tunisian: Gringou
Turkish: Mıgrı
Other names: Fiéla (Midi);
  Ugor (S.C.); Congre (Cat.)

RECIPES.
Congrio con Pasas y Piñones, p. 274.
Salade Antiboise, p. 293.

Congre Braisé p. 296.
Brudet, p. 384.

Flying Fish, Gar-Fish and Gadoid Fish

The next order, *Beloniformes*, provides two species in the family *Belonidae* and one in the family *Exocoetidae*. All the fish in this order are pelagic and of memorable appearance. Those listed are beaked or winged. There are also the half-beaks (not listed as they are rare in the Mediterranean) which have the lower but not the upper half of a beak.

Shoals of the skipper regularly visit British waters, and the gar-fish is also relatively common in British waters in the summer and early autumn. The flying fish, on the other hand, is unknown except possibly for stray and freak visits. North Americans have both Pacific and Atlantic saury, of which the latter is the same species as No. 72; many species of needlefish (gar-fish) and half-beaks; and a whole squadron of flying fish.

After these we turn to the order *Gadiformes*, which contains the important family *Gadidae*, the family of the cod, haddock, hake, ling and whiting.

The cod itself is missing in the Mediterranean (except in the form of salt cod which is widely consumed under such names as morue and baccalà), and so are the haddock and saithe (coalfish). The pollack is more or less unknown. Even so, the family is well represented. The hake, of particular importance in Spain and Italy and Yugoslavia, makes the best eating, while whiting is particularly easy to digest.

British and North American readers will be satisfied to note that they have in their own waters and shops a better array of gadoid fish than can be mustered in the Mediterranean. The north Atlantic is indeed the ocean where these fish have attained their greatest abundance and variety.

Gar-fish

Belone bellone (Linnaeus)
FAO 71

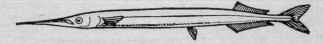

REMARKS. Maximum length 80 cm. The gar-fish is capable of leaping out of the water, is often found in shoals, and comes in from the deep waters towards the coast for the period of reproduction (February–May).

CUISINE. This fish has a backbone of a purple or greenish colour which turns bright green when the fish is cooked. This wrongly puts people off. In fact it is a wholesome and delicious fish which provides good bone-free fillets. (On the Atlantic coast of France its merits are recognized by the name bécassine de mer.) Fry in oil, cook in a court-bouillon, use in Tunisian couscous, or cook in a sauce made with tomatoes and onions and flavoured with oregano.

French: Aiguille, Orphie
Greek: Zargána
Italian: Aguglia
Spanish: Aguja
Tunisian: M'sella
Turkish: Zargana
Other names: Sauteur (Alg.); Bucellula (Corsica); Agulio (Provence); Agulla (Cat.); Iglica (S.C.)

Saury, Skipper

Scomberesox saurus (Walbaum)
FAO 72

REMARKS. Maximum length 40 cm. The back is blue-grey.

CUISINE. Like its close relation, the gar-fish, this is good to eat. It may be had salted.

French: Balaou
Greek: Zargána
Italian: Costardello
Spanish: Paparda
Tunisian: M'sella
Turkish: Zurna
Other names: Billfish;
    Gastaurello (It.);
    Gastadélo (Provence);
    Trumfau (Cat.)

Flying fish

Cypselurus rondeleti (Valenciennes)
Exocoetus rondeleti
FAO 75

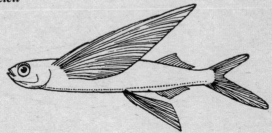

REMARKS. Maximum length 30 cm. May glide in the air for distances of up to 100 metres, reaching a height of seven or eight metres, thanks to its very large pectoral fins which amount almost to wings.

CUISINE. All right to eat, but I have no particular suggestions. A fish which arouses no general enthusiasm, although Palombi and Santarelli praise the flavour of its flesh and state that some fishmongers artfully trim down its 'wings' and pass it off as mackerel. It is certainly better than the other flying fish of the Mediterranean – *Dactylopterus volitans* (Linnaeus), the flying gurnard (French hirondelle, Italian pesce civetta, Spanish chicharra) which is bigger and has 'wings' prettily marked with blue but makes poor eating and is therefore not listed.

French: Poisson volant
Greek: Chelidonópsaro
Italian: Pesce volante
Spanish: Pez volador, Golondrina de mar
Tunisian: Khoutiffet el bahr, Khoutiffa
Turkish: Uçan balık
Other names: Rondinella (It.); Exocet, Hirondelle de mer (Fr.); Orenyola (Cat.)

Poor cod

Trisopterus minutus (Linnaeus)
Gadus minutus
FAO 76

REMARKS. Maximum length 32 cm.

CUISINE. This fish has a good flavour but must be eaten very fresh, and is rather bony.

French: Capelan
Greek: Bacaliaráki síko
Italian: Merluzzo cappellano
Spanish: Capellán
Tunisian: Nazalli
Turkish: Mezit balığı
Other names: Fico (Midi)

Whiting

Merlangius merlangus (Linnaeus)
Gadus merlangus
FAO 77

REMARKS. Maximum length 40 cm. Found in shallow inshore waters.

CUISINE. A rather tasteless fish, but the flesh is light and easily digestible. Fry or bake.

French: Merlan
Greek: Bacaliáros
Italian: Merlano
Spanish: Plegonero
Tunisian: Nazalli
Turkish: Mezit* balığı, Bakalyaro
Other names: Peix rei (Cat.); Gádos (Gr.)

RECIPE.
Merlan en Raïto, p. 300.

Boulettes de Merlan Pannées, p. 377.

*Or Mezcit.

Blue whiting

Micromesistius poutassou (Risso)
Gadus poutassou
FAO 78

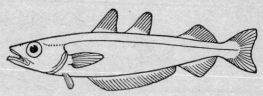

REMARKS. Maximum length 40 cm. An oceanic version of No. 77, found near the surface but only over deep water. Note the distance between the dorsal fins. The Greek name means little exile or refugee.

CUISINE. As No. 77. Consume very fresh.

French: Poutassou
Greek: Prosphygáki
Italian: Melú
Spanish: Bacaladilla
Tunisian: Nazalli
Turkish: Mezit balığı, Bakalyaro
Other names: Couch's whiting; Llúcera, Maire (Cat.); Peix rei (Bal.)

Hake

Merluccius merluccius (Linnaeus)
FAO 81

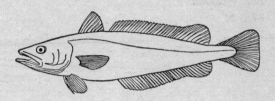

REMARKS. Maximum length 100 cm. or even more. A fine fish which is particularly plentiful in Spanish waters, where small specimens are known as pescadillas.

CUISINE. The best of the family. Easily deboned. Bake, poach, steam, make into fish balls.

Hake can also be good cold. The Italian dish Merluzzo in Carpione provides a good antipasto, and is made as follows. Chop a carrot, a celery stalk, a little fresh basil and an onion. Roughly chop a tomato. Cook all these with 2 teaspoonfuls of black peppercorns in undiluted vinegar for 15 minutes. Meanwhile fry pieces of hake, or whole small hake, in olive oil. Place them in a bowl and pour the marinade over them, with the addition of a bay leaf. Leave them thus overnight before eating them.

French: Merlu
Greek: Bacaliáros
Italian: Nasello, Merluzzo
Spanish: Merluza
Tunisian: Nazalli
Turkish: Berlam
Other names: Various misleading local names such as gros merlan or even colin (cod) in the Midi; Lluç (Cat.); Oslić (S. C.)

RECIPES.
Caldillo de Perro, p. 266.
Peix en es Forn, p. 269.
Merluza Rellena, p. 275.

Naselli alla Marchigiana, p. 338.
Biánco, p. 354.

Spanish ling, Mediterranean ling

Molva macrophthalma (Rafinesque)
Lota elongata
FAO 83

REMARKS. Maximum length 90 cm. Greyish. *Molva molva* (Linnaeus) is a similar Atlantic species which may be found in the western Mediterranean. It is larger and less elongated. It is the English ling and the Spanish maruca.

French: Lingue
Greek: Pentíki
Italian: Molva occhiona
Spanish: Arbitán
Other names: Julienne (Fr.);
    Escolà (Cat.)

CUISINE. Akin to whiting. Give it a good sauce, or try frying medallions cut from it.

Forkbeard

Phycis sp.
FAO 84, 85

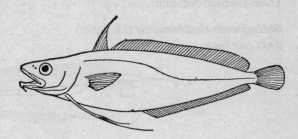

REMARKS. Maximum length 40 cm. The species *Phycis blennioides* (Brünnich) and *Phycis phycis* (Linnaeus) are very much alike, but the former is brownish and the latter greyish. The former (84) is illustrated, as it is the more commonly found in the markets.

CUISINE. As for No. 77, but frying is the preferred treatment for these comparatively small and delicate fish. An alternative procedure, to which Escudier gives the title Mostelle Méditerranée, is to cook the fish in a well-flavoured court-bouillon (which will not take long) and then to carry on as follows. Add to a prepared béchamel sauce a pinch of cayenne pepper and some grated parmesan, with a little of the liquid in which the fish was cooked. Use this sauce to coat the bottom of one of those long narrow oven dishes for fish, add the forkbeard, pour the rest of the sauce over it, sprinkle grated parmesan over all and brown in the oven.

French: Mostelle (de fond for 85)
Greek: Pontikós
Italian: Mustella
Spanish: Brótola (de roca for 85)
Other names: Moustelle (Alg.); Mòllera (Cat.); Petite lingue (Fr.)

Three-bearded rockling

Gaidropsarus mediterraneus (Linnaeus)
FAO (not listed)

REMARKS. Maximum length 50 cm. Not common, but found throughout the Mediterranean. A dark fish. The lighter, spotted version ***Gaidropsarus vulgaris*** (Cloquet) is found only at the western end of the Mediterranean, being an Atlantic species. It is the Spanish lota.

French: Motelle
Greek: Gaidourópsaro
Italian: Motella
Spanish: Bertorella
Turkish: Gelincik
Other names: Loche (de mer) (Fr.); Fura (Cat.)

CUISINE. Delicious, but spoils quickly. Clean at once and cook as for No. 77.

The John Dory

The family *Zeidae* (order *Zeiformes*) includes for our purposes only one species, but an interesting one.

These are all primitive spiny-finned fish, and the John Dory has these characteristics to a high degree. It bears the same relationship, in appearance, to a fish of more sophisticated design (like, say, the grey mullet) as does a motor car of the late nineteenth century to those of the mid twentieth century.

An interesting feature of the John Dory is the presence on either side of a dark spot, for which a number of explanations have been given. The most popular is that the marks were left by the fingers of Saint Peter, after he had thrown back into the sea a specimen which he had landed and which had provoked his sympathy by making distressed noises. (It is believed that this is the fish which Saint Peter took up, on the instructions of Christ, to find in its mouth the silver which he was to pay as tribute, but this belief has arisen as a result of confusion between the John Dory and a fresh-water species with somewhat similar markings.) An alternative explanation is that Saint Christopher, while he was carrying Jesus on his shoulder through the waters, stooped down and picked up a John Dory, on the sides of which his finger marks remained ever after.

The elder Pliny remarked that the John Dory was the favourite fish of the citizens of Cadiz, in a passage which clearly implies that it was not so honoured elsewhere. So far as I can judge, it nowadays holds a position of high, but not the highest, esteem in most of the Mediterranean area.

It is appropriate to mention here two species which are not given separate entries in the catalogue but which may be met in fish markets as ingredients for fish soups and which attract attention by their red or rosy colouring. These are *Hoplostethus mediterraneus* Valenciennes (the French poisson montre and Italian pesce specchie) and *Holocentrus ruber* Forskål which is found in the eastern Mediterranean.

John Dory, Dory

Zeus faber Linnaeus
FAO 98

REMARKS. Maximum length 50 cm. A distinctive fish, with ingenious extending jaws.

CUISINE. The large head and gut account for nearly two-thirds of the weight, so this fish is expensive. However, it has an exquisite taste and its firm white flesh separates easily into four fillets free of bone. Give the John Dory the same sort of treatment as you would choose for sole or turbot. Baby ones can go into the bouillabaisse.

French: Saint-Pierre
Greek: Christópsaro
Italian: Pesce San Pietro
Spanish: Pez de San Pedro
Tunisian: Hout sidi sliman
Turkish: Dülger (carpenter *)
Other names: Poule de mer, Dorée (Fr.); Gall (Cat.); Gal (Midi); Kovač (S.C.)

RECIPES.

Saint Pierre à la Parmentier, p. 306. Filetti di Pesce Gallo al Marsala, p. 339.

*Because the various bones resemble a set of carpenter's tools.

Perciformes: *Barracuda and Sand-Smelt*

The order *Perciformes* is a very large one in which the common feature is some degree of structural resemblance to the perch. Even a limited study such as this one involves the examination of about thirty families within the order.

The first two families are *Sphyraenidae* and *Atherinidae*, those of the barracuda and smelt.

In North American waters there is the Pacific barracuda, and a number of species (of which some are called guaguanche and sennet) on the Atlantic coast. But the barracuda is not found in British waters. *Sphyraena* was the classical Greek name for the barracuda, and *sudis* meaning a pointed stake was the Latin name. The French name spet, and the similar Spanish name, maintain the sense of the Latin name.

The sand-smelts are much smaller fish. Of the species listed one, No. 102, succeeded in establishing itself in the period 1955–63 in warm-water docks in Swansea and Barrow-in-Furness, and actually bred in the Swansea dock! But the species generally available in British waters is the related *Atherina presbyter* Valenciennes, which is thought to be superior to the Mediterranean species. A number of smelts are found in North American waters, but they belong to the family *Osmeridae* and so are outside this category.

The sand-smelts may be distinguished from the anchovy (No. 61) by their jaws and by the fact that they have two dorsal fins to the anchovy's one.

Barracuda

Sphyraena sphyraena (Linnaeus)
FAO 100

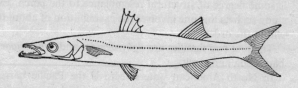

REMARKS. Maximum length 120 cm., but usually smaller. Bronze on top, silver-white underneath. It is the related species *Sphyraena barracuda* Walbaum (found in the tropical Atlantic and twice as big) which has the reputation of attacking human beings. The barracuda is a fish of the high seas which comes into coastal areas in the early summer.

French: Brochet de mer
Greek: Loútsos
Italian: Luccio marino
Spanish: Espetón
Tunisian: Moghzel, Ghzerma, Sh'bour
Turkish: Iskarmoz
Other names: Spet (Fr.); Espet (Cat.); Lizz (Malta)

CUISINE. Good fried (in pieces) or cooked whole in a court-bouillon.

Sand-smelt, Atherine

Atherina sp.
FAO 102–4

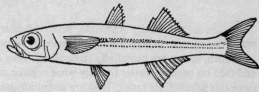

Species	*Atherina mochon* Cuvier	*Atherina hepsetus* Linnaeus	*Atherina boyeri* Risso
FAO	102	103	104
French:	Prêtre	Siouclet	Joël
Greek:	Atherína	Atherína	Atherína
Italian:	Latterino	Latterino sardaro	Latterino capoccione
Spanish:	Pejerrey	Chucleto	Abichón
Tunisian:		Bou chaïara	
Turkish:	Gümüş	Çamuka	
Other names:	Moixo (Cat.)	Sauclet (Fr.), Xanquet (Cat.)	Cabassoun (Marseille), Cabeçuda (Cat.)
Maximum length	14 cm.	15 cm.	18 cm.

REMARKS. These little fish are silver, with darker backs. Nos. 102 and 104 may be different forms of the same species. The illustration is of No. 102.

CUISINE. Fry. See also under Poutine, Nonnat and Melet (p. 292). Tiny sand-smelt, only 1 to 2 cm. long, are known as muccu at Syracuse, where (so Margaret Guido informs me) they are washed in a strainer, mixed with chopped parsley and garlic, made into flat round cakes about 5 cm. in diameter, floured and fried.

The Grey Mullets

There are in the family *Mugilidae* seven Mediterranean species, of which five concern us here. These fish, generally known as grey mullet or, in French, mulet, are beautifully streamlined. They have small mouths and feed on organic matter (exactly what organic matter is important, since this affects their taste). They are essentially coastal fish, and may be found in salt-water lakes, e.g. the Lake of Tunis, as well as in river estuaries.

They occur in British waters (Nos. 106, 107, 110) and in North American waters (No. 105, there known as the striped mullet or in Florida the black mullet, and No. 108 known as the liza, together with some other non-Mediterranean species).

The Greek poet Oppian, who was inclined to praise or blame fish according to their behaviour rather than judge them by their taste, had great admiration and sympathy for the grey mullet. Among all the nurslings of the sea, he believed, they had the most gentle and just disposition, harming neither each other nor any other creatures, never staining their lips with blood but in holy fashion feeding always on the green seaweed or mere mud. Oppian also believed that their exemplary behaviour brought its meet reward, in that baby grey mullet were not eaten by other fish.

The sympathies of Oppian are again evident when he is describing techniques for ensnaring male fish by using a captive female as lure. This technique is still used. But I have read no modern description to match the following passage (which I give in Mair's translation, which well conveys the original poetry):

A like doom does love bring upon the Grey Mullets; for they also are beguiled by a female trailed in the waves. She should be in good condition and fat of limb. For so, when they behold her, they gather around in countless numbers and wondrously overcome by her beauty they will not leave her. . . . But even as youths when they remark the face of a woman exceeding fair first gaze at her from afar, admiring her lovely form, and thereafter they draw near and, forgetting all, walk no more in their former ways but follow her with delight, beguiled by the sweet smells of Aphrodite: even so shalt thou behold the humid crowd of the Mullets passionately thronging.

Grey mullet

Mugil cephalus (Linnaeus)
FAO 105

REMARKS. Maximum length 75 cm. Easily distinguished from the other grey mullet by the transparent membranes which cover the eyes. Note that there are many names which are used of all the grey mullet. Mulet and muge (Fr.), mujol (Sp.), llissa (Cat.), muzao (Genoa), mulettu (Sicily) and bigeran (French Tunisian for small ones) are all used with general application.

French: Mulet cabot
Greek: Képhalos
Italian: Cefalo
Spanish: Pardete
Tunisian: Bouri
Turkish: Has kefal (true mullet)
Other names: Capitán (Sp.); Mazzerdu, Capocchio (Corsica)

CUISINE and RECIPES. See under No. 106 for material which applies to all five grey mullet.

Tito de Caraffa, in his essay on Corsican fish, says that it is usually grey mullet of the species listed on this page which gourmets at Bastia appreciate under the name cannuchiale. These are fish into whose gills a tiny eel has insinuated itself, which feeds on the fish's blood during the night. 'In the morning the bloodless fish, found almost dead, is to be eaten at once. Its flesh is very fine and has lost all bad taste.'

Thin-lipped grey mullet

Mugil capito Cuvier
Liza ramada
FAO 106

REMARKS. Maximum length 50 cm.

CUISINE for Nos. 105–110. Taken from clean water the grey mullet are all excellent to eat. They are relatively free of tiresome small bones. The small ones are best charcoal-grilled. Large ones may be baked, grilled (try putting a sprig of rosemary inside) or poached in a court-bouillon. Serve hot or cold. Good with couscous.

French: Mulet porc
Greek: Mavráki
Italian: Cefalo botolo, Botolo
Spanish: Morragute
Tunisian: Bitoum
Turkish: Pulatarina
Other names: Cirita (Corsica); Porqua (Languedoc)

The eggs of the female, removed in their intact membrane, salted, washed, pressed, dried in the sun and encased in wax, make the delicacy known as boutargue (Tunisia), poutargue (France), bottarga (Italy, especially Sardinia), putago (Turkey) and avgotáracho (Greece).

RECIPES for Nos. 105–110.
Mulet à la Martegale, p. 301.
Muggine al Sugo di Melagrana, p. 338.
Kefal Balığı Pilâkisi, p. 366.
Biánco, p. 354.

Stuffed Grey Mullet, p. 378.
Grey Mullet with Piquant Sauce, p. 379.
Mujol a la Sal, p. 277.
Athenaikí Mayonaísa, p. 353.

Golden grey mullet

Mugil auratus (Risso)
Liza auratus
FAO 107

REMARKS. Maximum length 40 cm. A couple of golden spots beside each eye account for the name. Also, the sides have a yellowish tint.

CUISINE. See No. 106. Highly esteemed. This species and No. 108 are smoked in Turkey and then known as likorinos. The method of smoking is as follows. The fish, neither cleaned nor scaled, are packed upside down in a barrel, in salt. The amount of salt is, in weight, one third that of the fish. A plank is laid over the top and weighted down, and the barrel is left thus for ten days. The fish are then taken out and washed once or twice in fresh water, then hung up to dry for two days and finally smoked over straw or wood shavings or sawdust.

French: Mulet doré
Greek: Mixinári
Italian: Cefalo dorato
Spanish: Galupe
Tunisian: Saffraya* or Mejil (Sfax), or Mazoul (South)
Turkish: Altınbaş kefal
Other names: Galta-roig (Cat.); Alifranciu (Corsica); Gaouto-rousso, Aurin, Mujou de roco (Midi); Lotregan (Venice) and Lustro (Naples)

*Or Safratouzen.

Mugil saliens (Risso)
Liza saliens
FAO 108

REMARKS. Maximum length 40 cm. Capable of an impressive leap.

CUISINE. See No. 106.

French: Mulet sauteur
Greek: Gástros
Italian: Cefalo verzelata, Verzelata
Spanish: Galúa
Tunisian: Karshou*
Turkish: Kobar, or Nobar
Other names: Acucu (Corsica)

*This (used in Sfax, the Kerkenna Islands, etc.) seems the best Arabic name, but bouri (cf. No. 105) is used in the north, ourhaghis is used in the south for small ones, and the French name cigare is also met.

Thick-lipped grey mullet

Crenimugil labrosus (Risso)
Mugil chelo
FAO 110

REMARKS. Maximum length 60 cm. To be recognized by the thick lips and by having a rounder body than the preceding species.

CUISINE. See under No. 106.

French: Mulet lippu
Greek: Velanítsa
Italian: Cefalo bosega, Bosega*
Spanish: Lisa
Tunisian: Kmiri (north), or Kahlayoun (black-eyed)
Turkish: Top baş kefal (round-head mullet)
Other names: Lissa and variants (Roussillon, Languedoc); Mujou labru (Provence); Cirita (Corsica)

*The Venetians exercise a remarkable degree of discrimination in naming the grey mullets. Thus they apply the name bosega to thick-lipped grey mullet in their third year. The names boseghetta and boseghin are used for specimens in the second and first year respectively.

The Family Serranidae

This family includes the bass, sea perch and grouper.

The bass, well-known in France as the bar or loup de mer, is fairly common on the southern and western coasts of England and the southern coast of Ireland. There have been lots of little ones in the Thames in 1968–70. The same species does not occur in North American waters, but there are many other related species there, mostly with the word bass in their names. Bass are attracted to inshore areas and highly regarded by anglers.

The wreckfish or stone bass is much deeper in the body. It is a fish of the high seas, which is met occasionally in British waters and occurs on the Atlantic coast of North America.

The four following species are kinds of grouper, of which there are many species in North American waters, but none to be found round Britain except for very occasional visits by No. 116. This is a pity, because these fish, well-known in France as the mérous, make splendid eating. Small quantities are imported by a firm in London, but if you want to know what happens to *them* turn to page 242.

The *orphos* mentioned by Aristotle and other ancient Greek authors is probably either the mérou or the wreckfish, or both. Some of the puzzles attending this identification are less baffling if one remembers that there are four species of mérou in the Mediterranean, presenting a wide range of colour schemes, and that ancient authors probably classed them together, perhaps with the wreckfish thrown in too. (Indeed there is another species, not listed because of its comparative rarity, which falls into the same category. This is *Mycteroperca rubra* (Bloch), which is close in size and general appearance to No. 116 but usually mottled with light patches on its reddish back and sides. It is the French abadèche rouge, Greek píga, Italian cernia cirenga and Spanish gitano.)

Of the two combers listed one, No. 122, comes as far north as the south-western tip of England. Neither is present in North American waters. Both, incidentally, are hermaphrodite. I do not list a third, the small brown comber, *Serranus hepatus* (Linnaeus), but mention here that the names tambour (French), sacchetto (Italian) and merillo (Spanish) refer to it.

Bass, Sea bass

Dicentrarchus labrax (Linnaeus)
Morone labrax
FAO 113

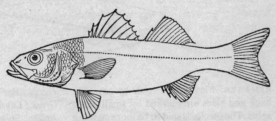

REMARKS. Maximum length 100 cm. May be found in salt-water lakes and the lower reaches of rivers as well as in the sea. The Romans preferred specimens taken in rivers ('*At in lupis, in amne capti praeferuntur*', wrote Pliny), but nowadays those taken in the sea are better. The basic colour is silver, with a darker back and a white belly.

French: Bar, Loup (de mer)
Greek: Lavráki
Italian: Spigola
Spanish: Lubina
Tunisian: Qarous
Turkish: Levrek
Other names: Loupassou (Midi); Llobarro, Llop (Cat.); Branzino, Spinola (It.); Smudut, Lubin (S.C.)

CUISINE. An admirable fish, which has a firm flesh, free of bone, and which holds its shape well when cooked. Little ones may be grilled or cooked en papillote. Big ones are best cooked in a court-bouillon and served with any of a variety of sauces, e.g. a green one made with spinach, chervil and chopped tarragon. You may also braise the fish in white wine. It is good served cold and is suited to decorative work.

Sea bass is popular in Turkey, but there is no Turkish recipe for it in the recipe section. So I mention here the simple Levrek Limon Salçalı, which is sea bass cooked in a court-bouillon (see p. 258; include celery tops and several chopped cloves of garlic) and served with a lemon sauce (beat together the juice of a large lemon, 1½ tablespoonfuls of olive oil and finely chopped parsley).

RECIPES.
Lubina en Salsa Verde, p. 275.
Loup de Mer Beurre de Montpellier, p. 299.
Denté Farci, etc., p. 298.
Spigola in Agrodolce, p. 344.

Spigola al Forno, p. 344.
Athenaiki Mayonaísa, p. 353.
Samak Kebab, p. 392.
Samak Yakhni, p. 393.

Dicentrarchus punctatus (Bloch)
FAO 114

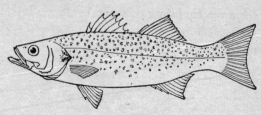

REMARKS. Maximum length 70 cm. The back and sides are marked by small black spots. The species is said to be more cunning and hard to catch than No. 113. It is found mostly in the southern parts of the Mediterranean, and is very common round Gibraltar, since it is basically an Atlantic species. It is imported frozen for the Italian market, where it is sold as spigola Atlantica.

French: Bar tacheté
Greek: Lavráki
Italian: Spigola macchiata
Spanish: Baila
Tunisian: Qarous bou nokta
Turkish: İspendik*
Other names: Loup tigré
   (Alg.)

CUISINE. As for No. 113.

*This may also be applied to small specimens of No. 113.

Wreckfish, Stone bass

Polyprion americanum (Bloch and Schneider)
Polyprion cernium
FAO 115

REMARKS. Maximum length 150 cm. Note the prominent cheekbone to the rear of the eye. The colour is generally dark. This species is not found in the eastern basin of the Mediterranean, and is not common in the market, as it has to be fished with a line and hook at a depth of 150 metres or so.

CUISINE. As for No. 116.

French: Cernier
Greek: Vláchos
Italian: Cernia di fondale
Spanish: Cherna
Tunisian: Shringi
Turkish: İskorpit hanisi
Other names: Dott (Malta);
  Pàmpol rascàs (Bal.);
  Rascàs (Cat.)

Grouper

Epinephelus guaza (Linnaeus)
Serranus gigas
FAO 116

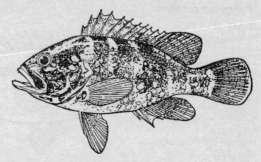

REMARKS. Maximum length 100 cm. The fish is usually a reddish or yellowish brown, with dark patches (*epinephelus* means 'with clouds upon it'). This is the most common species of mérou. Perhaps 60% of the fish of this name in the Mediterranean belong to this species, while 30% are mérou blanc (No. 118) and only 10% mérou noir (No. 119).

CUISINE. A delicious fish, which may be regarded as a North African speciality. The flesh is firm, delicately flavoured, free of bone and suited to all standard methods of cooking. Grill or bake steaks, preferably cut from amidships or the stern. Poach and serve cold, e.g. with a sauce incorporating some Bleu de Bresse.

French: Mérou
Greek: Rophós
Italian: Cernia
Spanish: Mero
Tunisian: Mennani ahmar
 (i.e. Mérou rouge, which
 is the French Tunisian
 name)
Turkish: Sarı hani, Orfoz*
Other names: Cerna
 (Malta); Anfós (Cat.);
 Anfounsou (Nice); Luxerna
 (Genoa, used also of No.
 115); Mérou serranier (Fr.);
 Kirnja (S.C.)

RECIPES.
Mero a la Naranja, p. 276.
Mérou au Bleu de Bresse, p. 301.
Zuppa di Pesce alla Barese, p. 318.
Cernia Ripiena, p. 336.
Mérou à la Sfaxienne, p. 377.

Mérou Cooked with Tunisian
 Pickles, p. 378.
Mérou, Sauce Rouge, p. 382.
Samaki Harra, p. 390.
Samkeh Mechwiyeh, p. 391.

*Also, e.g. around Izmir, variants of the Greek name, such as roufo. (cf. Latin *rufus*, meaning red.)

Epinephelus alexandrinus Valenciennes
FAO 117

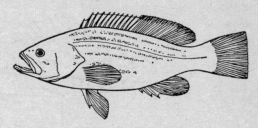

REMARKS. Maximum length 80 cm. The basic body colour is brown. Distinguished by five dark longitudinal stripes along the upper part of each side, at any rate in youth. The older fish may have a big yellow patch on each side. Frequent at the mouth of the Nile.* Common in the Aegean and throughout the eastern Mediterranean, and also found in Tunisian waters and around Sicily.

French: Badèche
Greek: Stíra
Italian: Cernia abadeco
Spanish: Falso abadejo
Tunisian: Mennani
Turkish: Taş hanisi

CUISINE. As No. 116, but less good, the flesh being rather fibrous.

*Hence *alexandrinus* in the scientific name. The Egyptian name for all mérous is, incidentally, wakar. The Lebanese name is loukos.

Epinephelus aeneas (Geoffroy Saint-Hilaire)
FAO 118

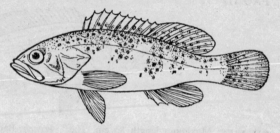

REMARKS. Maximum length 80 cm. Colour generally grey, but may be very pale (as the name mérou blanc would suggest) with rosy tints on the back. Most specimens have a couple of distinctive white lines across each cheek area. This is the most slender of the four mérous, and is found in the southern rather than the northern parts of the Mediterranean. Abundant around Cyprus.

French: Mérou blanc
Greek: Sphyrída
Italian: Cernia bianca
Spanish: Cherne de ley
Tunisian: Mennani adiad
Turkish: Lahoz

CUISINE. As No. 116. Good.

Epinephelus caninus (Valenciennes)
FAO 119

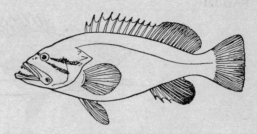

REMARKS. Maximum length 120 cm. This species is of a dark grey colour and has a bulky body like No. 116. It seems to be the least common of the four mérous in the Mediterranean, being found in Algerian and Tunisian waters but not often elsewhere. It may be met under the name mérou blanc, which is confusing (cf. No. 118).

French: Mérou noir
Greek: Rophós
Italian: Cernia nera
Tunisian: Mennani

CUISINE. As No. 116.

Serranus scriba (Linnaeus)
FAO 121

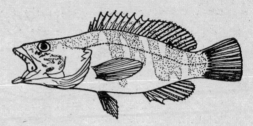

REMARKS. Maximum length 28 cm. Distinctively marked by what looks like scribbling. Hence the English name lettered perch, which is sometimes used.

CUISINE. Quite a good fish, which is often fried. Also used in fish soup.

RECIPE
Balık Çorbası, p. 363.

French: Serran écriture
Greek: Pérca
Italian: Sciarrano (scrittura)
Spanish: Serrano
Turksih: Yazılı hani
Tunisian: Burqash
Other names: Perche (Fr.);
Vaca (Cat.); Pirka (S. C.)

Comber

Serranus cabrilla (Linnaeus)
FAO 122

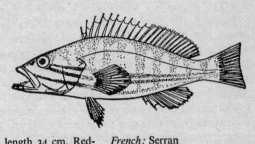

REMARKS. Maximum length 34 cm. Reddish, with horizontal yellow stripes along the lower sides, and vertical bands.

CUISINE. Best used in fish soup, although the rear, and less bony, half of a big one may be worth frying.

French: Serran
Greek: Chános
Italian: Perchia
Spanish: Cabrilla
Tunisian: Burqash
Turkish: Asıĺ hani
Other names: Serrà (Cat.);
   Serran chevrette (Fr.);
   Kanjac (S.C.)

RECIPE.
Balık Çorbası, p. 363.

The Breams

The family *Sparidae* is a large one. Twenty-one species are listed in the FAO catalogue.

No single English or French name covers the whole lot, but sea bream and brême de mer would be the least misleading collective names to use. To distinguish successfully between all of them one has to study their teeth, but for practical purposes it is sufficient to know the size and colouring of the species most often met, and the variations which they display of the standard bream shape (ovale, allongé, comprimé, as the French put it). The big members of the family are the dentex (No. 125) and the pagre (No. 129). The little one is the paclé (No. 137). The best to eat are the daurade (No. 128) and the dentex (No. 125).

In North American waters there are well over a dozen members of the family, mostly known there as porgies. As Wheeler says: 'The greatest number of species and the greatest abundance of sea breams in general occur in tropical and sub-tropical seas, and they are poorly represented in northern European waters. With two exceptions, all are rare vagrants north of the English Channel.' The two exceptions are Nos. 133 and 144, the red bream and the black bream. In addition the bogue, No. 141, occurs with moderate frequency in the English Channel. The prized dentex and daurade, alas, find British waters too cold.

The noble array of *Sparidae* once reviewed the reader will next find two species of the ill-favoured family *Centracanthidae*, the picarel, whose absence from both British and North American waters need cause no grief.

Dentex

Dentex dentex (Linnaeus)
FAO 125

REMARKS. Maximum length 100 cm. Colour varies according to age and may also change somewhat – e.g. spots disappearing – within a short time of death. Young adults normally have steel-blue backs and silver sides. The pectoral fins have a reddish tint. Very large specimens are apt to be of what Bini calls a vinous reddish hue.

French: Denté
Greek: Synagrída
Italian: Dentice
Spanish: Dentón
Tunisian: Dendiq (but Qattous in the south)
Turkish: Sinarit *
Other names: Denci (Malta); Déntol (Cat.); Dental (Venice, etc.); Zubatac (S.C.)

CUISINE. A fine fish. It is especially good if grilled and served with anchovy butter, but it may be presented in numerous ways, either filleted or whole. Large ones can be stuffed and baked.

RECIPES.
Denté Farci, Grillé, et Flambé à la Farigoulette, p. 298.
Dentice Farcito, p. 336.
Dentón al Horno, p. 274.
Synagrída Baked with Tomatoes, p. 388.
Sayadieh, p. 388.

*This and other similar fish which are sold in ready-cut thick slices may be presented under the name trança, which is simply a version of the French word 'tranche'.

Large-eyed dentex

Dentex macrophthalmus (Linnaeus)
FAO 126

REMARKS. Maximum length 35 cm. Has big eyes. Crimson in colour. Abundant in the Aegean. A smaller relation, *Dentex maroccanus* Valenciennes, is also crimson and is found only at the western end of the Mediterranean.

French: Denté aux gros yeux
Greek: Bálas
Italian: Dentice occhione
Spanish: Cachucho
Tunisian: Guerfal

CUISINE. As No. 125.

Dentex gibbosus (Rafinesque)
Dentex filosus
FAO 127

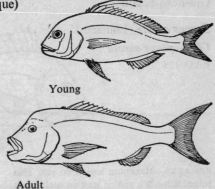

Young

Adult

REMARKS. Maximum length 90 cm. Not common and not found at all in the eastern Mediterranean. The third spine of the dorsal fin extends into a long filament. Old males develop a pronounced forehead, which gives them a quaintly intellectual air. Such a fish may be called denté bossu. (These are also apt to be called pagre (royal) in Tunisia and Algeria, which is confusing in relation to No. 129.) The general colour is rosy.

French: Gros denté rosé
Italian: Dentice corassiere
Spanish: Sama de pluma
Other names: Denté couronné (Fr.), and Faber recorded Dentale della corona in the Adriatic

CUISINE. As No. 125.

Gilt-head bream

Sparus aurata (Linnaeus)
Chrysophrys aurata
FAO 128

REMARKS. Maximum length 60 cm. This prized fish has a golden spot on each cheek and another one, crescent-shaped, between the eyes. It frequents salt-water lakes as well as the open sea. It was sacred to Aphrodite, whether because of its beauty or because it is hermaphrodite I do not know.

Tunisians call small specimens warka or sometimes sefif. Saouqueno is a name for young ones in the Midi.

French: Daurade
Greek: Tsipoúra
Italian: Orata
Spanish: Dorada
Tunisian: Jerraf, Ourata
Turkish: Çipura
Other names: The French is often spelled Dorade; Orada (Cat.); Palmata (Corsica); Komarča (S.C.)

CUISINE. An excellent fish, widely regarded as the best of the bream family. It may be divided into fillets or presented whole. A whole daurade may be grilled, cooked in court-bouillon, or baked in the oven, e.g. with white wine, mushrooms, etc., or suitably stuffed.

RECIPES.
Daurade à la Crème d'Oursins, p. 297.
Daurade à la Niçoise, p. 298.

Daurade aux Tomates, p. 297.
Daurade aux Citrons Confits, p. 381.
Orata alla Pugliese, p. 339.

Couch's sea bream, Sea bream

Pagrus pagrus (Linnaeus)
FAO 129

REMARKS. Maximum length 75 cm. This and the next species have rosy tints on their backs and sides. This one alone has white tips to the tail.

CUISINE. The pagre is not as delicate as the daurade (No. 128), but a good fish from which to cut steaks, or to be stuffed and baked.

French: Pagre commun
Greek: Fagrí
Italian: Pagro
Spanish: Pargo
Tunisian: Hamraia, or (?) Bourrass
Turkish: Sinarit
Other names: Praio (It.); Pagro (Sp.); Pagre (Cat.); Pàguera (Bal.); Farrideh (large) and Farrafir (small) are Lebanese names for this and No. 128

RECIPES.
Pagre aux Moules, p. 302.
Trancie di Pagro col Pesto, p. 339.

Samaki Harra, p. 390.

Pagrus auriga (Valenciennes)
Pagrus hurta
FAO 129-A

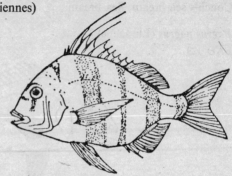

REMARKS. Maximum length 90 cm. Usually marked by four red-brown vertical bands. Fairly common in Tunisian and Algerian waters, but rare in most other parts of the Mediterranean. Some experts believe that this fish, as it grows older, turns from female to male, gains in size, loses all but traces of the vertical bands and emerges as what has hitherto been counted a separate species, *Sparus caeruleosticus* (Valenciennes), which is common in the eastern Atlantic and also found in the Mediterranean.

French: Sar royal
Italian: Pagro reale
Spanish: Hurta
Tunisian: Harous
Other names: Pagre royal (Fr.)

CUISINE. As No. 129.

Sea bream

Pagrus ehrenbergi (Valenciennes)
FAO 130

REMARKS. Maximum length 60 cm. This fish has a loftier brow than No. 129, but they are very alike. Sky-blue spots on the sides will disappear after death. The species is more Atlantic than Mediterranean (indeed in the Italian markets it may be sold as dentice Atlantico) but it is present in the southern parts of the Mediterranean.

CUISINE. As No. 129.

French: Pagre à points bleus
Greek: Fagrí
Italian: Pagro
Spanish: Zapata
Tunisian: Jeghali
Other names: Pagre bossu (Fr.)

Pandora

Pagellus erythrinus (Linnaeus)
FAO 131

REMARKS. Maximum length 50 cm. Of a markedly reddish tint, as the scientific and French names imply. The nomenclature of this genus is confusing. All these fish are liable to be called pagel or pageau in French. Pagell is a Catalan name.

CUISINE. Quite a good fish, which you may grill or bake with good results, but not worthy of the highest culinary attention.

French: Pageot rouge
Greek: Lithríni
Italian: Fragolino
Spanish: Breca
Tunisian: Murjane (means coral)
Turkish: Mercan
Other names: Arbun, Rumenac (S.C.); Luvasu and variants (Sicily, etc.)

Bronze bream, Spanish bream

Pagellus acarne Risso
FAO 132

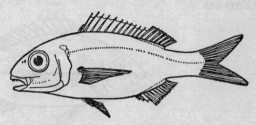

REMARKS. Maximum length 35 cm. Has large eyes. Silver, with a black spot where the pectoral fin joins the body.

CUISINE. As No. 131, but it is somewhat 'dry' for grilling. Escudier recommends preparing it for this by letting it stand in a marinade of olive oil (with salt) for a couple of hours. The treatment is all the more effective if executed in the sunshine, but may be assumed to be worth doing even on grey days.

French: Pageot blanc
Greek: Moúsmouli
Italian: Pagello bastardo
Spanish: Aligote
Tunisian: Murjane
Turkish: Kırma mercan
Other names: Bézuque (Provence); and variants elsewhere, e.g. Besuc (Cat.); Besugo (Sp.); Arbun, Rumenac (S.C.)

Red bream

Pagellus centrodontus (Delaroche)
FAO 133

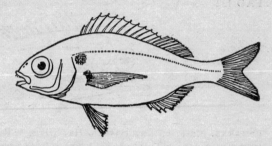

REMARKS. Maximum length 50 cm. Adults are marked by a large black spot on the shoulder. The back is usually grey or red-grey.

This is the only member of the family commonly found in northern European waters. Some authorities regard it as simply the adult version of No. 134, and not a separate species.

CUISINE. As No. 131.

French: Dorade commune
Greek: Lithríni
Italian: Occhialone
Spanish: Besugo
Tunisian: Murjane
Turkish: Mandagöz mercan
Other names: Rousseau, Gros yeux, Fausse daurade, Daurade de l'océan, Belugo (all Fr.); Quelet (Cat.); Arbun, Rumenac (S.C.)

RECIPES.
Dorade au Fenouil et au Vin Blanc, p. 307.

Besugo con Almendras, p. 272.

Blue-spotted bream

Pagellus bogaraveo (Brünnich)
FAO 134

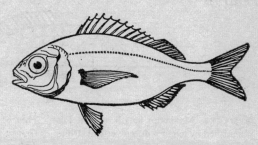

REMARKS. Maximum length 25 cm. Prettily marked by blue spots on its back.

CUISINE. I have seen these fish marketed in the island of Djerba and was told that they could be grilled or used in fish soup, according to size.

French: Bogaravelle
Greek: Lithríni
Italian: Rovello
Spanish: Goraz
Tunisian: Murjane
Other names: Bogaravell (Cat.); Arbun, Rumenac (S.C.)

Striped bream

Lithognathus mormyrus (Linnaeus)
FAO 135

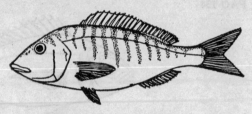

REMARKS. Maximum length 50 cm. Distinguished by ten or a dozen vertical stripes.

CUISINE. Grilling is recommended. An excellent fish.

French: Marbré
Greek: Mourmoúra
Italian: Marmora
Spanish: Herrera
Tunisian: Menkous
Turkish: Çizgili mercan
Other names: Morme (Fr.); Mabre (Cat.); Ajula and variants (Sicily); Ovčica (S.C.)

Sheepshead bream

Puntazzo puntazzo (Cetti)
Charax puntazzo
FAO 136

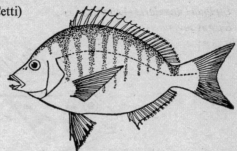

REMARKS. Maximum length 48 cm. Note the shape, the stripes and the snout.

CUISINE. A somewhat bony and not especially good fish. See No. 128.

French: Sar tambour
Greek: Mytáki
Italian: Sarago pizzuto
Spanish: Morruda, Sargo picudo
Tunisian: Maïza
Turkish: Sivriburun karagöz
Other names: Mouré pountchou (Marseille), Mourre agut (Nice); Šiljac, Pic (S.C.)

Annular bream

Diplodus annularis (Linnaeus)
Sargus annularis
FAO 137

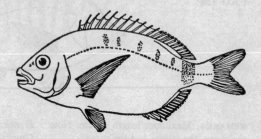

REMARKS. Maximum length 18 cm. The general colour is yellowish. There are often, but not always, darker vertical bands, as hinted in the drawing. There is a distinctive dark band round the junction of tail and body, and this is the ring to which *annularis* refers.

CUISINE. Used in fish soups, and an essential ingredient of the Sfax version.

RECIPE.
Marka, p. 372.

French: Sparaillon
Greek: Spáros
Italian: Sparaglione
Spanish: Raspallón
Tunisian: Sibri, Sbars, Sbares
Turkish: İspari
Other names: Sparlot, Pataclé (Midi, also in Tunisia); Esparrall (Cat.); Squirlu (Corsica); Spar (S. C.)

Diplodus sargus (Linnaeus)
Sargus sargus
Sargus rondeletii
FAO 138

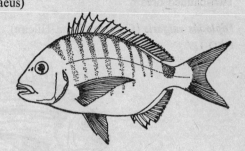

REMARKS. Maximum length 45 cm. Brown/ grey back and sides, marked by seven or eight thin vertical stripes.

CUISINE. Grill or bake. An excellent fish.

French: Sar commun, Sar
Greek: Sargós
Italian: Sarago maggiore
Spanish: Sargo
Tunisian: Fouliya (or Sargi, from the French)
Turkish: Karagöz
Other names: Sargue, Sar rayé (both Fr.); Sargo (It.); Sargu (Malta); Sard (Cat.)

RECIPES.
Sar au Fenouil et au Vin Blanc, p. 307.

Sayadieh, p. 388.

Two-banded bream

Diplodus vulgaris (Geoffroy Saint-Hilaire)

FAO 139

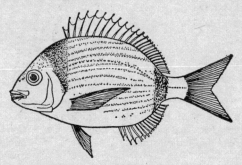

REMARKS. Maximum length 25 cm. The numerous thin horizontal lines are yellowish. The two vertical bands, fore and aft, are very noticeable. There is also a larger species, *Diplodus trifasciatus* (Rafinesque), which has five or six vertical bands and unusually large lips. It may be found in the western Mediterranean (sargo breado or sargo soldado in Spain, sar à grosses lèvres in France).

French: Sar doré
Greek: Spáros
Italian: Sarago fasciato
Spanish: Mojarra
Tunisian: Shergou, Ktef, Timar (south)
Turkish: Karagöz, or (?) Sarıgöz (cf. No. 144)
Other names: Variada (Cat.); Fratar (S. C.)

CUISINE. Another excellent fish which may be grilled or baked. Small ones go in the fish soup. I mention here, although it is suited to several and indeed requires at least two kinds of bream, the Tuscan dish Arrosto di Paraghi e Saraghi. Paragho is a Tuscan name applied to various members of the bream family, notably Nos. 131, 133 and 134; while saragho is a name for two-banded bream or No. 138. To make the dish, buy small bream (4 or 5 to the kilo) of these species, clean them and open them up sufficiently to permit extraction of the backbones, but without splitting the fish completely apart. Insert into each a thin piece of raw ham or bacon and a small sprig of rosemary, and sprinkle the inside with salt and pepper. Close the fish over again carefully and thread them on to the spit, alternately with pieces of toast and sprigs of sage. The fish are then spit-roasted on a lively fire. Baste them every now and then with their own juices collected from a dripping-pan and mixed with a little olive oil and Marsala or white wine. Once the fish are cooked and golden, take them off the spit very carefully and serve them with a squeeze of lemon juice. (Based on the instructions in *Cacciucco* by Maria Nenciolli, who writes with especial expertise on Tuscan fish dishes.)

Bogue

Boops boops (Linnaeus)
FAO 141

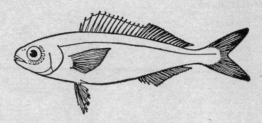

REMARKS. Maximum length 35 cm. The name *boops* signifies having big (literally, ox-) eyes. The colour is mainly silver, with yellowish tints. This is one of the species which account for a high proportion of the Maltese catches.

French: Bogue
Greek: Gópa
Italian: Boga
Spanish: Boga
Tunisian: Sbouga or Bouga
Turkish: Gupa, Kupes
Other names: Boba, Vopa (Italy, Malta, whence also the name Voppi in Tunisia), and Vuopa, Uopa (Sicily); Bukva (S.C.)

CUISINE. Wheeler observes that the flesh of the bogue seems to vary in quality, no doubt in response to the type of food which the fish consume. Maybe I shall come across one some day which has consistently eaten with good judgement. But according to my experience so far and the general repute of the fish, the bogue is not particularly good, although it can be given any of the standard treatments.

Salema

Boops salpa (Linnaeus)
Box salpa
FAO 142

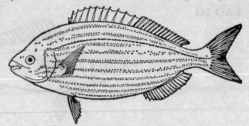

REMARKS. Maximum length 45 cm. An easy fish to recognize, with ten or eleven golden-yellow horizontal stripes.

Saupe are to be found among banks of seaweed, on which they feed. Their herbivorous habits have, I am told, earned them the name chèvre (goat) in Algeria.

French: Saupe
Greek: Sálpa
Italian: Salpa, Sarpa
Spanish: Salema
Tunisian: Shelba
Turkish: Çitari, Sarpa
Other names: Zilpa (Malta); Salpa (Cat.), Saupa (Sp.); Saoupo (Provence); Zlatopružica (S.C.)

CUISINE. The Kerkenna islanders eat a lot of this fish, grilled. The Tunisian saying; '*shelba wa maiet el anba*', means that it is at its best during the vendange (grape harvest). When it is not at its best it may be improved by marinading before cooking.

According to Euzière a distinction is to be made between the 'saupes sédentaires' which live off the south coast of France all year round and tend to be bony and to taste of mud, and the 'saupes de passage' which appear in October and November and are bigger and better-tasting.

RECIPE.
Kousha, p. 374.

Saddled bream

Oblada melanura (Linnaeus)
FAO 143

REMARKS. Maximum length 30 cm. A big-eyed fish with a noticeable black band round the junction of body and tail. Predominantly grey.

CUISINE. Good to eat, especially if one takes the advice of the saying, '*L'oblade se mange quand elle ronronne l'abeille*', and eats it in the spring. Best grilled or cooked à la meunière.

RECIPE.
Sopa de Peix, p. 267.

French: Oblade
Greek: Melanoúri
Italian: Occhiata
Spanish: Oblada
Tunisian: Kahlaia
Turkish: Melanurya
Other names: Blade and kindred names (Provence); Kahlija (Malta); Crnorep, Ušata (S.C.)

Black bream

Spondyliosoma cantharus (Linnaeus)
Cantharus lineatus
Cantharus griseus
FAO 144

REMARKS. Maximum length 50 cm., but not often found so big. Found in the eastern Atlantic as well as throughout the Mediterranean. The back is dark grey, the sides bear many golden-yellow longitudinal stripes. The fish was described as monogamous by Oppian; and Aelian commented that a black bream would fight for its mate as Menelaus fought with Paris.

CUISINE. One of the better bream, to be treated like a daurade (No. 128). But it is not esteemed in the south of France: a Provençal proverb, '*La tanudo ni cuecho ni crudo*', suggests that one should not eat it either raw (understandable) or cooked.

French: Griset
Greek: Scathári
Italian: Tanuta
Spanish: Chopa
Tunisian: E'houdiya (meaning Jew) or Zargaïa
Turkish: *
Other names: Canthare, Canthère (Fr.); Tanudo (Provence); Old wife (Eng.); Charbonnier (Alg.); Kannouta (Tun.); Càntera (Cat.); Kantar (S.C.)

*Here the researcher meets chaos. This species has a black eye. It is therefore hard to believe, as the FAO catalogue suggests, that its Turkish name is sarıgöz, meaning 'yellow eye'. But the name karagöz, meaning 'black eye' seems to be applied in practice to Nos. 138 and 139, whose eyes are yellow! It seems possible that the name fırtına balığı (storm fish) reported from Izmir applies to this species; but just as likely that no such tidy solution exists.

Picarel

Maena maena (Linnaeus)
FAO 145

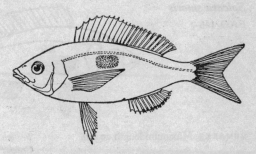

REMARKS. Maximum length 25 cm. Has a blotch on the side, as has No. 146. The male of this species is particularly easy to confuse with No. 146.

CUISINE. Not considered very good. Thus in Venice you could insult someone by calling him a picarel-eater; and at Port Vendres and some other places in France the fish is

French: Mendole commune
Greek: Ménoula
Italian: Mennola
Spanish: Chucla
Tunisian: Zmeimra
Turksih: İzmarit
Other names: Xucla (Cat.);
 Gira (S.C., also No. 146)

known as mata-soldat, or kill-soldier. (This last name is Catalan.) But the picarel can be quite good fried. See also under No. 146.

Faber, writing in 1883, recorded that '. . . it is a common mode of derision to accuse a person of eating this class of fish . . .' I do not know whether modern Venetians wither one another's reputations with similar charges.

RECIPE.
Sopa de Peix, p. 267.

Picarel

Maena smaris (Linnaeus)
Spicara smaris
FAO 146

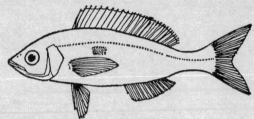

REMARKS. Maximum length 20 cm.

CUISINE. As No. 145. But in certain parts of southern Italy, notably Apulia, this fish is esteemed. And salted young picarel are delicious. This is a local speciality, known as Slana Gira, of the stretch of Dalmatian coast which runs from the island of Hvar south to Dubrovnik. Young fish of up to about 4 inches are gutted and salted, to be eaten later as the occasion arises. The occasion arose for me in the house of Mr Lozica Dinko in Lombarda in the island of Korcula, and his family instructed me in the correct procedure. First remove the head. Then delicately peel the the skin off each side in turn, and lift the fins off back and belly. Holding the little picarel, thus stripped, by the tail, dip it into a dressing of olive oil and vinegar and then lower it into the mouth. Bread and wine accompany these morsels, of which a surprisingly large number may be eaten at a sitting.

French: Picarel
Greek: Marída
Italian: Zerro
Spanish: Caramel
Tunisian: Zmeimra
Turkish: Strongiloz
Other names: Gerret (Cat.);
Jarret, Varlet de ville
(Marseille); Arznella,
Mungara (Malta);
Asineddu (Sicily)

The Red Mullet

The family *Mullidae* is chiefly represented in the Mediterranean by the two species listed below, for both of which red mullet is the basic name – or rouget in French and triglia in Italian. The crimson colour is distinctive, the taste delicate and unique. There are tiny bones, but the enthusiast quickly learns how to eat his red mullet without this disturbing him.

The family also includes a couple of exotic members in the eastern Mediterranean: *Upeneus tragula* Richardson, the black-striped goatfish, and *Upeneus moluccensis* (Bleeker), the golden-banded goatfish. These goatfish are Indo-pacific species which have migrated into the Mediterranean from the Red Sea through the Suez Canal. The members of the family which occur in North American waters are also called goatfish. The name is appropriate because the erectile barbels under the fish's chin, when in the 'down' position, give it a goatlike appearance. *Mullus barbatus* does not come as far north as Britain, but *Mullus surmuletus* does; it is taken in fair quantities in the summer off the south coast of England, and indeed is present in the English Channel as a breeding population.

In antiquity the red mullet was one of the most famous and valued fish. Its name was *trigle* in Greek, *mullus* in Latin.* The Greeks displayed a proper respect for and interest in the fish, and regarded it as sacred to Hecate, but they did not go mad over it as the Romans seem to have done during the first century A.D. Cicero, Horace, Juvenal, Martial, Pliny, Seneca and Suetonius have left abundant and interesting testimony to the red mullet fever which began to affect wealthy Romans during the last years of the Republic and really gripped them in the early Empire. The main symptoms were a preoccupation with size, the consequent rise to absurd heights of the prices of large specimens, a habit of keeping red mullet in captivity, and the enjoyment of the highly specialized aesthetic experience induced by watching the colour of the dying fish change. This was a strange pastime. It is not clear that many actually engaged in it. Pliny had evidently never witnessed such a scene when he wrote: 'The leaders in gastronomy say that a

*An interesting source of confusion arose when the great naturalist Linnaeus, finding that the red mullet had been classed with the gurnards in a single genus, rightly decided to separate them. In doing so he left the name *mullus* to the red mullets, and transferred *trigla* to the gurnards (see p. 163), contrary to the ancient usage. The two families are very different, but the red colour gives them a superficial resemblance and in French, for example, the name rouget is often applied to gurnards as well as to red mullets.

dying mullet shows a large variety of changing colours, turning pale with a complicated modification of blushing scales, at all events if it is looked at when in a glass bowl.' The other famous passage on this subject is in Seneca (Q.N. III, 18), who writes as though he had taken part in one of these 'Come-through-and-watch-the-mullet-die-before we-sit-down-to-eat' exercises; but he was to open his own veins and may have had a morbid fascination even beforehand for the pallor which he described as the colour of between life and death.

As to size, the largest red mullet caught nowadays measure no more than 40 cm. in length and weigh about 3½ or 4 pounds. It is therefore mildly surprising on the one hand to read in Pliny that a red mullet of 2 pounds is rare and to find Horace (Satires II, 2) branding as madness the enthusiasm of a gourmet for 3-pound specimens. On the other hand it is startling to find references to red mullet of 5 pounds or more. Juvenal (IV, 15) mentions one of nearly 6 pounds, which was sold for 6,000 sesterces. Finally, when three red mullet sold together fetched 30,000 sesterces (say £100 each, although many scholars would deny that it is feasible to make such a monetary translation) the emperor Tiberius was impelled to impose a sumptuary tax on the fish market, which may have contributed to the decline of the fever. Macrobius, writing a few centuries later, commented with quiet satisfaction that in his day it was not difficult to find a red mullet of more than 2 pounds but that the crazy prices of earlier days were quite unknown.

Red Mullet

Mullus barbatus (Linnaeus)
FAO 147

REMARKS. Maximum length 25 cm. The colour may vary, but the fish is generally rosy, and pale by comparison with No. 148. In Tunisia the palest ones may be called white (rouget blanc, or the Italian/Arabic hybrid name trilia beidha). The basic Italian name triglia is by the way subject to many local variations – tregghia in the south, trigghia in Sicily, treggh at Bari, etc.

French: Rouget barbet
Greek: Koutsomoúra
Italian: Triglia di fango
Spanish: Salmonete de fango
Tunisian: Mellou, or Bouqit (south)
Turkish: Barbunya
Other names: Moll de fang (Cat.); Trlja (S.C.); Rouget de vase (Tun.); Sultan Ibrahim ramleh (Leb.)

CUISINE for Nos. 147 and 148. See under No. 148.

RECIPES for Nos. 147 and 148.
Rougets à la Niçoise, p. 304.
Rougets au Safran, p. 305.
Rougets aux Feuilles de Vigne, p. 306.
Rougets en Papillote 'Baumanière,' p. 305.
Salmonetes con Salsa Romesco, p. 279.

Triglie alla Ligure, p. 346.
Triglie alla Livornese, p. 346.
Triglie Fredde con Salsa di Menta, p. 347.
Barboúnia Stó Hartí, p. 357.
Psitó Psári, p. 355.

Red mullet

Mullus surmuletus (Linnaeus)
FAO 148

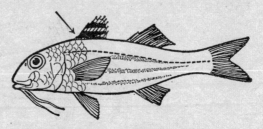

REMARKS. Maximum length 40 cm. Most easily distinguished from No. 147 by the stripes on the first dorsal fin. This species may also have horizontal yellow stripes on its flanks. The colouring varies under the water to match the surroundings, but out of the water the fish is generally redder than No. 147. Scaling a freshly caught specimen will make it even redder.

French: Rouget de roche
Greek: Barboúni
Italian: Triglia di scoglio
Spanish: Salmonete de roca
Tunisian: Mellou, Bouqit
Turkish: Tekir
Other names: Moll roquer (Cat.); Trlja (S.C.); Trilia hamra, Trilia hajar (Tun., hamra means red, hajar of the rocks); Sultan Ibrahim sakhri (Leb.)

CUISINE for Nos. 147 and 148. The red mullet, especially No. 148, is one of the most prized fish in the Mediterranean, and one of the few which are commonly cooked whole (not gutted). May be grilled, fried or cooked in the oven, but not poached or steamed. A standard Greek method is to leave the cleaned red mullet for a while with salt and lemon juice sprinkled over them, then to coat them lightly with flour and fry them in a pan of hot olive oil. At Kelibia on Cap Bon they draw out the gut through the gills, leave the fish unscaled but coated all over with fine salt, and grill them. In the Naples area very small red mullet are known as fragaglie and fried whole. Triglie alla Siciliana is a dish of red mullet which have been marinated for half an hour in seasoned olive oil and are then grilled whole and served with an orange sauce (unusual – cf. the Spanish recipe for mérou on p. 276).

RECIPES for Nos. 147 and 148. See under No. 147.

Meagre and Ombrine, Blue Fish, Horse Mackerel and Scad, Amberjack, Pilot Fish, Liche and Pompano

Still in the order *Perciformes* we come now to three families, *Sciaenidae*, *Pomatomidae*, *Carangidae*, which include a number of sizeable and important fish.

The meagre, No. 151, may be found as far north as the south coast of England, but the corb and ombrine stay in warmer waters. The sciaenid fish are basically fish of the warm temperate and tropical seas. They are noted for having large otoliths (stones in the ears) and sizeable air bladders which males can cause to resonate, thus producing a noticeable and characteristic noise. The many species which inhabit North American waters are for this reason mostly called croakers and drums or drumfish.

The blue fish, No. 154, is not present in British waters, but is found on the Atlantic coast of North America. It is a large and excellent fish, which is highly esteemed in Turkey, but is not so well known in many other Mediterranean countries where the opportunities for catching it are less good.

The family *Carangidae* is a mixed group – mixed, anyway, to the layman's eye – in which we find the genera *Trachurus* (a sort of bogus mackerel, but not as bad as one might think from some of their uncomplimentary names), *Seriola* (the splendid amberjack), *Lichia*, *Trachinotus* and *Naucrates* (the pilot fish). A common feature is the presence – obvious or unobtrusive – of two little spines in front of the anal fin. The *Carangidae* are widely distributed in all the tropical and temperate oceans, and are at their most abundant and diverse in the warmest waters. Of the species listed, only the horse mackerel, No. 155, is common in British waters. The pilot fish, No. 162, is an occasional visitor. It is also to be found on both the Pacific and Atlantic coasts of North America. And North Americans generally have a large variety of *Carangidae* available, to which the common names scad and jack, amberjack, pilot fish and pompano apply.

Meagre

Argyrosomus regium (Asso)
Sciaena aquila
FAO 151

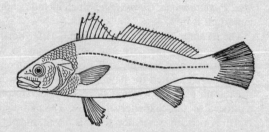

REMARKS. Maximum length 200 cm. A large, hungry fish, which makes a noise in the water. *Sciaena* is a Greek word indicating a dark colour, while *aquila* (eagle) stands for voracity. The Italian and Turkish names refer to the characteristic golden throat of this fish.

CUISINE. The cook may treat this fish like a particularly large sea bass (No. 113) which it resembles. The flesh is white and free of bones, and good cold as well as hot.

French: Maigre
Greek: Mayático
Italian: Bocca d'oro
Spanish: Corvina
Tunisian: Lej
Turkish: Sarıağız
Other names: Sciène (Fr.); Aetós (Gr.); Pei rei (Languedoc); Figoun (Provence); Reig (Cat.)

Corvina nigra (Bloch)
Sciaena umbra
FAO 152

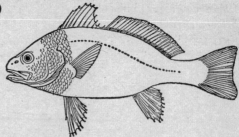

REMARKS. Maximum length 75 cm. A smaller fish than No. 151, but deeper in the body. In Turkey they extract two white balls (otoliths) from the head and use them as an old wives' remedy for urinary troubles. A French friend prefers to collect otoliths from No. 153, and makes them into necklaces.

French: Corb
Greek: Skiós
Italian: Corvo
Spanish: Corvallo
Tunisian: Ghrab
Turkish: Eşkina
Other names: Corbeau, Cotère, Poisson juif, Peï coua (all Fr.); Corba (Cat.); Escorball (Bal.)

CUISINE. Good fried in slices. Try serving with a béchamel sauce with egg yolk, lemon juice and chopped tarragon beaten in.

It is not often that one hears of a recipe being invented. But such a claim is recorded by Maria Nencioli, in *Cacciucco*, on behalf of an Italian naval officer. 'With this simple but delicious recipe of his own creation the Commandante della Corvetta Marcello Bertini used to cook corb obtained by trawler fishermen of the Isola del Giglio, while minesweeping in the insidious and fishy seas.' Disarmed by this evocative introduction, the reader will be willing by intuition or experiment to invest the brief instructions which follow with the necessary precision. Take one good corb steak for each person. Fry a good quantity of onion in plenty of olive oil and place the steaks therein. Wet them with some really good broth and a moderate amount of white wine. Add salt and pepper. Cook until done. Serve the result as it is, or with a piquant sauce of your choice and with mashed potatoes and green peas or lentils.

Umbrina cirrosa (Linnaeus)
Sciaena cirrosa
FAO 153

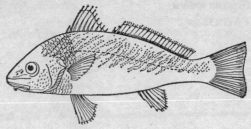

REMARKS. Maximum lenth 100 cm. Has a yellowish back and sides, with up to thirty thin diagonal wavy lines, blue bordered with black, on each side. The smaller species **Umbrina canariensis** Valenciennes has a deeper body and big eyes, and may be encountered in the western Mediterranean, and along the southern coast.

CUISINE. A good fish, which may be compared to (or substituted for) sea bass (No. 113). Grill, fry in slices, bake, or use in a fish couscous.

French: Ombrine
Greek: Mylokópi
Italian: Ombrina
Spanish: Verrugato
Tunisian: Kharbo, or Baghla (south)
Turkish: Minakop
Other names: Chraù or Dainé (Midi); Lumbrina (Corsica); Corball (Cat.)

Blue fish

Pomatomus saltator (Linnaeus)
FAO 154

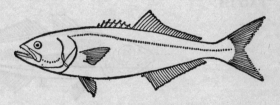

REMARKS. Maximum length 180 or even 200 cm. The back is blue-green. A fish of the high seas which approaches the coasts in summer. The Spanish (and similar Portuguese) name can cause confusion – a London importer once took a consignment of blue fish under the impression that they were two-pound anchovies!

French: Tassergal
Greek: Gofári
Italian: Pesce serra
Spanish: Anjova
Tunisian: Karradh
Turkish: Lüfer*
Other names: Serre (Tun.)

CUISINE. As No. 161, but not quite so good. The Turkish practice is to grill the fish on charcoal and serve it with a sauce of lemon and parsley, or to cook smaller specimens en papillote with finely chopped onion, tomato slices, a squeeze of lemon juice, olive oil, a bay leaf and seasoning.

*There are five Turkish names for this fish, bestowed according to size, thus: – tiny: defne yaprak (bay leaf); small: çinakop; larger: sarı kanat (yellow wing); at its prime: lüfer; very large: kofana. This precise nomenclature reflects the fact that the fish is well known in Turkey. It is sometimes taken in great quantities near Istanbul in January, but the regular season for it is the period of the southward migration, i.e. October to December, when it is fished with line and lamp.

Scad, Horse mackerel

Trachurus trachurus (Linnaeus)

FAO 155

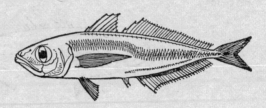

REMARKS. Maximum length 50 cm. Note the large eyes and the prominent, stepped lateral line, which is marked by a row of lozenge-shaped scales. The back is a fairly light greenish-blue. The species *Trachurus mediterraneus* Steindachner is almost indistinguishable from this one. The eastern Atlantic species *Trachurus picturatus* (Bowdich) is also found in the Mediterranean, although it is not common. It has a much darker back than *Trachurus trachurus*, and may grow slightly bigger. Its names in Spanish and Italian are chicharro and sugarello pittato.

French: Saurel
Greek: Savrídi
Italian: Suro
Spanish: Jurel
Tunisian: Shourou
Turkish: İstavrit
Other names: Jack mackerel (Eng.); Sorell (Cat.); Estrangle belle-mère (Toulon); Séveran, Sévereau, Chien, Succagnene (Provence); Cudaspru (Corsica); Sawrella (Malta); Šnjur, Trnobok (S. C.)

CUISINE. Generally, fry or treat like a mackerel. It is not as good, but easier to digest. The lateral line may be lifted off with the point of a knife before cooking. Escudier recommends Sévereaux aux Petits Pois, a dish which involves cooking tender young peas in a casserole and adding cleaned scad to them fifteen minutes before they are ready.

Amberjack

Seriola dumerili (Risso)
FAO 161

REMARKS. Maximum length 125 cm. A fine-looking fish, with a dark bluish back and a yellow streak running along each side from cheek to tail. Young specimens show some vertical stripes.

CUISINE. Quite good. Grill or bake, or cook in a court-bouillon.

French: Sériole
Greek: Mayático
Italian: Ricciola
Spanish: Pez de limón
Tunisian: Jerriwa (? south only), or Saffraya (but cf. No. 107) or Thirnab (uncertain)
Turkish: Sarıkuyruk
Other names: Yellow tail; Poisson limon (Fr. and Tun.); Cervia, and Verderol for young ones (Cat.); Serviola (Bal.); Aċċola (Malta); Parme (Provence); Leccia (It.)

RECIPES.
Mayático Skorthaliá, p. 358.   Athenaikí Mayonaísa, p. 353.

Pilot fish

Naucrates ductor (Linnaeus)
FAO 162

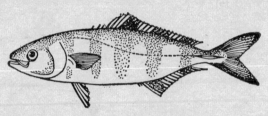

REMARKS. Maximum length 60 cm. Not very common, although taken in large numbers round Malta. Apt to follow ships or to swim in front of sharks, whence the name. Faber (*Fisheries of the Adriatic*, 1883) recorded that on one occasion a vessel arrived in Fiume accompanied by no fewer than twenty pilot fish. Perhaps they were mostly young ones, on a training exercise.

French: Poisson pilote
Greek: Kolaoúzos
Italian: Pesce pilota
Spanish: Pez piloto
Turkish: Malta palamuḍu
Other names: Pàmpol (Bal.);
    Vairó (Cat.);
    Fanfre (Provence);
    Fanfano, Fanfaru (It.);
    Fan fru (Malta)

CUISINE. Reputed to be excellent, with white flesh suitable for grilling. Maltese fishermen cook it in sea water with good results. Cavanna's advice is to treat the pilot fish like mackerel (see p. 140).

Lichia amia (Linnaeus)
FAO 163

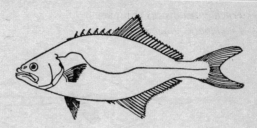

REMARKS. Maximum length 130 cm.

CUISINE. Another good fish (not, however, highly esteemed in Turkey), which can be prepared in a variety of ways depending on its size. The flesh is firm, not unlike that of the tunny. When Jean Tapu, the Tahitian champion of under-water fishing, wished to demonstrate to French friends the Tahitian technique of eating fish raw (but marinaded in lemon juice for one hour) he selected a liche for this purpose.

French: Liche
Greek: Lítsa
Italian: Leccia
Spanish: Palometón
Tunisian: Shabata, or Sh'rab (?)
Turkish: Akya
Other names: Palomida (Cat.); Lissa (Venice, also of related species)

Pompano*

Trachinotus ovatus (Linnaeus)
Trachinotus glaucus
FAO 164

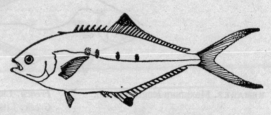

REMARKS. Maximum length 50 cm. Has a much more regular lateral line than No. 163, and may also be distinguished by its markedly V-shaped tail.

CUISINE. As No. 163. Excellent fillets can be taken from head to tail.

French: Palomine
Greek: Lítsa
Italian: Leccia stella
Spanish: Palometa blanca
Tunisian: Shelbout
Turkish: Yaladerma
Other names: Liche glauque, Palomète (Fr.)

*The American name – there is no current English name, although some early books on British fish give derbio.

The Dolphin Fish and Ray's Bream

These fish belong respectively to the families *Coryphaenidae* and *Bramidae*.

The dolphin fish is to be found on both the Pacific and Atlantic coasts of North America, but not in British waters.

Ray's bream also occurs on both North American coasts, where it is known as the pomfret, and migrates annually into northern European waters in the autumn and winter, sometimes in sufficient numbers to make it almost common, although it is not marketed frequently despite the excellence of its flesh.

The dolphin fish is almost certainly the *hippurus* of Aristotle, Pliny, Ovid and Oppian. Oppian observes that it congregates around the floating timbers of a wreck and may be caught in the neighbourhood of bundles of reeds set out to attract it, all of which is true and confirmed by the unusual kannizzati fishery practised in Malta. Although this only takes place in the autumn and is directed only at two species, the dolphin fish and the pilot fish (No. 162), it accounts for a third by weight of the whole year's landings in Malta. Anchored floats are set up by the fishermen at intervals along courses running out into the deep waters west of Malta. The dolphin fish and pilot fish collect under and around the floats and are then taken in an encircling seine net.

A couple of fish which would appear hereabouts in the catalogue if their gastronomic value warranted it are *Cepola rubescens* (Linnaeus) and *Chromis chromis* (Linnaeus). The former is a long ribbon-like fish, pink in colour and worth using in fish soups. It is the French cépole rougeâtre, the Italian cepola and the Greek kordélla. The latter is a small bream-type fish which may be met in France as the petite castagnole and in Italy as the castagnola.

Dolphin fish

Coryphaena hippurus (Linnaeus)

FAO 166

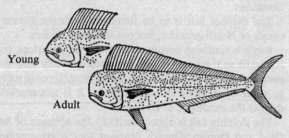

Young

Adult

REMARKS. Maximum length 100 cm. An attractive fish of silver and gold colouring.

The name dolphin by itself should properly be used only for the mammal dolphin, which is of course a much bigger and quite different creature. But *Coryphaena hippurus* is sometimes referred to incorrectly as a dolphin or a porpoise.

CUISINE. The dolphin fish is good to eat and has a full flavour. It responds well to baking, but may also be fried (cut fillets about three inches long, roll them in seasoned flour, coat with egg and fry in oil in a pan) or grilled (take steaks about one inch thick and soak them first in a mixture of olive oil, lemon juice, salt, pepper and a little crushed garlic).

French: Coriphène
Greek: Kynigós
Italian: Lampuga
Spanish: Lampuga
Tunisian: *
Other names: Lampougue (Alg.); Llampuga (Cat.); Dorade (Midi, but cf. Nos. 128 and 133); Dorado (Sp.); Capuni (Sicily); Lampuka (Malta)

RECIPES.
Lampuki Pie, p. 386.

Capone Apparecchiato, p. 335.

*One of the problems in Tunisian nomenclature. Lampouga (from the Italian) and the French name bille are used, but there is also evidence for herba and bouma.

Ray's bream

Brama brama (Bonnaterre)
Brama rayi
FAO 167

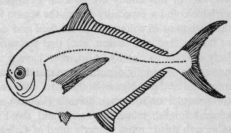

REMARKS. Maximum length 70 cm. A brown-grey deep-water fish which appears at the surface during the summer. Found in many seas, but in the Mediterranean is restricted to the centre and west.

CUISINE. A good fish, which may be treated as a member of the bream family.

French: Brème de mer
Italian: Pesce castagna
Spanish: Japuta
Other names: Castanyola (Cat.); Castagnole (Midi); Pisci luna (Sicily); Palometa negra (Sp.)

Fillets may be fried. Or follow this recipe devised by Marilyn Wailes at her house in Spain. Simmer fillets for twenty minutes in white wine to cover, with slivers of onion, chopped parsley and salt and pepper. Keep the fillets hot while mixing the cooking liquid with an equal quantity of milk, turning it into a roux with butter and flour and adding a chopped hard-boiled egg. Cover the fillets with this sauce and brown the whole under the grill. Call it Castanyola Almoster. These are not the only possibilities. The Italian expert Cavanna, who called the fish rondino, favoured poaching or grilling it.

The Wrasses and Kindred Fish

The fish of this family are striking in appearance, with bright and variable colours, especially during the season for reproduction. Indeed the variations in colour are so marked and depend on such a variety of factors (age, sex, season, etc.) that the various species are particularly difficult to classify. Also, they have a wide variety of popular names, some usually denoting one member but others being used for any or all of them. Names in the latter class are the Provençal roucaou (or rouquier or rouquas), donzela (Venice), sabonero (Algeria). The general English name is wrasse, and the French equivalent vieille (although this is most properly used of *Labrus bergylta* Ascanius, the ballan wrasse, not listed as it is less common in the Mediterranean). A general Turkish name is ot balıkları (grass- or seaweed fish).

The Mediterranean species do not occur in North American waters, but there is an abundance of related species, mostly called damselfish, wrasse and parrotfish. In British waters Nos. 170 and 173, the cuckoo wrasse and ballan wrasse, are respectively common and abundant. The latter is one of the few fish which build nests; and is fished by anglers. British chefs in search of small fish for a Mediterranean-type fish soup may also take advantage of the presence of the corkwing, *Crenilabrus melops* (Linnaeus), and the goldsinny, *Ctenolabrus rupestris* (Linnaeus); also, especially in Scotland, the rock cook, *Centrolabrus exoletus* (Linnaeus).

Generally speaking the fish in this group of families are of little interest as food. But if, as seems likely, the Latin name *scarus* is to be taken as referring generally to them and particularly to the parrotfish, we should note that this last species – *Euscarus cretensis* (Linnaeus), not listed – enjoyed a remarkable vogue at one time in the Roman Empire. Indeed after the Roman admiral Optatus had collected some from the Carpathian Sea and established them as a breeding population on the west coast of Italy they became for a time the fish most prized by Roman gourmets. They are still plentiful in the Aegean, and may be met in Malta under the name marzpan; but no one now esteems them so highly. This is puzzling. Perhaps the Roman enthusiasm was based on their vivid colouring (often bright green) and novelty.

Cuckoo wrasse

Labrus mixtus Linnaeus
Labrus bimaculatus
FAO 170

REMARKS. Maximum length 24 cm. The variable colours are particularly bright on the males. The female may be brown, having a light patch on the back close to the tail with a row of three dark spots on it.

CUISINE. Best used in fish soup.

French: Vieille coquette
Greek: Chiloú
Italian: Tordo fischietto
Spanish: Gallano
Tunisian: Kheddir
Turkish: Ördek balığı
Other names: Demoiselle (Fr.); Pastenaga, female, and Lloro, male (Cat.)

Labrus turdus (Linnaeus)
Labrus viridis
FAO 171

REMARKS. Maximum length 55 cm. Often has a dark green back, but the colour is variable and a red back with white spots occurs too.

CUISINE. Big enough to be cooked by itself, but best used in fish soup.

French: Labre vert
Greek: Chiloú
Italian: Tordo
Spanish: Tordo
Tunisian: Kheddir, or Sh'rif
Turkish: Lapina
Other names: Vieille (Fr.) and Limbert (Marseille) or Tourdre (Midi); Grivia, Massot (Cat.)

Labrus merula (Linnaeus)
FAO 172

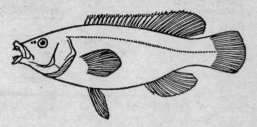

REMARKS. Maximum length 50 cm. The colour may be anything from dark green to reddish brown, the latter being the more common. This species is confined to the Mediterranean.

CUISINE. As No. 171.

French: Merle
Greek: Chiloú
Italian: Tordo nero
Spanish: Merlo
Tunisian: Kheddir
Turkish: Lapina
Other names: Merlo marino
   (It.); Vrana (S. C.)

Wrasse, Corkwing

Crenilabrus sp.
FAO 174, 175, 176

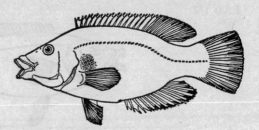

REMARKS. Most have a maximum length of only 10 to 15 cm. It is hardly worthwhile distinguishing between these little fish, which are very alike. But the largest, **Crenilabrus tinca** (Linnaeus), which is known as the peacock wrasse and is the one illustrated (176), may be up to 30 cm. long.

CUISINE. Mostly for fish soup, although one friend reports that a large one, fished at Aegina, was very good steamed.

French: Crénilabre
Greek: Chiloú
Italian: Tordo
Spanish: Tordo
Tunisian: *
Turkish: Curçur, Çırçır
Other names: Crenilabrus tinca is known as the Lucrèce at Marseille and Toulon;

*I have met a number of Tunisian names for the *Crenilabrus* species. Aroussa (meaning bride) and soultan are used, also hajla. In addition kheddir and (in the north) zankour, names applying also to the *Labrus* species, are used.

Rainbow wrasse

Coris julis (Linnaeus)
FAO 177

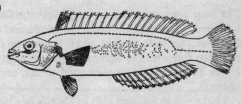

REMARKS. Maximum length 25 cm. One of several species which may be lumped in with the crénilabres. A longitudinal orange band (in the shape of lozenges merging into each other) is not uncommon.

CUISINE. For fish soup, or possibly fry full-size ones, whole or filleted. These fish are comparatively bone-free and have a good flavour.

French: Girelle
Greek: Ghýlos
Italian: Donzella
Spanish: Julia, Doncella
Tunisian: (See footnote to preceding entry)
Turkish: Gün balığı
Other names: Donzella (Cat.)

The Weevers, the Star-Gazer and the Scabbard Fish

The three weevers, which here represent the family *Trachinidae*, have venomous spines on their backs and heads, and need careful handling. However, they taste all right, and it is even said that their fillets may be mistaken for sole. The star-gazer, the fetchingly ugly member of the family *Uranoscopidae*, is also good to eat, and lacks the venomous spines.

I have not so far been able to identify any North American equivalents to the weevers, but there are several varieties of star-gazer available on the Atlantic coast, and one on the Pacific coast. The greater weever and the lesser weever (see catalogue entry No. 182) are both present in British waters. The former is fished by continental fishermen and marketed on the continent but not, so far anyway, in Britain. The star-gazer is not to be found in British waters – but this does not matter since anything it could do for the cook the greater weever can do just as well, and the healing capabilities attributed in classical times to its disproportionately large gall have long since, I assume, been overtaken by the progress of medical research.

The scabbard fish belongs to the family *Trichiuridae*, in which fortunate North Americans have a choice of three species, the Atlantic cutlass fish and, on the Pacific side, the Pacific cutlass fish and the scabbard fish *Lepidopus xantusi* Goode and Bean, a close relation of the Mediterranean species. The Mediterranean species, unfortunately, has hardly ever been recorded in British waters during this century, and the related black scabbard fish (*Aphanopus carbo* Lowe) also normally shuns British waters, although it is caught in deep water to the west of the British Isles.

Scabbard fish have no scales and are rather delicate, so that specimens taken in the trawl are often damaged.

It is strange that, so far as I can discover, no references to this fish in classical literature have been identified. As it is so good to eat, and of a dramatic appearance, one would suppose that the Greeks and Romans would have known about it. Perhaps it escaped attention in classical times because it is a fish of the open sea and middle-depth waters which may not readily have fallen prey to the fishing devices then available.

Trachinus araneus Cuvier
FAO 181

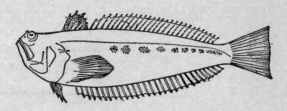

REMARKS. Maximum length 40 cm. Has a brownish-grey body, with a darker head and back marked by lots of brown spots and faint diagonal lines. Not found in the eastern Mediterranean.

CUISINE. The firm flesh makes the weevers good for bouillabaisse, but the bigger ones are worth cooking in other ways too. For example, dip fillets in batter, deep fry and serve with a tomato sauce. Have the poisonous spines cut off when you buy the fish.

French: Vive araignée
Greek: Drákena
Italian: Tracina ragno
Spanish: Araña
Tunisian: Billem
Other names: Araignée by itself is used in Algeria of all the weevers; similarly names like Iragno, Aragno, Araignée, Dragena (Midi); Aranya fragata (Cat.); Pauk (S. C.)

Madame Audollent, who performed the startling feat of providing twenty-four out of forty-eight prize-winning recipes at a congress held by the French Oceanographic Institute in 1926, suggests grilling weevers after marinading them in a mixture of olive oil, salt and pepper, chopped parsley and chopped shallots. (This was one of the twenty-four.)

Greater weever*

Trachinus draco Linnaeus
FAO 182

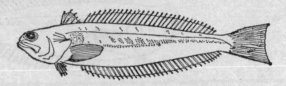

REMARKS. Maximum length 37 cm. The greyish body has blue tints and is marked by thin diagonal lines.

CUISINE. As No. 181.

French: Grande vive
Greek: Drákena
Italian: Tracina drago
Spanish: Escorpión
Tunisian: Billem kbir
Turkish: Trakonya
Other names: Aranya blanca (Cat.); Pauk (S.C.)

*The reader may notice that although this species has names like greater weever and grande vive it is the smallest of the three listed. The explanation is that it is accounted greater in relation to the small and unlisted *Trachinus vipera* Cuvier (the lesser weever, French petite vive, Spanish salvariego, Italian tracina vipera, Turkish varsam and Tunisian billem sghir or lefâa – viper). It earns names like viper by its habit of almost burying itself viper-fashion in the sand, where it is a hazard for barefoot bathers.

Trachinus radiatus Cuvier*

FAO 183

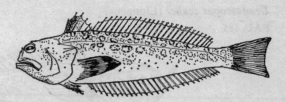

REMARKS. Maximum length 40–50 cm., but usually smaller. Yellowish, with brown spots which form a row of rings, more or less distinct, along the sides.

CUISINE. As No. 181.

French: Vive rayée
Greek: Drákena
Italian: Tracina raggiata
Spanish: Víbora
Tunisian: Billem
Turkish: Çarpan †
Other names: Aranya de
    cap negre and variants
    (Cat.); Pauk (S. C.)

*All three weevers catalogued have been given the name *Trachinus lineatus* by one naturalist or another.

†This weever is found in the Bay of Sinop, in the Black Sea, and the name given may be a local one. Elsewhere the Turkish name might very well be trakonya.

Star-gazer

Uranoscopus scaber (Linnaeus)
FAO 185

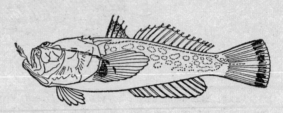

REMARKS. Maximum length 29 cm. Common all over the Mediterranean. The fish has eyes set permanently skywards, and is constructed to provide the maximum reception area for what it eats. Said to be the fish with the gall of which Tobias recovered his sight, although it seems improbable that a star-gazer should have leapt out of the River Tigris and have appeared large enough to devour him.

CUISINE. For fish soups.

French: Bœuf, Rat
Greek: Lýchnos
Italian: Pesce prete
Spanish: Rata
Tunisian: *
Turkish: Kurbağ balığı (frog-fish)
Other names: Saltabardissa (Cat.); Miou, Muou (Provence, Nice); Bocca-in-cielo, Boca in cao, Cocciu (It.)

*A puzzle. The fish is often caught in Tunisian waters, but there is no clearly established name. Tunisian sources generally reject the name bouma, cited by some, but suggest no plausible alternative except billem, the name of the weevers.

Scabbard fish

Lepidopus caudatus (Euphrasen)
FAO 188

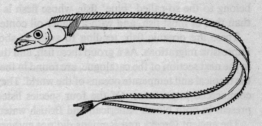

REMARKS. Maximum length 200 cm. Freshly caught, it is a lovely silver colour. The body is like a scabbard, the head voracious-looking with plenty of teeth and big eyes, rather like a stage villain. This fish is not common in Mediterranean markets, although it is brought up in the trawl from time to time. (The related species known as the black scabbard fish is common off the Portuguese coast and is the most important fish in the Madeira market.)

French: Sabre
Greek: Spathópsaro
Italian: Pesce sciabola
Spanish: Pez cinto
Tunisian: Sbata
Turkish: Çatal kuyruk
Other names: Pesce argentin (Genoa) and variants elsewhere in Italy refer to the silver colour; Sabre (Cat.)

CUISINE. An excellent fish. Wipe, cut into 3-inch sections, fry these pieces in the pan and serve with wedges of lemon and brown Arab bread. Nothing else is needed, although a tomato sauce is a good accompaniment.

Mackerel and Bonito

The families *Scombridae* and *Scomberomoridae*. The species listed here belong to the so-called 'blue' fish, whose flesh is so to speak meatier than that of most fish, and with a higher oil content.

These are oceanic fish, tending to swim in shoals and to perform impressive migrations. As a group these fish, and the tunas which follow in the next section of the catalogue, are found in the surface waters of all the tropical and temperate oceans of the world. They are of considerable commercial importance. Of the four species listed the first three are present in both North American and British waters.

The ancient Greeks and Romans did not enthuse over the mackerel, although they knew it well. They regarded it as an inferior substitute for tunny. It was often used only for the production of garum (see p. 246); and Catullus and Martial both use a turn of phrase about poems providing tunics for mackerel, which may have meant that sheets of dud Latin poetry went to the fishmonger for wrapping up fish, of which an inferior sort was cited to emphasize the ignominy of this fate. Dr Richmond has pointed out to me in correspondence that the phrase '*tunica molesta*' which is used in this context has another and dreadful meaning – a sort of pitch-impregnated strait-jacket which was used under Nero for burning Christians alive. He suggests, plausibly in my opinion, that Martial may therefore have been referring not to the mere wrapping up of fish for carriage but to their being wrapped in papyrus in preparation for being cooked en papillote. The traditional Greek Tsirosaláta (see next page) involves this technique.

Bonito on the other hand was admired and recognized as being especially good in the Black Sea, which it still is today.

Atlantic mackerel

Scomber scombrus Linnaeus
FAO 189

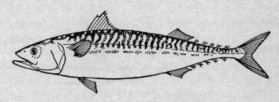

REMARKS. Maximum length 50 cm. Dark blue back, with dark blue wavy lines running part of the way down the sides, which are green. Found throughout the Mediterranean and in the Black Sea. This species and No. 190 are not always distinguished in popular nomenclature. The Algerian name cavallo is used of both, and so is the Roman maccarello.

French: Maquereau
Greek: Scoumbrí
Italian: Sgombro
Spanish: Caballa
Tunisian: Skoumbri
Turkish: Uskumru
Other names: Verat (Cat.);
    Auriou (Provence);
    Lacerto and variants (w.
    It. coast); Skuša (S.C.)

CUISINE. For general remarks and recipes see under No. 190. Here I mention that after mackerel have spawned in the spring they are called tsíros in Greek and çiroz in Turkish. These mackerel are cleaned, soaked in brine and hung up in the sun until they are quite dry. Both Greeks and Turks have ways of preparing these dried mackerel. The Greeks hold the fish over a flame until the skin blisters and breaks, then remove and shred the flesh, which they wrap up in cooking paper (en papillote). The packages are dipped in water, sprinkled with vinegar and left at the side of the oven until they are dry. Then the flesh is removed and put in a dressing of olive oil and vinegar, with a little water added, and finely chopped parsley and dill. This is Tsirosaláta.

Chub mackerel

Scomber japonicus colias Gmelin
FAO 190

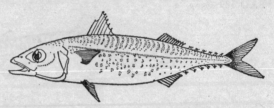

REMARKS. Maximum length 50 cm. Very similar to No. 189, but with more discreet markings on the back, dusky spots on the underside and bigger eyes. Also found throughout the Mediterranean, and in the Black Sea. One of the fish taken in large quantities by Maltese fishermen.

French: Maquereau espagnol
Greek: Koliós
Italian: Lanzado
Spanish: Estornino
Tunisian: Skoumbri
Turkish: Kolyoz
Other names: Bis, Bisso (Cat.); Occhi-grossi (Sicily); Cavalla (Genoa); Kavall (Malta); Cavallo (Alg.); Plavica (S. C.)

CUISINE for Nos. 189 and 190. The flesh of mackerel is very nutritious, and has a comparatively high oil content, so that some find it rather heavy and indigestible. It is best grilled; or cooked en papillote; or poached in a court-bouillon; or baked. It is also good cold, for example in the well-known French dish Maquereaux au Vin Blanc (put cleaned mackerel in an enamel baking dish with a carrot and onion and lemon, sliced, and a bouquet garni with 3 wineglassfuls of white wine and 1 of vinegar, bring to the boil and then simmer very gently for 5 minutes or so before leaving to cool).

RECIPES for Nos. 189 and 190.
Petits Maquereaux, p. 300.
Psári Spetsiótiko, p. 357.

Uskumru Dolmasi, p. 369.
Skuše Marinirane, p. 385.

Bonito, Atlantic bonito

Sarda sarda (Bloch)
Pelamys sarda
FAO 191

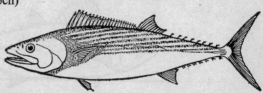

REMARKS. Maximum length 70 cm. The upper sides are marked by distinctive slanting longitudinal stripes. This fish is found throughout the Mediterranean, and in the Black Sea (whence it migrates south in the last three months of the year, returning in the period April to June).

CUISINE. cf. Nos. 192 (tuna) and 189 (mackerel). The bonito comes in between. It is often sold in the form of steaks ready for grilling. In Turkey only the small specimens are eaten fresh (grilled). These are the smaller palamut (the smallest of all are called çingene palamudu). The larger fish, i.e. the torik, are canned or preserved as lakerda (cut in thick slices, deboned, soaked in sea water or brine for a few hours, then salted lightly and kept in a barrel, weighted down, for a week, after which rinsed free of salt and eaten with lemon juice).

French: Bonite à dos rayé
Greek: Palamída
Italian: Palamita
Spanish: Bonito
Tunisian: Balamit
Turkish: Palamut (up to 2½ lbs.) and Torik (3 to 12 lbs.)
Other names: Bonítol (Cat.); Pelamide (Fr.); Polanda (S. C.)

Algerians used to preserve bonito for a week or so, when they had a glut of it during the season, by preparing Bonite à l'Escabèche. (cf. the Spanish recipe on page 270.) Doctoresse Olivier-Fauchier recorded the recipe, some forty years ago, as follows. Take 1 kilo of bonito steaks about 3 centimetres thick, roll them in flour and fry them in very hot oil. Put them aside, once cooked, in a salad bowl. Chop a large onion finely and fry it gently in the same oil, until it begins to turn brown. Add 2 very large cloves of garlic, into which you have stuck a few cloves (the kind used as a spice), one hot red pepper, a few sprigs of thyme, a bay leaf, one sprig of parsley, a pinch of salt and two of paprika, and 1½ wineglassfuls of tarragon vinegar made from wild tarragon. Cook for 15 minutes, taking care that the sauce does not reduce too much. Then pour it over the bonito steaks so that they are completely covered. The dish may be eaten afterwards either hot or cold.

RECIPES.
Palamut Papaz Yahnisi, p. 368.

Orcynopsis unicolor Geoffroy Saint-Hilaire
FAO 191A

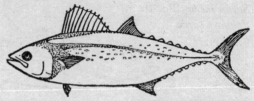

REMARKS. Maximum length 80 cm. or possibly a little more. Uncommon in the Mediterranean generally, though not a rarity along the North African coast as far as and just beyond Tunisian waters. Its Latin name indicates the absence of markings, although it is usually possible faintly to discern traces of tunny-type marbling and some horizontal stripes. However, the general effect is of a silver fish with touches of gold in the fins. The fish is comparatively thin.

CUISINE. Greatly esteemed by the inhabitants of Tunis, who most often fry it (cut into steaks) or use it for fish couscous. Indeed it is so sought after in Tunis that it commands twice the price of kindred species. I hope some day to apply to this excellent fish the advice of Archestratus on cooking bonito – to wrap it in fig leaves with some marjoram and cook it under the hot ashes.

French: Palomète
Italian: Palamita bianca
Spanish: Tasarte
Tunisian: Qalaqt
Other names: Dieuzeide gives the names Casarte (Mauritania) and Kallach (Tripolitania) which look like versions of the Spanish and Tunisian names. The Spanish name is in fact from the Canary Islands, and the fish seems to be unknown on the Mediterranean coast of Spain. Also Bonite blanche, Bonite plate.

The Family Thunnidae

The Mediterranean contains a wide selection of fish in the tunny family, ranging from the huge blue-fin tuna down to the frigate mackerel, which being no bigger than the two mackerel already listed is naturally enough called a mackerel in popular nomenclature, but for technical reasons (such as having a corselet of larger scales) counts as a tuna. The yellow-fin tuna is the most notable absentee. Of the species listed, only the blue-fin tuna enters British waters. But all, and others too, are found in American waters.

The tuna fisheries in the Mediterranean are of considerable commercial importance and great antiquity. Blue-fin tuna are caught in large numbers in special tuna traps during their breeding migrations. Although the number of these traps has diminished in recent centuries, and the size of the catch is dwindling, there are still about a hundred left, including many in Sicily and substantial numbers in Spain, other parts of Italy, Yugoslavia, Greece, Turkey, Libya, Tunisia, Algeria and Morocco. There is evidence that comparable traps were used in neolithic times, and certainly in classical times.

A Mediterranean tuna trap consists of a long net stretching out to sea which intercepts the migrating fish and diverts them into a series of pounds (the trap proper, French madrague, Italian isola) ending in the 'death chamber' (Italian camera della morte) or lift net where the fish are finally captured when the net is hauled up far enough to allow them to be taken with gaffs. 'It is the first tuna of the catch that are most difficult to heave aboard. After ten minutes or so the rest of the fish in the death chamber either kill each other in their struggles or can be taken half dead' (*The Sicilian Tuna Trap*, a detailed and fascinating study by Dr Vito Fodera). This horrendous and bloody scene (to which Aeschylus likened the slaughter of the Persians at Salamis) is the famous mattanza of Sicily.

The migratory movements of the tuna are still not fully understood and charted. Aristotle's view was that they came in from the Atlantic in the spring, travelled east along the North African coast to spawning grounds in the eastern Mediterranean and the Black Sea and then returned via Greece, Italy, the south coast of France and Spain to the Atlantic. Only in the nineteenth century was evidence marshalled to show that for once Aristotle had not been correct. It now seems that the majority of tuna in the Mediterranean stay there throughout the year and that they do not perform the arduous Mediterranean tour, or obstacle race past the traps, which Aristotle postulated, but instead make more localized migratory movements for the purpose of spawning, coming inshore during the early summer (on their way to spawn, when they are known in Italy as tonni di corso) and again in the late summer and autumn (tonni di ritorno), when they are evidently returning from the spawning ground. The partial mystery surrounding their movements is to be explained by the great difficulty of tagging them. Not only are they too large and active to be tagged easily, but they are also so valuable that it is extremely expensive – and incomprehensible to the fishermen – to release a captured tunny, with a tag on it which may of course never be seen again. However it is possible to make accurate observations from certain vantage points. For example the tuna pass the Golden Horn in great numbers when migrating northwards into the Black Sea for summer spawning, and the numbers coming out again in the autumn and winter can be checked too. Pliny believed that the name Golden Horn was given to mark their abundance; and they certainly occur on many Byzantine coins.

Dr Pasquale Arena has given an interesting account of a 'caravan' of tunny which he observed spawning not far from the Aeolian Islands. It was a kilometre in length and 20 metres wide. Some tunny were swimming on the surface, some as far down as 10 metres. The average distance between the tunny was about 2 metres. So (his arithmetic, not mine) there were 10,000 of them. Each weighed about 200–300 kilogrammes. As they swam, a dozen or so at a time would turn off to their left sides, whereupon another dozen from behind would swish forward, on their right sides, and rub bellies with the first lot as they passed. The caravan, incidentally, was not heading for some predetermined destination, like a flock of migratory birds: it turned almost right about on reaching a mass of water which was slightly warmer. It is plausible to suppose, on the basis of this kind of evidence, that the migratory movements of the tunny are mainly governed by water temperatures and by the movements of other fish on which the tunny feed.

Tunny, Bluefin tuna

Thunnus thynnus (Linnaeus)
Orcynnus thynnus
FAO 192

REMARKS. Maximum length 200 cm. The biggest member of the family, and a rapid, powerful swimmer. The back is dark blue.

CUISINE. The flesh of the tunny is very firm and compact, and rather heavy. The best part is what the Italians and Spaniards call *ventresca*. It is most commonly bought in tins, but may also be cooked fresh. For example, steaks may be grilled, or braised in white wine with shallots, tomatoes, garlic, etc. The eggs, salted and pressed, make a good boutargue. One method of cooking which might work well with small specimens of other species of this family is to cook them en papillote, sealed up in aluminium foil or greaseproof paper with butter and herbs.

French: Thon rouge
Greek: Tónnos
Italian: Tonno
Spanish: Atún
Tunisian: Toun ahmar
Turkish: Orkinos
Other names: Tonyina (Cat.); Tonn (Malta); Toun (Midi); Tunj (S. C.)

RECIPES.
Petits Pâtés au Thon, p. 308
Thon en Chartreuse, p. 309.
Tunisian Tunny Salads, p. 380.
Brik à l'Oeuf au Thon, p. 379.

Ragu di Tonno, p. 345.
Tonno alla Genovese, p. 345.
Conchas de Atún, p. 272.
Tunj Kao Pašticada, p. 386.

Albacore, Longfin tunny

Thunnus alalunga (Bonnaterre)
FAO 193

REMARKS. Maximum length 100 cm. A fish of the seven seas, but not so common in the Mediterranean. Easily recognized by its long pectoral fins (to which the name *alalunga* refers). The back is dark blue, the flesh lighter in colour than that of No. 192. In the U.S.A. this is the only tunny which can be tinned as 'white meat tuna'. (Other species provide 'light meat tuna'.)

French: Germon
Greek: Tónnos macrópteros
Italian: Alalonga
Spanish: Albacora
Tunisian: Ghzel
Turkish: Yazılı orkinos
Other names: Thon blanc (Fr.)

CUISINE. As No. 192. The albacore is generally, but not universally, considered better.

Little tunny

Euthynnus alletteratus (Rafinesque)
Thynnus thunnina
FAO 194

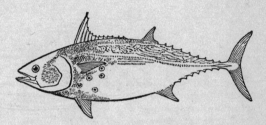

REMARKS. Maximum length 80 cm. *Alletteratus* refers to the marks like scribbling on the fish's back. This is also the meaning of the Turkish name – literally, written-upon tunny – and is indicated in numerous local Italian names such as letterato (Adriatic coast).

CUISINE. As No. 192.

French: Thonine
Greek: Karvoúni
Italian: Tonnetto
Spanish: Bacoreta
Tunisian: Toun sghir
Turkish: Yazılı orkinos
Other names: Bacorète (Alg.); Tunnaġġ (Malta, according to Burdon, although Lanfranco reserves the name for the young specimens of No. 192); Tonyina (Cat.)

Skipjack, Oceanic bonito

Katsuwonus pelamis (Linnaeus)
Euthynnus pelamis
FAO 195

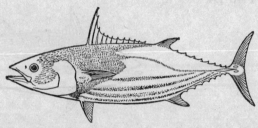

REMARKS. Maximum length 80 cm. This species is more common in the Atlantic and Pacific than in the Mediterranean, where it is mainly to be found along the North African coast. To be recognized by the parallel dark blue stripes running fore and aft along its belly. Katsuwo is the name of this fish in Japan, where it is very common.

French: Bonite à ventre rayé
Italian: Tonnetto listato
Spanish: Listado
Tunisian: Balamit
Other names: Palomida (Cat.); Bonita (It.)

CUISINE. As No. 192.

Frigate mackerel

Auxis thazard (Lacépède)
FAO 196

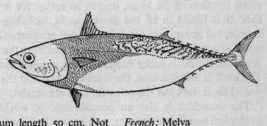

REMARKS. Maximum length 50 cm. Not unlike No. 194, but smaller and with more of a gap between the two dorsal fins.

CUISINE. The flesh is markedly red and somewhat indigestible. Otherwise as No. 192.

French: Melva
Greek: Kopáni
Italian: Tombarello
Spanish: Melva
Tunisian: Tebrelli
Turkish: Gobene
Other names: Mèlvera (Bal.);
  Bonitou (Midi)

The Luvar and the Swordfish

We move now to the families *Luvaridae* and *Xiphiidae*. I could not resist mentioning the luvar, despite its rarity, for it is such a splendid fish. It is found in all the great oceans, including the Atlantic and Pacific, but occurs very rarely in the northern part of the Atlantic and is not at all common in the Mediterranean (and is not therefore catalogued). The reader who is lucky enough to see one will not forget the sight. The back is metallic blue, the sides pink-red and the belly silvery; the dorsal fin is dark but the other fin rays are scarlet.

The swordfish is also an oceanic fish, of worldwide distribution in tropical and temperate seas, well known to North Americans and an occasional visitor to British waters. The sailfish, marlin and spearfish are of similar construction and familiar to Americans but are not found in the Mediterranean except for the comparatively rare *Tetrapturus belone* Rafinesque (Spanish marlín, Italian aguglia imperiale, English spearfish, American longbill spearfish).

Classical authors, as well as modern ones, have made much of stories about swordfish embedding their swords deep into the timbers of ships. And in classical times, as now, the swordfish was mostly hunted by harpoon or caught in the tunny traps. A traveller in Sicily in the eighteenth century recorded that the Sicilian fishermen used a Greek sentence as a charm to lure the swordfish to their boats: if the fish overheard a word of Italian he would plunge under water at once and make off.

Swordfish

Xiphias gladius Linnaeus
FAO 199

REMARKS. Maximum length 400 cm. The sword is reputedly used for flailing around among banks of smaller fish, which are thus killed or stunned. The swordfish is found throughout the Mediterranean and in the Black Sea, whither it migrates in the spring, to return in August.

CUISINE. Swordfish steaks, familiar to Americans, are delicious grilled. Dress with a thread of wine vinegar, nothing more. They may also be cooked à la meunière. Turkish smoked swordfish are prepared thus: wash them, then salt them well and keep them in wood for eighteen hours or so. Next take them out and wash them in seawater or mild brine, and leave them to air in a draught. Finally, smoke them over oak shavings for ten to twelve hours.

French: Espadon
Greek: Xiphiós
Italian: Pesce spada
Spanish: Pez espada
Tunisian: Bou sif
Turkish: Kılıç balığı
Other names: Empereur (and variations such as the Spanish Emperador); Peix espada (Cat.)

RECIPES.
Impanata di Pesce Spada, p. 340.　　Kılıç Domatesli, p. 366.
Kılıç Şişte, p. 367.

The Pomfret, the Sand-eel, the Blennies and the Gobies

We shall now consider the families *Stromateidae*, *Ammodytidae*, *Blenniidae* and *Gobiidae*. The *Stromateidae* are not represented in British waters, but an array of them including the Pacific pompano and the butterfish of the Atlantic coast are available in North American waters.

The *Ammodytidae* or sand-eels are not of much direct interest to human fish-eaters, but they are of considerable indirect interest, since they are essential to the diet of many important food fishes. The Third Fisherman in Shakespeare's Pericles asks: 'Master, I marvel how the fishes live in the sea.' The First Fisherman replies: 'Why, as men do on land; the great ones eat up the little ones.' We have to remember that the creatures of the oceans supply food for each other on a far greater scale than for us. European North Atlantic waters are rich in sand-eels, and North Americans have three species which are called sand-lances.

Blennies too, for what they are worth (not very much), occur in wide variety in British and North American waters. So do gobies, of which there are over forty North American species and over a dozen northern European ones. The gobies are interesting fish for the ichthyologist, but even the bigger and edible species are not generally thought of as exciting food. 'The gobies are not food for the gods but for very ordinary men' was an ancient Greek opinion which most Mediterranean people would endorse today. Latin authors contrasted the goby with luxury fish like tunny, but a dissenting Venetian view was recorded by Martial:

> 'At Venice,* famed for dainty dishes,
> The Gobies rank the first of fishes.'

There is also evidence of particular interest in gobies around the Black Sea, where, according to Pliny, 'the fish most frequently caught in the ice is the goby, which is only made to reveal the movement of life by the heat of the saucepan'. This local interest is maintained today by Turks.

*The reference is to the province of Venice, not to the city, which had not been established when Martial wrote.

Pomfret

Stromateus fiatola (Linnaeus)
FAO 201

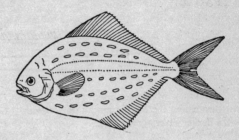

REMARKS. Maximum length 35 cm. Grey, with oval golden marks running in interrupted bands from front to back. Not very common, and seems to be absent from the north-east Mediterranean.

CUISINE. Not especially good, but they can be grilled, and should be all right fried.

French: Fiatole
Italian: Fieto
Spanish: Pámpano
Tunisian: Elmiss
Other names: Pudenta (Cat.); Stromatée (Fr.); Figue (Alg.); Figa, Fica, etc. in various parts of Italy

Sand-eel

Gymnammodytes cicerellus (Rafinesque)
FAO 204

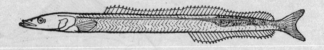

REMARKS. Maximum length 18 cm. Found throughout the Mediterranean. Silver, with a darker silvery-green back.

CUISINE. Worth frying.

French: Cicerelle
Greek: Loutsáki
Italian: Cicerello
Spanish: Barrinaire
Turkish: Kum balığı
Other names: Lançon,
   Équille (Fr., both used
   more of the Atlantic
   species); Sonso (Cat.)
   and Enfú (Bal.

Blenny

***Blennius* sp.**
FAO 205–8

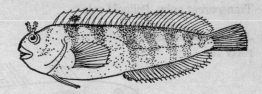

REMARKS. A collection of small fish, whose maximum lengths run from 8 to 20 cm., which come in black, grey and red colour schemes. The one illustrated is ***Blennius gattorugine*** Brunnich, the tompot or rock blenny (207).

CUISINE. Normally used for fish soups.

French: Baveuse
Greek: Saliára
Italian: Bavosa
Spanish: Torillo, Baboso
Tunisian: Senegaless, or (?) Mrel
Turkish: Horozbina
Other names: Bavosa (Cat.); Raboa (Bal.)

Transparent goby, Pellucid sole

Aphia minuta (Risso)
FAO 212

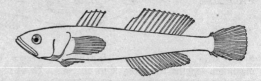

REMARKS. Maximum length 5 or 6 cm. This tiny fish belongs to the family of gobies (see next entry) and is presented here by itself since it is unusual in being virtually without colour.

French: Nounat
Greek: Goviodáki
Italian: Rossetto
Spanish: Chanquete
Other names: The Italian name Nonnati is a variant of the French name.

CUISINE. Despite its small size the transparent goby is eaten with enthusiasm in various parts of the Mediterranean. They are a popular dish at Málaga, fried in batter, golden brown with the eyes standing out as tiny dots, and served with lemon. According to Faber they are good baked in milk.

RECIPES.

See under Poutine, Nonnat and Melet, p. 291.

Chanquetes and Aladroch, p. 273.

Goby

Gobius sp.
FAO 213–15

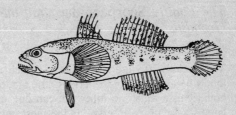

REMARKS. Maximum length mostly about 15 cm. Dieuzeide lists sixteen different species to be found off the coast of Algeria. Only a few gobies are big enough to be worth eating.

The illustration is of *Gobius niger* Linnaeus, the black goby (213).

CUISINE. Fry.

French: Gobie
Greek: Goviós
Italian: Ghiozzo
Spanish: Cabot
Tunisian: Boughill, or (?) Zankour
Turkish: Kaya*
Other names: Gòbit (Cat.); Goujon, Chabot (Fr.)

*The general name, to which various additions are made according to the species. Thus kumurcun kayası and saz kayası ... a dozen or more. The Turks are discriminating and enthusiastic over the goby.

The Family Scorpaenidae, *and the Gurnards or Grondins*

The rascasses (to use the familiar French name) are an important family because three of them (Nos. 216, 217, 218) can do something for bouillabaisse which no other fish can do; and for me at least a fine large scarlet rascasse serves as the most apt and memorable symbol of Mediterranean fish generally, and for this reason appeared on the cover of the original version of this book when it was published in Tunis. The three 'genuine' rascasses are not matched in British waters (but see the note on No. 219), and I simply do not know what the position is in North American waters where there are no fewer than six dozen members of the family to be found. Someone would have to experiment with all these species in order to discover which, if any, could claim the properties of their Mediterranean relations; and so far as I can discover this research has not yet been carried out.

Next come the families *Triglidae* and *Peristediidae*. In the first family I catalogue five from a septet of Mediterranean species, while the second consists only of the armed gurnard. There are half a dozen species in British waters and about twenty in North American waters (where they are known as sea-robins).

Gurnards are gregarious fish and can keep in touch with one another by producing audible grunts (a feat performed by muscle contractions acting on the swim bladder). This characteristic was described by Aristotle and other ancient authors, and accounts for many of the common names applied to members of the family, for example the English piper, the Marseillais grognant and the Neapolitan cuoccio.

The gurnards are scaly, even armoured, fish, with disproportionately big heads (which do not, incidentally, weigh much). Perhaps because of this outward aspect they are often dismissed as mere 'bouillabaisse'. Or the red ones may hopefully be presented as 'rougets' or 'rouget-grondins'. It is however wrong either to despise them or to imply that they are comparable with red mullet.

Scorpaena porcus Linnaeus
FAO 216

REMARKS. Maximum length 25 cm. A brown fish with darker markings reminiscent of camouflage – which is indeed their purpose and accounts for their being variable. Common throughout the Mediterranean, in shallow water.

French: Rascasse noire
Greek: Scórpena
Italian: Scorfano nero
Spanish: Rascacio
Tunisian: Bou keshesh aghel
Turkish: İskorpit
Other names: Rascasse brune (Fr.); Bodeč, Škrpun (S. C.)

CUISINE. See No. 217. This is presumably the species of which Méry wrote:

> 'La rascasse, poisson, certes, des plus vulgaires.
> Isolé sur un gril, on ne l'estime guère,
> Mais dans la bouillabaisse aussitôt il répand
> De merveilleux parfums d'où le succès dépend.
> La rascasse, nourrie aux crevasses des syrtes
> Dans les golfes couverts de lauriers et de myrtes,
> Ou devant un rocher garni de fleurs de thym.'

One sympathizes with the implication that the rascasse manages to absorb the flavours of the aromatic herbs on the cliffs, although nowadays these have to contend more and more with non-aromatic pollutants in the water.

Scorpion fish

Scorpaena scrofa Linnaeus
FAO 217

REMARKS. Maximum length 55 cm. Red or orange is the dominant colour, but this is variable. Like No. 216 this species is found all over the Mediterranean, but in deeper water (20 fathoms or more).

CUISINE. This and No. 216 are the two best rascasses for bouillabaisse, and this is their principal use. But a large rascasse rouge may be successfully baked (baste often with butter) and will then present a dramatic appearance at table, providing good helpings of remarkably firm white flesh – not unlike that of the lobster. Do not neglect to eat the cheeks.

French: Rascasse rouge
Greek: Scórpena
Italian: Scorfano rosso
Spanish: Cabracho
Tunisian: Bou keshesh ahmar
Turkish: Lipsos, Kırmızı
  iskorpit
Other names: Cap roig (Bal.);
  Chapon, Capoun (Midi);
  Bodeljka, Škrpina (S. C.)

RECIPES.
Cassoulet de Rascasse à la Suffren,
  p. 303.

Cap-roig con Salsa de Almendra,
  p. 273.
Brudet, p. 384.

Scorpaena notata Rafinesque
Scorpaena ustulata
FAO 218

REMARKS. Maximum length 18 cm. *Ustulata* means with burn-like marks upon it. Brownish. May be found throughout the Mediterranean, but is a good deal less common than the two preceding species.

CUISINE. For bouillabaisse and other fish soups.

French: Petite rascasse
Greek: Scorpiós
Italian: Scorfanotto
Spanish: Escórpora *
Tunisian: Bou keshesh sghir
Turkish: İskorpit
Other names: Garde-écueil (Fr.)

*The official Spanish name, but the species is rare in Spanish waters and the name is more often used of Nos. 216 and 217.

Blue-mouth

Helicolenus dactylopterus (Delaroche)
Sebastes dactyloptera
Scorpaena dactyloptera
FAO 219

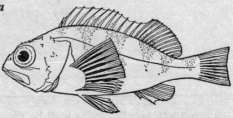

REMARKS. Maximum length 30 cm. Reddish brown in colour. This member of the family is available in North American waters (see the researches described by A. J. Liebling in the *New Yorker* of 27 October 1962), and in British waters. In the Mediterranean it is found in the western and central parts.

French: Rascasse de fond
Greek: Sevastós
Italian: Scorfano di fondale
Spanish: Gallineta
Tunisian: Bou keshesh
Other names: Chèvre (Fr., Alg.); Badasco (Marseille); Cordonniero (Nice); Panegall (Cat.)

CUISINE. The French allow that this is a rascasse, and one may treat it so (see No. 217). But from the point of view of the cook it really seems closer to two other members of the family which are found in Scottish and North Atlantic waters but not in the Mediterranean: *Sebastes viviparus* Kroyer (the Norway haddock) and *Sebastes marinus* (Linnaeus) (the red-fish, often also referred to as Norway haddock). And these last species are in demand for the manufacture of fish fingers rather than for incorporation in bouillabaisse! I judge it best to treat the blue-mouth as you would a member of the bream family. It is indeed sometimes called, incorrectly, red bream in Britain.

Piper

Trigla lyra (Linnaeus)
FAO 220

REMARKS. Maximum length 50 cm. Red back, rosy sides, silvery belly. Lives in comparatively deep water.

CUISINE. A sizeable member of the family. These larger gurnards have firm white flesh, easy to digest, of good flavour and comparatively free of troublesome bones, but tending to be rather dry. They may be cooked whole, in fillets or cut into sections. A large one, gutted and seasoned, may be baked in the oven with white wine, chopped mushrooms and slices of lemon. Or it may be simmered in water, left to cool and dressed with mayonnaise (a method popular in Turkey). Epicharmus (of Sicily) recommended that gurnards be fried in oil, spiced and served in vinegar, a procedure which some authors believe to have survived in the cuoccio marinato or soused gurnard of Naples.

French: Grondin lyre
Greek: Capóni
Italian: Capone lira
Spanish: Garneo
Tunisian: Djaje, or Serdouk
Turkish: Öksüz
Other names: Garneu (Cat.)

RECIPE.
Gurnard with Almond Sauce, p. 367.

Tub gurnard, Tub-fish

Trigla hirundo (Linnaeus)
Trigla lucerna
FAO 221

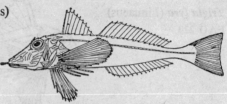

REMARKS. Maximum length 60 cm. The back is usually of a yellowish or greyish rose. The pectoral fins (red with peacock-blue and green spots and margin) provide an instant recognition point.

CUISINE. The largest member of the family and one of the best. See No. 220.

French: Grondin galinette, Galinette
Greek: Capóni
Italian: Capone gallinella
Spanish: Bejel
Tunisian: Djaje, or Serdouk
Turkish: Kırlangıç balığı
Other names: Perlon (Provence)

Streaked gurnard

Trigla lineata (Pennant)
Trigloporus lastoviza
FAO 222

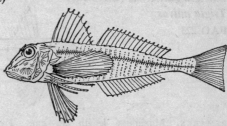

REMARKS. Maximum length 35 cm. Bright red – hence the French imbriago, which means drunkard. The lines slanting across the body are a distinguishing feature which account for the Latin and English names.

CUISINE. Another good one. See No. 220.

French: Grondin imbriago
Greek: Capóni
Italian: Capone ubriaco
Spanish: Rubio
Tunisian: Djaje, or Serdouk
Turkish: Mazak
Other names: Camard (Fr.); Lluerna (Cat.); Kokot (S. C.)

Grey gurnard

Eutrigla gurnardus (Linnaeus)
Trigla milvus
FAO 223

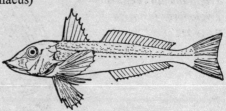

REMARKS. Maximum length 40 cm. Usually grey, with little white spots. This is the most common gurnard in British waters, and it is sometimes landed and marketed.

CUISINE. Fairly good. See No. 220.

French: Grondin gris
Greek: Capóni
Italian: Capone gurno
Spanish: Borracho*
Tunisian: Djaje, or Serdouk
Turkish: Benekli kırlangıç
Other names: Oriola vera (Bal.)

* This name means drunkard and in some places it is used, as one would expect, for the preceding species. Spanish nomenclature for the gurnards is particularly confusing.

Red gurnard

Aspitrigla cuculus (Linnaeus)*
Trigla pini
FAO 224

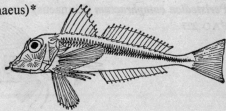

REMARKS Maximum length 40 cm. Deep red in colour. Note the pronounced lateral line, which reminded the naturalist Bloch of pine leaves (hence *Trigla pini*) and the marked taper to the tail. Common in British waters.

CUISINE. Again, a good one. See No. 220.

French: Grondin
Greek: Capóni
Italian: Capone coccio
Spanish: Arete
Tunisian: Djaje, or Serdouk
Turkish: Kırlangıç balığı
Other names: Gallineta (Cat.); Peix de San Rafel (Bal.)

*I have now catalogued five species of the family *Triglidae*, which is quite enough. But I mention here two others. *Aspitrigla obscura* (Linnaeus), the long-finned gurnard, is reddish grey in colour with a pearly pink lateral line and a very long spine at the front of the first dorsal fin. It is less common than the preceding species. *Lepidotrigla cavillone* (Lacépède) is the smallest Mediterranean gurnard (maximum length 15 cm.) and suitable only for use in fish soups. The usual gurnard names are applied to it; also caviglione (Italian), cabete (Spanish) and capet (Catalan).

Armed gurnard

Peristedion cataphractum (Linnaeus)

FAO 227

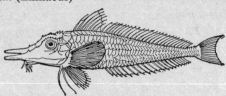

REMARKS. Maximum length 25 cm. The forked snout of this fish makes it quite unmistakable. Red in colour. A very occasional visitor to southern British waters in the time of Queen Victoria, but not more recently.

CUISINE. See No. 220. I particularly enjoyed a malarmat cooked aboard the Tunisian trawler which was commanded by Captain Luigi Drago. The fish was taken straight from the trawl, gutted and skinned and cut into sections – which were then simmered in water with herbs and seasoning, and served with a freshly made tomato sauce.

French: Malarmat
Greek: Capóni keratás
Italian: Pesce forca
Spanish: Armado
Tunisian: Serdouk (preferred to Djaje in this instance)
Turkish: Dikenli öksüz
Other names: Peï furco (Provence); Armat, Ase (Bal.)

Flatfish: 1 Sinistral

Here we pass to the order *Heterosomata*, which is the order of flatfish. The king of flatfish, the halibut, is not found in the Mediterranean, but sole, turbot, and other good species are. Generally speaking, both British and North American waters offer a range as good as or better than the Mediterranean one. But hideous complications attend any attempt to draw up comparative lists, since American popular nomenclature is differently based (see p. 244).

Flatfish start life upright, but when they are still tiny they turn over on to one side, which then becomes the belly and stays white, or anyway pale. The eye and the nostril on the belly side move up over the head and join the other eye and nostril on what has now become the back of the fish. The mouth changes shape, and the back takes on a colouring which matches the sea bottom and camouflages the fish.

Some flatfish have their eyes on the left side, some on the right. They are called sinistral or dextral accordingly, and this helps identification (although it is well to remember that the phenomenon known as reversal happens from time to time, which results in some flatfish turning out the wrong way round).

Our review of the Mediterranean flatfish begins with the sinistral ones, which are congregated in the family *Bothidae*. Eight species are listed, of which the brill and turbot (Nos. 230 and 231) are the biggest, the finest to eat and the best known. Both are landed at British ports, and the turbot fishery in particular is important in value, if less so in volume, since many people count the turbot as the best-flavoured of all sea fish and its price is correspondingly high. It is highly esteemed in the Mediterranean, and especially in Turkey. There are interesting Black Sea varieties of the species, and the fishmongers of Istanbul make magnificent and dramatic backdrops to their fish displays by hanging up turbot, with their nail-like protuberances and rosy glow, in a row at the back. The turbot was also a prized fish in classical times, and Juvenal's Fourth Satire is devoted to the story of an enormous turbot which was netted at Ancona on the Adriatic.

Of the other sinistral flatfish listed little need be said. Many are present in British waters and closely matched in North American waters; but the tribes of fausses limandes and scaldfish lack the qualities which excite epicures.

Citharus linguatula (Linnaeus)
FAO 229

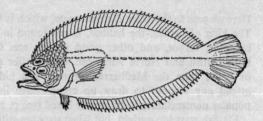

REMARKS. Maximum length 30 cm. The back is straw-coloured or a light greyish colour. The snout is darker.

CUISINE. Fry.

French: Fausse limande
Greek: Glossáki
Italian: Linguattola
Spanish: Solleta
Tunisian: Balay
Turkish: Pisi*
Other names: Palaia rossa (Cat.)

*See footnote on page 171.

Brill

Scophthalmus rhombus (Linnaeus)
Rhombus laevis
FAO 230

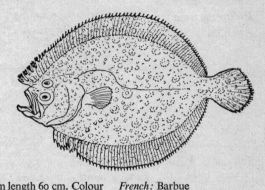

REMARKS. Maximum length 60 cm. Colour variable, but dark on top and without the protuberances of the turbot (hence the Turkish name, which means 'nail-less turbot', and the second of the scientific names shown above, which means 'smooth turbot').

CUISINE. An excellent fish, very like the turbot but with more delicate flesh. Directions given for No. 231 apply.

French: Barbue
Greek: Rómbos-pissí
Italian: Rombo liscio
Spanish: Rémol
Tunisian: M'dess moussa
Turkish: Çivisiz kalkan, Pisi*
Other names: Names like Rhum, Roun and Roumbou in the Midi

*The name pisi (or pissi or pisi balığı) is a difficult one. Having conveyed to the British Museum a fish from Istanbul which had been identified indubitably on the spot as a pisi I learned that it was, equally indubitably, a young brill. But there is evidence for associating the name also with Nos. 229 and 232. A likely explanation is that in popular usage these two other species and young brill (which are all about the same size) share the name.

Turbot

Scophthalmus maximus (Linnaeus)
Rhombus maximus
Psetta maxima
FAO 231

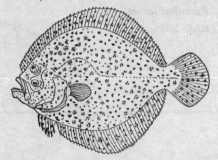

REMARKS. Maximum length 80 cm. or perhaps more. The back is usually a brownish or yellowish grey, spotted with little black and white spots and covered with bony protuberances like nail-heads, very noticeable in the Black Sea variety which appears around the Bosphorus in the Spring – *Scophthalmus maeoticus* (Pallas).

French: Turbot
Greek: Kalkáni
Italian: Rombo chiodato, Rombo
Spanish: Rodaballo
Tunisian: M'dess moussa
Turkish: Kalkan, Kalkan balığı

CUISINE. An excellent fish, which has given its name to the turbotière, a metal cooking-vessel shaped to take the fish whole. The fish may be cooked simmering in water in this and served with, for example, a sauce hollandaise; or cut crosswise into slices and fried, to be served with a sauce tartare; or grilled and served with a sauce béarnaise; or cut into pieces and cooked à la Dugléré (i.e. poached in white wine, which you then use to complete a tomato sauce); or filleted, after which you may use any of the numerous recipes for fillets of sole. Best in winter.

RECIPES.
Suquillo, p. 268.

Elmalı ve Soğanlı Balık, p. 364.

Megrim, Sail-fluke*, Whiff

Lepidorhombus whiffiagonis (Walbaum)
Pleuronectes megastoma
FAO (not given)

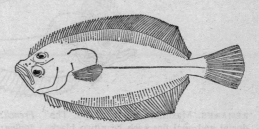

REMARKS. Maximum length 50 cm. This species is to be found only in the western part of the Mediterranean. It is however widely distributed in the eastern Atlantic.

CUISINE. Fry or bake. Medium quality.

French: Cardine
Italian: Rombo giallo
Spanish: Lliseria
Other names: Palaia bruixa (Cat., also for No. 232) and Cappelà (Bal.)

*The peculiar English name sail-fluke is said to reflect a tale from the Orkneys according to which this fish has the habit of up-ending itself, with its tail sticking out of the water and acting as a sail. Some nineteenth-century naturalists accepted the story and one even gave the fish a scientific name, *Zeugopterus velivolans*, which reflects it.

Lepidorhombus boscii (Risso)
Pleuronectes boscii
FAO 232

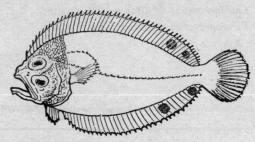

REMARKS. Maximum length 25 cm. The dorsal and anal fins each bear two black spots, not always very noticeable. The back is generally of a pale yellowish translucent colour. Found in the western Mediterranean, but not common, although it is present in fairly large numbers in the Ligurian Sea.

French: Fausse limande
Italian: Rombo quattrocchi
Spanish: Gallo
Tunisian: Balay
Turkish: Pisi*
Other names: Petro
   (Marseille); Petrale (Genoa)

CUISINE. Fry. Medium quality.

* See Footnote on page 171.

Bothus podas (Delaroche)
FAO 233

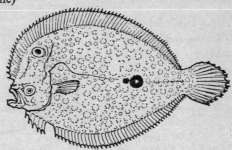

REMARKS. Maximum length 20 cm. Note the wide-spaced eyes and the two dark spots on the back. There may also be quite a lot of lighter spots, bluish and distributed all over the back. The general colour of the back is variable, but grey or a brown-grey is usual.

CUISINE. Fry.

Greek: Píssi
Italian: Rombo di rena
Spanish: Podás
Other names: Puput (Cat.); Pedaç (Bal.)

Scaldfish

Arnoglossus laterna (Walbaum)
Pleuronectes laterna
FAO 235

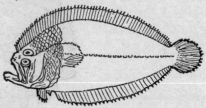

REMARKS. Maximum length 17 cm. The back is an uneven brown in colour. The name scaldfish is derived from the appearance of the fish when caught (scales and skin rub off). Other scaldfish in the Mediterranean include the slightly smaller *Arnoglossus thori* Kyle (Spanish peluda, Catalan palaia rossa, Italian suacia mora). This is a family in which the classification of the various species is still uncertain.

French: Fausse limande
Greek: Arnóglossa
Italian: Suacia
Spanish: Serrandell
Other names: Palaia misèries (Cat.)

CUISINE. Fry.

Flatfish: 2 Dextral

The dextral flatfish in the Mediterranean belong to the families *Pleur-onectidae* and *Soleidae*.

The first of these families includes the plaice and the flounder. The former, *Pleuronectes platessa* Linnaeus, the French plie and Italian passera, is not really a Mediterranean fish, although it may be met at the western end and specimens are occasionally taken in Italian waters. I have not listed it separately, but the reader who comes across one will know it at once by the combination of numerous orange or red spots on its back with a generally flounder-like shape. The dabs and lemon sole familiar to the British do not occur at all in the Mediterranean.

The other family, *Soleidae*, is represented in the Mediterranean by *Solea solea*, which is *the* sole, and by the three other species of which details are given below. All these are good, and of a reasonable size when adult. There are some other species with the same general characteristics which are too small to be of real interest, notably **Solea lutea** Risso (the French petite sole jaune), **Monochirus hispidus** Rafinesque (the French sole velue, an almost shaggy little fish) and **Microchirus variegatus** (Donovan) (a small banded sole found in the western Mediterranean, the Spanish golleta*). There is surprisingly little precision in the nomenclature of members of this family. In many languages one name tends to do for the lot. Perhaps this is a tribute to the efforts which fishmongers and restaurateurs have no doubt been making for thousands of years, as they still do, to invest the inferior members of the family, in the eyes of purchasers, with the merits of the best members. Certainly the reader should not expect his fishmonger to offer him, say, 'sole de Klein', and although for interest I have given correct specific names where these exist it is well to remember that the names which one will meet are (in the familiar order) sole, sole, glóssa, sogliola, lenguado, m'dess and dil.

Solea solea (No. 238) is the species known as 'Dover sole' in Britain. Any idea that most members of the species congregate near Dover is quite wrong. They are wide-ranging and adaptable fish, found anywhere from the eastern Mediterranean to Norway, in inshore and offshore waters.

*The same as the British thickback sole, but a good deal smaller in the Mediterranean and therefore less interesting for the cook.

Flounder

Platichthys flesus (Linnaeus)
Pleuronectes flesus
FAO 237

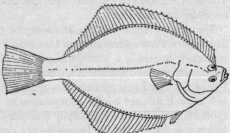

REMARKS. Maximum length 45 cm. There may be two sub-species here – *Platichthys flesus flesus* and *Platichthys flesus italicus*. According to those who make the distinction the former is found in the western Mediterranean only, while the latter is more generally distributed, although most plentiful in the Adriatic. The back is brown, grey

French: Flet
Greek: Chematída
Italian: Passera pianuzza
Spanish: Platija
Turkish: Dere pisisi
Other names: Rèmol de
riu (Cat.); Fluke (Eng.)

or olive, sometimes spotted with black or orange; or a plain green-black.

CUISINE. Fry, if small. Otherwise cook them whole or in fillets according to your choice. One method is to score them in both directions and put them in a shallow oven dish with seasoning, parsley, a little white wine and knobs of butter – then cook in a fast oven to brown them.

Sole

Solea solea (Linnaeus)
FAO 238

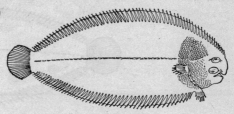

REMARKS. Maximum length 47 cm. The back is usually brown or a yellowish grey.

Incidentally, this is one of the species with a wide range of local names in Italy, e.g. lengua (Genoa), palaia (Naples, etc.), sfoglia (Ancona), sfogio (Venice) and linguata (Sicily).

French: Sole
Greek: Glóssa
Italian: Sogliola
Spanish: Lenguado
Tunisian: M'dess
Turkish: Dil, Dil balığı
Other names: List (S. C.)

CUISINE. A fish renowned for its delicacy and versatility. There is no end to the good recipes which may be employed. The sole is excellent grilled whole, fried, prepared à la meunière, or cooked in court-bouillon. Alternatively it will provide four good fillets with which many culinary feats may be performed.

The preparation of a sole should be carried out as follows. Cut off the head slantwise (because the flesh extends further forward on one side) and then make an incision in the skin of the back at the tail. Grasp the raised skin with a cloth and rip it off in one firm movement. Cut off the lateral fins, then gut, wash and dry the fish. To fillet it you take off the skin of the underside as well, then cut along the line of the spine and ease the fillets off the bone with a flexible knife.

RECIPES.
Sole à la Provençale, p. 308.
Filetti di Sfoglia, Veri e Falsi,
    p. 343.

Sogliole alla Parmigiana, p. 343.

Solea ocellata (Linnaeus)
FAO 239

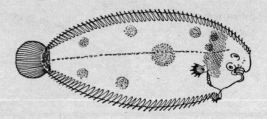

REMARKS. Maximum length 25 cm. The large dark spots are distinctive. The general colour of the back is brown.

CUISINE. See No. 238. Very good.

French: Sole ocellée
Greek: Glóssa
Italian: Sogliola occhiuta
Spanish: Tambor real
Tunisian: M'dess
Turkish: Dil, Dil balığı
Other names: Soldat (Cat.);
   Pégouse (Fr.)

French sole, Lascar

Pegusa lascaris (Risso)
Solea lascaris
FAO 241

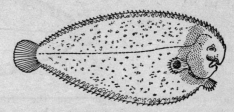

REMARKS. Maximum length 35 cm. Variable in colour. The spot on the pectoral fin is distinctive, but the whole back is usually patched and spotted.

CUISINE. See No. 238. Also good.

French: Sole à pectorale ocellée
Italian: Sogliola dal porro
Spanish: Sortija, Lenguado
Tunisian: M'dess
Turkish: Dil, Dil balığı

Solea kleini (Risso)
FAO 242

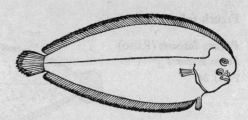

REMARKS. Maximum length 25 cm. The black rim on the fins is distinctive. Klein was an eighteenth-century German naturalist.

CUISINE. See No. 238. This one is small but good.

French: Sole de Klein, Sole tachetée
Greek: Glóssa
Italian: Sogliola turca
Spanish: Suela, Lenguado
Tunisian: M'dess
Turkish: Dil, Dil balığı
Other names: Palaia petit (Cat. also for No. 241)

Trigger-Fish and Angler-Fish

Finally we have the order *Plectognathi* containing the family *Balistidae* which features the trigger-fish, and the order *Pediculati* containing the family *Lophiidae* of which the angler-fish is a member.

The order *Plectognathi* contains some remarkable fish with inflatable prickle-covered bellies, but these do not concern us here. The trigger-fish, which does, occurs in North American waters (where it is known as the grey trigger-fish) along with many close relations, and is occasionally taken in British waters. 'The name trigger-fish and indeed its generic name *Balistes* are given to these fish because of the curious structure of the spiny dorsal fin. The large first dorsal spine, when erected, locks into position and cannot be lowered manually. The small third spine, however, acts as a trigger, and when this is depressed the locking apparatus on the first spine base is released and the fin folds down.' (Wheeler.)

The angler-fish is found in northern European waters and has recently become an important commercial fish, of which Britain and Spain take the largest share. A close relation of our species is found in the American Atlantic (this is *Lophius americanus* Valenciennes, the goosefish). The angler-fish is aptly named, since it really does angle. Its habit is to excavate and settle into a shallow depression on the bottom. By the time sand particles disturbed by this process have drifted down over the angler it is almost invisible and ready to start 'angling'. The technique captures a wide variety of prey, and its very success brought down on this fish the disapproval of Oppian (*Halieutica* II, 199) who referred to it as the day-sleeper, observing that

he knows no satiety of food nor any measure, but in his shameless belly he nurses gluttony, rabid and endless, nor would he cease from feeding if the food were at hand till his belly itself burst utterly in the midst and himself fall flat upon his back . . .

There is a lesson to be drawn here for man, as Oppian does not fail to point out. I again use Mair's translation.

Hear, ye generations of men, what manner of issue there is to gluttonous folly, what pain follows upon excessive eating. Let a man therefore drive far from heart and hand idleness that delights in evil pleasure, and observe measure in eating. . . . For many such there be among men who hold the reins loose and allow all rope to their belly. But let a man behold and avoid the end of the day-sleeper.*

This is excellent advice although characteristically presented with too much emphasis for modern ears.

Some readers may notice the absence, from this part of the catalogue, of an entry for the shark sucker, **Remora remora** (Linnaeus) of the family *Echeneididae* in the order *Discocephali*. Aristotle and the elder Pling both dismissed it as unfit for eating; and in modern times too it is indeed a rarity in the market or on the table. However, Pliny did admit that it could be beneficial for pregnant women, and more recently the Italian expert Cavanna thought it worth poaching or stewing; on which basis, and because it is a curiosity of marine life, I mention it here.

The shark sucker, which is no bigger than 40 cm., has a disc on top of its head, by which it can attach itself to sharks and other large fish and even to boats. Its classical Greek name *echeneis* means literally 'ship-holder', and many classical writers from Ovid onwards dealt with this theme. Here is Philemon Holland's version of a passage in Pliny:

The current of the sea is great, the tide much, and more than that, ores and sails withal . . . are mighty and powerful; and yet there is one little sillie fish, named Echeneis, that checketh, scorneth and arresteth them all. Let the winds blow as much as they will, rage the storms and tempests what they can, yet this little fish commandeth their fury, restraineth their puissance, and . . . compelleth ships to stand still.

Antony's ship was said to have been held so at Actium; and Caligula's on his way to Antium, although he had 400 lusty rowers on board. Such tales recur in later literature. Thus Spenser in *Visions of the Worlds Vanitie*, writing of a proud sailing ship: 'All sodainely there clove unto her keele A little fish, that men call Remora, Which stopt her course, and held her by the heele. . . .' It is true that small ships do sometimes lose way unaccountably, as if gripped from below. But Nansen's experience of this phenomenon on his polar voyages led to an explanation which absolved the shark sucker from responsibility.

*I should explain that I definitely take Oppian's day-sleeper to be the angler-fish. The suggestion that the star-gazer (No. 185) is meant here is defensible by academic argument but quite inappropriate. The name 'day-sleeper' had, incidentally, already been used by Hesiod with reference to burglars.

Trigger-fish

Balistes carolinensis Gmelin
Balistes capriscus
FAO 246

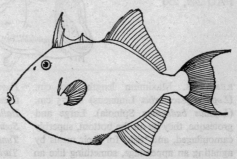

REMARKS. Maximum length 40 cm. A strange fish, with strong teeth. They are said to swim around in pairs. If you hook one pull it in quickly or the other will bite through the line.

Although the trigger-fish is known throughout the Mediterranean it is more common in the southerly parts. Thus it is regularly taken in Tunisian waters, but rarely off the Italian mainland. Not found in the Black Sea.

French: Baliste
Greek: Gourounópsaro
Italian: Pesce balestra
Spanish: Pez ballesta
Tunisian: Hallouf bahr (pig of the sea)
Turkish: Çotira balığı
Other names: Cochon de mer (Fr.); Pisci porcu (Sicily); Bot (Cat.) and Surer (Bal.)

CUISINE. The skin of this fish is very tough and must be removed before cooking. Esteemed by some, including the author, disdained by others. Let the hesitant note that Professor Bini, tasting the fish for the first time, in Tunisia, thought it very good.

RECIPE.
Baliste, Sauce aux Olives, p. 376.

Angler-fish

Lophius sp.
FAO 249, 250

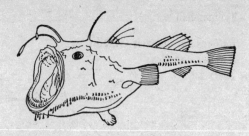

REMARKS. Maximum length 150 cm. (*Lophius piscatorius* Linnaeus) or 75 cm. (*Lophius budegassa* Spinola). Large and grotesque, they lie on the bottom, superbly camouflaged, and 'fish' for their meals by agitating an appendage, something like an angler's rod, over their mouths. When they open their mouths the little fish which have come to investigate are engulfed.

The illustration is of No. 249, the larger of the two species.

French: Baudroie
Greek: Vatrachópsaro
Italian: Rana pescatrice
Spanish: Rape
Tunisian: Ra'asha
Turkish: Fener (lamp)*
　balığı
Other names: Monkfish,
　Monk (but cf. No. 26);
　Rap (Cat.); Lotte (Fr.);
　Rospo (It.); Budicu
　(Corsica); Grdobina (S. C.)

CUISINE. The tail is good to eat – firm, white and lobster-like. Coda di Rospo is a prized dish in Venice.

RECIPES.
Flan de Baudroie, p. 296.
Coda di Rospo, p. 341.

Rape, Spanish Ways with Angler-Fish, p. 278.

*With reference to the shape of ancient oil-lamps.

3. Catalogue of Crustaceans Molluscs, etc.

(1) THE CRUSTACEANS

The crustaceans are not, strictly speaking, shell-fish, although often so described. They are members of the animal phylum *Arthropoda*, which also includes the spiders, scorpions and insects. Like these other creatures they are covered with hard, horny carapaces which are jointed for movement and sloughed from time to time as their owners grow. Many have a characteristic change of colour when cooked, for example the blue-black lobster which turns scarlet and the semi-transparent shrimp which turns pink and white.

I deal here successively with the three orders *Decapoda Natantia*, *Decapoda Reptantia* and *Stomatopoda*, that is to say 'ten-legged swimmers', 'ten-legged crawlers' and 'mouth-feet'. In the first category are prawns, shrimp, lobster, etc. The second consists of the crabs. In the third there is only the peculiar mantis shrimp.

First, however, some points which apply generally to all these orders. It is to be noted that crustaceans are at their best when the ovaries are well developed. There are also grounds for selecting specimens whose carapaces are encrusted and therefore old. It may be assumed that the occupant has had plenty of time to grow into and fill the carapace, whereas the occupant of a soft new carapace will probably still be too small for it. (But see p. 202 on soft-shell crabs.)

Finally, I should mention the question of killing crustaceans humanely. This is particularly difficult for the lobster and its relations, since these creatures have a markedly diffuse nervous system, which cannot feasibly be put out of action by stabbing. Splitting a lobster from head to tail by a single blow kills it at once, but most people are disinclined to adopt this technique, and it tends to be messy. Some have recommended putting the live lobster in cold water and raising the heat gradually, on the ground that his process induces first a stupor and then, at the relatively low temperature of 40° C or so, death. On the other hand, the Universities Federation for Animal Welfare in Britain

(UFAW) advocate plunging the live creature into a gallon of rapidly boiling water, and cite experimental evidence to support the view that this brings about a quick death (probably in fewer than 15 seconds) and may be regarded as less inhumane than any other practicable method. Crabs may, however, be tackled in a different way, since their nervous systems have only two centres. Two stabs with a pin (for little crabs) or something more substantial (for big ones) will therefore suffice. Both should be delivered from below. One is to pierce the ventral nerve centre, while the second penetrates the front nerve centre. You could ask a fishmonger or other expert to indicate the right spots. It is better still to have handy the UFAW pamphlet: *The Humane Killing of Lobsters and Crabs*, which contains helpful drawings, and (for those who regularly kill large crabs) to buy from UFAW their special awl for piercing crabs.

Prawns and Shrimp

Here we are dealing with the families *Penaeidae*, *Palaemonidae* and *Crangonidae*, and I must at once draw attention to a pitfall for visitors from North America and those who would converse or deal with them about the members of these families. North Americans call shrimp (or jumbo shrimp) what Europeans call prawns.

I have listed below those prawns which are most commonly brought to market in the Mediterranean. These are by no means all. But too much detail would be confusing; and even the species listed are not often differentiated in popular nomenclature – although the Italians, as usual, and the French can muster separate names for each.

Prawns and shrimps are frequently sold cooked. But it is possible to buy them uncooked, for example in fish markets. If you do, you may first peel them and then cook them gently for five minutes or so in simmering water (sea water is best, otherwise salted water) to which a flavour may be imparted (as is done in Provence) by for example garlic, bay leaves, thyme.

Alternatively, or in succession to the above operation, the peeled prawns can be deep-fried quickly in hot oil, a process for which they are prepared by either a dusting with flour or the egg-and-breadcrumb treatment or a coating of butter.

Prawns may also be grilled, as in the well-known Spanish dish Gambas a la Plancha. Mix olive oil with a little lemon juice in a saucer, adding salt and pepper. Put the prawns, complete and unpeeled, directly on to the grill. As they cook use a sprig of parsley to brush them with the olive oil and lemon juice mixture. The whole process takes about 20 minutes.

The largest prawns (or of course the true scampi – see p. 199) may be grilled on skewers. First bathe the prawns, peeled, for an hour in olive oil, salt and pepper. This will give you plenty of time in which to acquire and sharpen some suitable thin sticks, preferably of tamarisk wood. Spear the prawns on these, interspersing sage leaves, and grill over a moderate fire, basting with the marinade liquid. Serve hot, with lemon juice.

Finally, you can stew the prawns (or scampi) by following the Italian method of preparing Scampi in Umido. Peel the prawns first. Heat some olive oil in a small thick pan and cook the prawns gently in this. When they are nearly cooked (about 10 minutes) add some chopped garlic, a lot of parsley, a few capers and a little lemon juice. Finish the cooking and serve the prawns in the sauce from the pan.

Aristeus antennatus (Risso)
FAO 500

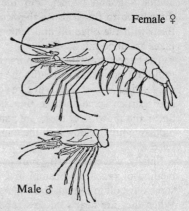

Female ♀

Male ♂

REMARKS. Maximum length 20 cm. Light red body with a mauve headpiece. There is a similar species **Aristeomorpha foliacea** (Risso) of which the male may attain 23 cm. Its colours are darker (blood-red body, violet headpiece). It is gambero rosso in Italian and langostino moruno in Spanish. Otherwise the names are the same.

French: Crevette rouge
Greek: Garída
Italian: Gambero rosso chiaro
Spanish: Carabinero
Tunisian: *
Other names: Gamba rosada (Cat.)

CUISINE. See p. 188. Both the prawns mentioned on this page are excellent.

*This species and the other referred to under *Remarks* are fished in Algerian but not in Tunisian waters. When marketed in Tunisia they would be gembri or crevettes.

Penaeus kerathurus (Forskål)
Penaeus caramote
FAO 502

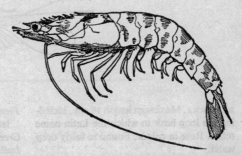

REMARKS. Maximum length 22 cm. Brown, with reddish tints.

CUISINE. See p. 188. One of the best prawns.

French: Caramote
Greek: Garída
Italian: Mazzancolla
Spanish: Langostino
Tunisian: Gembri kbir
Turkish: Karides
Other names: Crevette royale (often used in Tunisia), Grosse crevette (Fr.); Spanocchio, Gambero imperiale (one better than 'royale'!) (It.); Llagostí (Cat.)

Parapenaeus longirostris (Lucas)
FAO 503

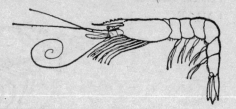

REMARKS. Maximum length 16 cm., including the long beak to which the Latin name refers. Rose in colour. Found in fairly deep water.

CUISINE. See p. 188. One of the best prawns.

French: Crevette rose du large
Greek: Garidáki
Italian: Gambero rosa
Spanish: Gamba
Tunisian: Gembri sghir
Other names: Kozica (S. C.)

Common prawn

Palaemon serratus (Pennant)
FAO 504

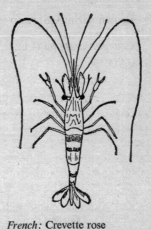

REMARKS. Maximum length 9 cm., with a comparatively short body. A prawn of shallow inshore waters.

CUISINE. See p. 188.

French: Crevette rose
Greek: Garidáki
Italian: Gamberello
Spanish: Quisquilla, Camarón
Tunisian: Gembri*
Other names: Gambeta (Cat.); Bouquet, Boucot (Fr.); Ammiru (Sicily) – all being general names.

RECIPE.
Garidopílafo, p. 359.

*This name, formed from the Italian, is the general Tunisian name for prawns, but the two species fished and marketed in large quantities by the Tunisians are Nos. 502 and 503 – the latter being called little (sghir) in relation to the former, not in relation to No. 504.

Brown shrimp, Shrimp

Crangon crangon (Linnaeus)
FAO 506

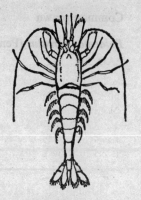

REMARKS. Maximum length 9 cm., i.e. the same as the smallest prawn listed. In colour a semi-transparent grey with dark spots. The same species is fished in British waters. It is a burrowing species which likes muddy sand, usually in shallow inshore waters.

CUISINE. See p. 188.

French: Crevette grise
Greek: Psilí garída
Italian: Gamberetto grigio, Gambera della sabbia,
Spanish: Quisquilla gris
Tunisian: B'rgouth bahr* (flea of the sea)
Turkish: Tekke, Çalı karides
Other names: Gamba d'esquer (Cat.)

RECIPE.
Schile Agio e Ogio, p. 347.

* May also be used of the smallest prawns.

Lobsters and Related Creatures

The lobster is the largest of the Mediterranean crustaceans, but the langouste or crawfish may be nearly as large. The langoustine is much smaller. Broadly speaking, the same methods of preparation may be applied to all. But the langouste and langoustine, so many people hold, have the more delicate flavour (which should not be masked).

Lobster are to be bought either alive or ready cooked. They may be presented simply or after complicated and costly processes. Elizabeth David has given the following advice: 'When all is said and done, plain freshly boiled lobster or crawfish served either hot or cold is infinitely superior to all the fancy and showy dishes such as Newburg, à l'américaine and the rest. In towns, lobsters are seldom sold alive, nor would one wish to have to carry one home, struggling and clacking their claws in the most alarming way. Having done this job in seaside villages in Cornwall and in the west of Scotland, in Greece and in Provence, having manoeuvred them into cauldrons of cold water, brought them gradually to the boil in the way recommended by the R.S.P.C.A.* and eaten them in the freshest possible condition I think I would still rather buy them from a reliable fishmonger, who will choose good ones, split them, crack the claws and send them more or less ready to serve.'

I do not give Homard à l'Américaine, although its ingredients suggest that it is a recipe of Mediterranean origin. But I reproduce Elizabeth David's Langouste comme chez Nenette (p. 309) which is a recipe from the Port of Sète in the Languedoc, of the same descent as the more famous recipe but free of the misleading name (whether one prefers américaine or armoricaine is immaterial: both are inappropriate and lack historical basis or even plausibility).

To return, however, to more simple preparations, I suggest the following:

(1) Serve the lobster cold, with a mayonnaise into which you have worked the pounded coral (if you are dealing with a hen lobster, otherwise there won't be one).

(2) Serve it as the Greeks do, cold and with an oil and lemon sauce (made by beating one part of lemon juice with five of olive oil, and seasoning) and a sprinkling of parsley or oregano.

(3) A very similar method, perhaps more prevalent in Turkey, is to serve the cold lobster with a simple dressing of olive oil and lemon juice (not beaten, just mixed) with chopped parsley.

*Author's footnote. See also comments on p. 187.

Spiny lobster

Palinurus elephas (Fabricius)
Palinurus vulgaris
FAO 507

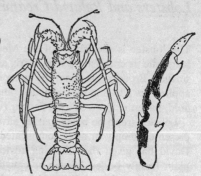

REMARKS. Maximum length 50 cm. This prized creature finds congenial conditions in a number of places in the Mediterranean. Those of Menorca are famous in Spain. Another favoured haunt is the island of Galita, off the the north coast of Tunisia, where only about a hundred people live, using a wrecked tank-landing ship from the Second World War as a jetty, and linked

French: Langouste
Greek: Astakós
Italian: Aragosta
Spanish: Langosta
Turkish: Böcek (beetle)
Other names: Crawfish, Rock lobster (Eng.); Jastog (S. C.); Llagosta (Cat.)

to the mainland by weekly visits from the langouste boat. Voyaging in this I found that the hold did not have a solid bottom, but a grid which lets the sea water in and makes of it a large storage tank. Thus the langoustes, having been caught in wicker traps by the islanders, are installed in their own element, if not in comfort, for the journey to Bizerta.

A less common species, ***Palinurus mauritanicus*** Gruvel, has a somewhat broader body. This is the Spanish langosta mora.

The langouste is reddish brown or red in colour, with yellow and white markings.

CUISINE. Some would hold the langouste, especially the pieces from its tail, superior to the lobster, but ways of preparing the latter apply to the former too. See p. 195.

RECIPE.
Langouste comme chez Nenette,
p. 309.

Flat lobster

Scyllarides latus (Latreille)
FAO 510

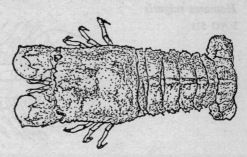

REMARKS. Maximum length 45 cm. Colour chestnut. The most obvious difference between the cigale and the lobster is of course that the claws of the cigale are very short. The back is covered with tiny protuberances.

There is also a petite cigale, *Scyllarides arctus* (Linnaeus), which only reaches a length of 14 cm.

The cigales owe their French name to the fact that they make a snapping cricket-like noise in the water, plainly audible to under-water fishermen.

French: Grande cigale
Greek: Lýra
Italian: Magnosa, Cicala
Spanish: Cigarra
Tunisian: Ziz el bahr
Turkish: Ayı ıstakozu
Other names: Macieta (Midi); Cigala (Cat.); Xigala (Bal.); Kuka (S. C.)

CUISINE. The petite cigale is used mainly in fish soups. The grande cigale, from the point of view of the cook, may be treated in the same ways as a langouste or a lobster. See p. 195.

Lobster

Homarus gammarus (Linnaeus)
Homarus vulgaris
FAO 511

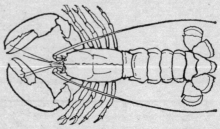

REMARKS. The largest crustacean in the Mediterranean, attaining a length of 60 cm. Dark blue in colour. The lobster is not plentiful in the Mediterranean, and not easily fished, for its size means that lobster pots must be large, and they have to be placed in suitably rocky spots at a fair depth. The high price of the lobster should not therefore cause surprise.

CUISINE. See p. 195.

French: Homard
Greek: Astakós, Karavída megáli
Italian: Astice, Elefante di mare
Spanish: Bogavante
Tunisian: Saratan el bahr
Turkish: Istakoz
Other names: Hlap (S. C.); Llamantol (Cat.); Grimalt (Bal.)

Dublin Bay prawn

Nephrops norvegicus (Linnaeus)
FAO 512

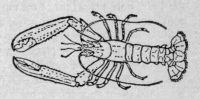

REMARKS. Maximum length 25 cm., i.e. a shade more than the largest crevettes. Rose-grey in colour. Not common in the Mediterranean, although there is a substantial colony in the Adriatic. British fishermen used to discard Dublin Bay prawns, but the growth in demand since the early 1950s has now made them a profitable catch. The best grounds are Scottish and Northumbrian, and also of course the area between the Isle of Man and the Irish coast (whence the English name).

French: Langoustine
Greek: Karavída
Italian: Scampo* (plural Scampi)
Spanish: Cigala
Tunisian: Jarradh el bahr
Other names: Norway lobster (Eng.); Skamp (S. C.); Escamarlà (Cat.)

CUISINE. As for the crevettes (p. 188). Often eaten cold. Elizabeth David has said that the delicate flavour of scampi is perhaps best savoured if the tails are cooked, still in their shells, in salted water for ten minutes and then served hot with melted butter.

RECIPE.
Rižot od Škampi, p. 385.

*This name is used loosely in (and outside!) Italy. Scampi in a restaurant are not necessarily Dublin Bay prawns, although they should be in Britain, where a labelling of food regulation restricts the use of the name.

Crabs and the Mantis Shrimp

Here we are concerned with a number of families and many species, but I give only a short list of the most common varieties, for I am not convinced that there is much to be gained by a comprehensive study. I do not list *Macropipus* sp., a group of small crabs, including what the French call the étrille or crabe nageur, the Spaniards nécora and the Turks çalpara, nor the equally tiny but furred *Dromia vulgaris* Milne Edwards which is the bear crab (Ayı pavuryası) in Turkey, although the last could claim attention for being cute as well as edible.

Crabs are often bought cooked. Otherwise they should be bought alive (preference being given to those which feel heavy for their size) and cooked in boiling salted water or a court-bouillon (p. 258) for a period of five to twenty minutes according to the size of the crabs (which can vary very considerably). Before cooking the crabs be sure to plug any holes in their carapaces (body or legs) with a compressed piece of bread. Once the cooking is done let them cool in the cooking water, then remove them and begin the tedious but rewarding business of extracting all the edible meat. First twist off the legs and claws. They are to be cracked and the meat taken out. Then, with the crab on its back, prise the body out. Discard guts and gills, but nothing else. Clean up the shell and return the meat to it in any number of ways either as a cold dish or for heating in the oven or under the grill.

Of course small crabs will not be given this treatment but will go into a soup. Favouilles (No. 516) are favoured for this purpose in the South of France, although they are often big enough to be prepared in other ways too.

Oppian (*Halieutica* II, 167–80) pays tribute to the cunning and the good taste of the crab:

And one who observes a Crab among the mossy ledges will praise and admire him for his cunning art. For to him also hath Heaven given wisdom to feed on Oysters, a sweet and unlaborious food. The Oysters open the bars of their doors and lick the mud, and, in their desire for water, sit wide open in the arms of the rocks. The Crab on the other hand takes a pebble from the beach and, moving sideways, carries it clutched in his sharp claws. Stealthily he draws near and puts the stone in the middle of the Oyster. Then he sits by and makes a pleasant feast. And the Oyster, though fain, is unable to shut his two valves, but gapes perforce until he dies and gluts his captor.

Edible crab

Cancer pagurus Linnaeus
FAO 515

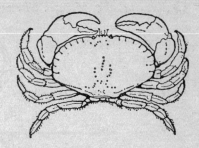

REMARKS. A large crab which can measure well over 20 cm. and which has extremely powerful, indeed dangerous, front claws. The only other Mediterranean crab of this size is ***Callinectes sapidus*** Rathbun, the blue crab, which is less esteemed and seems to be found only in the eastern Mediterranean. *Cancer pagurus* is the only species of crab fished in British waters for human consumption. It is found all round the British coast.

French: Tourteau
Greek: Siderokávouras
Italian: Granciporro
Spanish: Buey
Turkish: Pavurya
Other names: Dormeur (Fr.)

CUISINE. Mr Whittall in Istanbul suggests the following. First, cook the pavurya in brine which you boil gently and to which you add vinegar just before they are ready (perhaps half an hour). Next, separate all the meat from the body, claws and legs and chop it up; pour the liquid from the shell over the meat and mix in also the soft yellow matter from the shell and red spawn if any, as well as a pinch each of salt, pepper and cayenne. Beat up the mixture with olive oil and lemon juice and serve on small squares of bread.

Shore crab

Carcinus mediterraneus
   Czerniavsky
Carcinus maenas
FAO 516

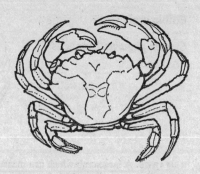

REMARKS. Length about 7 cm. Back greenish. This is the soft crab which has been cultivated in the Lagoon of Venice since the eighteenth century.* The object is to market the crabs immediately after they have moulted. If a crab which has moulted is allowed to stay in the water its new skin will by a process of calcification become hard within a matter of hours. So timing is very important. The crabs are kept in hatcheries as the moulting season approaches and inspected several times daily so that they can be taken out at the right moment. Males and females both moult in the spring. The males alone moult again in the autumn.

French: Crabe vert
Greek: Kávouras
Italian: Granchio commune
Spanish: Cangrejo de mar
Tunisian: Aghreb bahr
   (scorpion of the sea)
Turkish: Çingene
Other names: Cranc verd
   (Cat.); Yengeç (the
   general Turkish name for
   crabs); Favou and
   Favouille (Midi)

CUISINE. This species, in the soft state, provides a Venetian speciality for which a recipe is given. Generally, as this crab is not too highly flavoured, it is well suited to the preparation of crab soups.

RECIPES.

Moleche a la Muranese, p. 348.
Zuppa di Granchi/Favolli, p. 320.

Riz aux Favouilles, p. 310.
Soupes aux Crabes, p. 289.

*Varagnolo, in his interesting study of this fishery, explains the local names as follows. Granzi matti or falsi are normal hard crabs, not regarded as edible. Granzi boni are crabs near to moulting. They turn grey and are known as spiantani when they are within a few days of moulting. Immediately after moulting the soft crabs are moleche. As they become hard again (5 to 10 hours later) they are known as strussi, and are still saleable. The females which are eaten in the hard state in the autumn are masanette.

Eriphia verrucosa (Forskål)
Eriphia spinifrons
FAO 521

REMARKS. Maximum size about 10 cm. A somewhat furry creature, with noticeably powerful pincers. It lives in shallow waters close to the shore.

CUISINE. This is perhaps the most sought after crab in the south of France, where its flavour is considered very good indeed.

French: Ériphie
Italian: Favollo
Spanish: Cangrejo moruno
Other names: Cranc pelut (Cat.); Pélou (Nice); Fiou pelan (Provence); Granzoporo (Venice)

RECIPES.
Soupe de Pélous, p. 289.

Zuppa di Favolli, p. 320.

Spider crab

Maja squinado (Herbst)
FAO 523

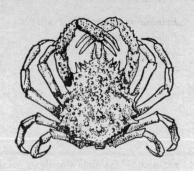

REMARKS. Maximum length 20 cm. The layout of the legs suggests a spider. The colour varies from yellowish red to rose or chestnut. The carapace is covered with protuberances. The smaller female is the better buy, and is best bought in January or February when she is carrying eggs. Look for the eggs under the 'tail'.

French: Araignée
Greek: Kavouromána
Italian: Grancevola, Granzeola
Spanish: Centolla
Tunisian: R'tila bahr
Turkish: Ayna
Other names: Cabra (Cat.); Squinado, Esquinadoun, etc. (Midi); Rakovica (S. C.)

CUISINE. Highly regarded at the northern end of the Adriatic, where Grancevola alla Veneziana is a well-known dish. The first step is to put them in water and bring it to the boil. Once the crabs are cooked and have been allowed to cool take off the upper shells (reserving them for use in serving the dressed crab) and extract and chop all the meat and coral. Dress this with olive oil, pepper and lemon juice and arrange it in the upper shells. Another possibility is to combine the crab meat with peeled and pounded small prawns, and mix it all into a mayonnaise (which should not be too stiff, and made slightly piquant with paprika or pepper). However you proceed, plan on the basis of one crab per person, and serve in the upper shells.

Mantis shrimp

Squilla mantis (Linnaeus)
FAO 525

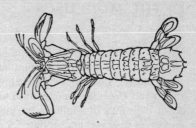

REMARKS. Up to 25 cm. in length. Brown-grey in colour.

This strange creature is singled out by several characteristics, of which the most striking is that his front 'legs' are extensions of his mouth. He is the marine counterpart of the insect known as the praying mantis.

French: Squille
Greek: Skoulíki
Italian: Pannocchia, Cannocchia
Spanish: Galera
Other names: Mante; Prega-diou (Midi)

CUISINE. At their best (when the ovaries are full and the flesh firm) these creatures are quite good, and may be treated like the cigale. They may also be used in fish soups, for some versions of which Italians regard them as essential. Cavanna suggests steaming them. (Put the bodies, shorn of all projecting parts like antennae and claws, in a casserole with herbs; cover the casserole with a folded cloth soaked in salt water; jam the lid on; and cook thus for a few minutes only.)

The Romagna is one part of Italy where the mantis shrimp is a speciality. Caminiti, Pasquini and Quondamatteo, in *Mangiari di Romagna*, give instructions for frying them in two ways. Remove heads, legs and fins, flour the bodies and fry them in plenty of oil. Alternatively, remove the carapaces first. This is done by simmering them in water for 10 minutes, cooling them and then taking off the carapace (top first, underside second). The bodies, thus peeled, are then dipped in a mixture of egg, flour, a little white wine, water, a little olive oil and seasoning, and fried thus. I also have a recipe from Signora Luciana Ricciardi of Cattolica for Brodetto di Cannocchie. (Buy 2 kilos of cannocchie when they are with eggs. Cut off the legs and cut round the body of each so that when you come to eat them, which you do with your fingers, it will be easy to open the carapaces. Wash them and put them in a big pan with almost $1\frac{1}{2}$ wineglassfuls olive oil, 250 grammes tinned tomatoes, 1 tablespoonful tomato paste, 4 chopped cloves of garlic, lots of chopped parsley, the peel of a lemon and seasoning. They will themselves supply additional liquid. Bring all this to the boil, then lower the heat and cook gently for 20 minutes.)

(2) THE MOLLUSCS

Various classifications into orders have been recommended for these creatures. I like the basic division into *Gastropoda* (creatures living in single shells), *Lamellibranchiata* (bivalves, creatures living in double shells) and *Cephalopoda* (creatures like the octopus), and will proceed down the ranks of Molluscs on this basis, conducting a less formal inspection than was appropriate for other categories of sea-food.

The Gastropoda, *Inhabitants of Single Shells*

A modest collection, claiming edibility but – most of them – little more. Some of the names are interesting.

The first species listed in this section is the Mediterranean counter-part of the famous abalone of the Pacific coast of North America.

Some of the species of the escargot de mer type, for example No. 529, bequeath their shells to a curious marine partnership involving the hermit crab (Bernard l'Ermite as the French call him) and the sea anemone. The hermit crab takes over an empty escargot de mer shell and turns it into his movable home. Sea anemones establish themselves on the outside of the shell, affording protection to the hermit crab and benefiting from the fact that the hermit crab will move his house from place to place and thus provide them with a series of new fishing grounds which they would not enjoy if they were anchored to a rock. The hermit crab is edible, but apparently not worth marketing, and certainly not as good as the original owners of the shells which he appropriates.

Ormer, Abalone

Haliotis tuberculata (Linnaeus)
FAO 526

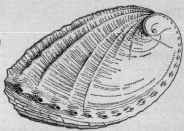

REMARKS. May be 10 cm. long. As many of the names indicate (including the curiously precise Provençal oreille de Saint Pierre, and auriglia de San Pietro said to be used in Monaco, and aoureillo de cat, at Agde) the shell looks like an ear. Note the row of holes. The inside of the shell is pearly, the outside rough and brown or greenish.

French: Ormeau
Greek: Aliótis
Italian: Orecchia marina
Spanish: Oreja de mar
Turkish: Deniz kulağı
Other names: Orella de mar (Cat.); Oreille de mer (Fr. and Tunisian); Six yeux (Fr.)

The species is indigenous in the Channel Islands, but not elsewhere in British waters, although a community of them has been established at Hunterston in Scotland for the purpose of keeping clean the fish hatchery tanks there, a task which they perform very well.

CUISINE. Remove and clean the white 'foot', beat it with a wooden mallet and then cook it by braising or frying. Garlic helps, and the result is quite good. It may also be eaten raw with lemon juice.

Top-shell

Monodonta turbinata (Born)
Trochocochlea turbinata
FAO 527

REMARKS. Only 3 cm. long, dark in colour with broken lines following the course of the spirals.

Many of the names for this and other gastropods which can move around like snails are words meaning snail.

CUISINE. Bring some sea or salted water to the boil, preferably with black pepper, thyme and a bay leaf, and cook the bigorneaux in this for about quarter of an hour. They may then be taken out of their shells easily on the point of a pin. Good. May also be used in bouillabaisse.

French: Bigorneau
Greek: Tróchos
Italian: Chiocciola marina
Spanish: Caracol gris, Caramujo
Other names: Baldufa (Cat.); Escargot de mer (Fr. – a name also used of *Murex* sp., e.g. No. 529, and of No. 533); Caragolo (Venice); Biou (Midi, a general name)

In the island of Murano near Venice they are known as bodoletti, and the procedure is as follows. Put a wineglassful of olive oil, bay leaves and salt into a fireproof dish. Lay the bodoletti in this (still in their shells), cover the dish and put it in a medium oven for twenty minutes or so. The bodoletti may then be winkled out of their shells and eaten as an appetizer.

Limpet

Patella caerulea (Linnaeus)
FAO 528

REMARKS. The shell is conical and more or less symmetrical, with a pearly inside, and is normally no more than 4–5 cm. long, although I have heard of giants up to 8 cm. in the Corsican isle of Cavalho, with flesh as hard as leather.

CUISINE. The first three months of the year are reputedly the best season for limpets, which are normally eaten raw. I am told that some Greeks make a soup with them. They may also be cooked briefly with a little butter placed in the shell. The big ones with yellow flesh are best. But the results are not such as to warrant the marketing of limpets.

French: Patelle
Greek: Petalída
Italian: Patella
Spanish: Lapa
Tunisian: N'lat
Turkish: Deniz kulağı
Other names: Chapeau Chinois, also Arapède, Alepedo and variants in the Midi; Barretet (Cat.)

Murex brandaris (Linnaeus)
FAO 529

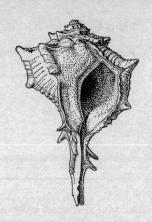

REMARKS. Up to 9 cm. long. *Murex trunculus* (Linnaeus) is a similar species (rocher à pourpre in French) and *Murex erinaceus* (Linnaeus) is a smaller one (perceur in French, murice riccio in Italian). The murex was the source of a famous purple dye in antiquity – see note below.

CUISINE. As No. 527. Rather tough. Cavanna commented that *Murex brandaris* is less tough than the other two species mentioned above, but that the other two were popular in the Adriatic. He referred to *Murex erinaceus* as the ginocchiello.

French: Rocher épineux
Greek: Porphýra
Italian: Murice
Spanish: Cañadilla
Turkish: Dikenli salyangoz
Other names: Escargot de mer (Alg. and Tun.); Buccuni (Sicily and Sardinia); Garuzolo (Venice) and Sconciglio (Naples, where 'ugly as a sconciglio' is a telling insult); Cornet amb pues (Cat.); Volak (S. C.)

NOTE ON THE PURPLE DYE OF MUREX. The production of purple dyes from the murex was a major industry in antiquity. d'Arcy Thompson, in a learned note, lists the sixteen main centres of the industry. Tyre and Sidon were the best known, but Laconia had an almost equally high reputation. It was still possible in the last century to see huge heaps of used shells at Tyre and Sidon (where they were shells of *Murex trunculus*) and similar accumulations at Tarentum and on the Laconian coast (where *Murex brandaris* had been used). These were not the only relics of the industry. The Latin name murex is said to survive in the Provençal burez; and the ancient Greek name porphýra not only continues in modern Greek but also lingers on in the form porpora on the Italian Adriatic coast.

The Tyrian legend of the discovery of the dye is that Heracles (or Bacchus, or a nameless shepherd) saw his dog's mouth stained purple by the shell, and realizing the possibilities proceeded to dye a ribbon purple for a lover's gift.

Purple was the imperial colour, and one thinks of, say, Caesar's purple robe or the purple sails of Cleopatra's warship at the Battle of Actium. But the colour was used for many purposes (a small purple rag was placed in sore ears to heal them), and there were many variants of it, depending on the place and method of preparation. The range went from what seems to have been a blood-red to a colour which was nearly black. The art of mixing and preparing the dye was a highly developed one, and was still practised up to the time of the fall of Constantinople. Some ancient purple vestments are still preserved; and modern scholars have occasionally collected specimens of the murex and sought to extract the vital vein and mix the dye therefrom. But long gone, and presumably for ever, are the days when as Pliny explains one took 200 pounds of one kind of murex and 100 of another, and worked with huge leaden vats for days on end to dye 1000 pounds of fleece.

The liquid in the vein is, incidentally, usually whitish when first revealed. It assumes the purple colour on exposure to sunlight, in a process observed and agreeably described by Cole in his account in *Purpura lapillus* (1685):

... in the heat of the day, in Summer, the colours will come on so fast, that the succession of each colour will scarce be distinguisht; next to the first 'light green', it will appear 'deep green'; and in a few minutes change into a full 'Sea-green'; after which, in a few minutes more, it will alter into a 'Watchet-blew'; from that, in a little more, it will be of a 'Purplish red'; after which, lying an hour or two (supposing the Sun still shining), it will be of a very 'deep Purple red', beyond which the Sun can do no more.

Horn-shell

Cerithium vulgatum (Bruguière)
FAO 533

REMARKS. Length up to 7 cm. Rather like an ice-cream cone with an opening bent over sideways. Of a brown or greenish colour, but this is variable, as is the size.

CUISINE. As No. 527. In the Romagna a special soup is made of these creatures, called Zuppa di Garagoli. The same soup may be prepared with *Aporrhais pes-pelecani* (Linnaeus) (Italian crocetta or pie di pelicano), which is a similar creature, distinguished by the fact that one lip of its shell fans out into a shape like a webbed foot. This second species is available in British waters, e.g. off the Northumbrian coast.

French: Cornet
Greek: Kerátios
Italian: Torricella
Spanish: Cuerno
Tunisian: Zarbout
Turkish: Şeytan minaresi
Other names: Caragolo longo and variants (Venice); Escargot de mer (Fr.); Pada (Cat.)

The Bivalves

The edible bivalves are numerous and classified in many orders and families. Some of them are excellent, for example the oyster. Others have a less wide appeal. Many are eaten raw. Those listed below are the ones most likely to be found on sale in the Mediterranean area.

The English are traditionally bivalve-eaters, and we Londoners more so than most. The latter title I claim by adoption, having set up home at the World's End, where there is an excellent and busy stall of the kind which sells winkles and jellied eel, and having Whitehall, within scenting distance of Tower Bridge and Billingsgate, as the node of my official life. But I must deplore the gentle decline of mussel-eating which I lately perceive at home, even at the World's End. Living in Brussels for a time has brought home to me how low our enthusiasm for this delicacy is waning beside the Belgian passion which seems in contrast to wax from year to year.

The pilgrim scallop of the Mediterranean is, incidentally, quite like the British scallops and those found in North American waters. The fact that North Americans do not normally eat the coral in addition to the white muscle, as Europeans do, does not arise from any difference between the species of scallops but reflects different levels of gastronomic development within the human species.

However, North Americans can claim to be well advanced in the appreciation of clams; and may wonder how their clams are related to the Mediterranean species listed in this section, from No. 557 to No. 562. The answer is that the species are quite closely related, for example in the genus *Tapes* which includes the clovisse in the Mediterranean and the Japanese littleneck clam in California, and the genus *Donax* which includes the wedge shell in the Mediterranean and the bean and wedge clams in North America. But there are many more species in North America.

Noah's Ark

Arca noae (Linnaeus)
FAO 536

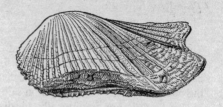

REMARKS. Maximum length 9 cm. I suppose that it *does* look like Noah's Ark?

CUISINE. Usually eaten raw. All right, but not suitable fare for those with shaky digestive systems.

French: Arche de Noé
Greek: Kalógnomi
Italian: Arca di Noè
Spanish: Arca de Nóe
Other names: Peu de cabrit (Cat.)

Dog-cockle

Glycymeris glycymeris (Linnaeus)
FAO 538

REMARKS. May be 7 cm. long. The exterior of the shell is marked by both radiating and concentric striations.

CUISINE. Eat raw, but they are not tender.

French: Amande de mer
Greek: Melokídono
Italian: Pie d'asino
Spanish: Almendra de mar
Tunisian: Mahar
Other names: Petxinot (Cat.)

Oyster

Ostrea edulis (Linnaeus)
FAO 539

REMARKS. Maximum length 12 cm. The oyster needs no explanation, except to say that there are a number of local varieties of this species in the Mediterranean, and that the other, elongated, species *Crassostrea angulata* (Lamarck) (the Portuguese oyster) is not unknown, for example in Spain where it is called ostión. (It is illustrated above left, along with *Ostrea edulis*.)

French: Huître
Greek: Strídi
Italian: Ostrica
Spanish: Ostra
Tunisian: Istridia
Turkish: İstiridye
Other names: Huître plate (Fr.); Kamenica (S. C.)

CUISINE. Lavish your money on these delectable creatures, open them, cool them on a bed of ice and, having sprinkled lemon juice, go to it. It is possible to do other things, such as frying or even grilling them, not to mention including them in steak and kidney pies, but in my belief they are best eaten as they are, and to do otherwise is mistaken and even blameworthy.

Oysters are not normally available during the summer months (the months without an 'r'), but they can perfectly well be eaten then, if you can get at any. The only difference is that they are what the French call 'laiteuses', i.e. with eggs, which gives them a fatter look and taste.

Pilgrim scallop

Pecten jacobaeus (Linnaeus)
FAO 541

REMARKS. The shells, which run up to 14 cm., are often used as dishes for small servings of fish gratiné.

The scallops swim around by opening and closing their shells so that the expulsion of the water drives them along. The muscle joining the two halves of the shell is therefore large and powerful.

The great scallop has two smaller relations. Whereas it has fourteen to sixteen prominent ribs on the shell, *Chlamys opercularis* (Linnaeus) has about 20, and *Chlama varia* (Linnaeus) about thirty. The names of these two smaller relations are (French) vanneau and pétoncle, (Italian) pettine and canestrello, (Spanish) volandeira and zamburiña. Both are found in British waters.

French: Coquille Saint-Jacques
Greek: Kténi
Italian: Ventaglio
Spanish: Concha de peregrino
Turkish: Tarak
Other names: Vano, Petxina de pelegrí (Cat.); Peigne, Pèlerine (Fr.); Cappa santa (Venice)

CUISINE. The main edible part is the large white muscle. Otherwise only the orange-yellow 'tongue' or coral can be eaten. It is usually quite easy to buy these edible parts ready prepared. But if you buy whole coquilles and have to open them, just put them in a casserole over a flame for a few moments. Then take out the edible parts and wash them. Methods of cooking are numerous. Cook them à la meunière; sauté them; cook them en brochette with bits of bacon, tomato, mushroom, etc.; wrap them in foil with herbs and cook them in the oven. Or, as in Turkey, put the edible parts in the deeper of the two shells with olive oil poured over and a sprinkling of breadcrumbs and cook them in the oven thus.

RECIPES.
Coquilles Saint-Jacques à la Provençale, p. 313.

Cape Sante in Tecia, p. 348.

Mussel

Mytilus galloprovincialis (Lamarck)
FAO 545

REMARKS. The bluish-black mussel shells clinging in clusters to rocks are familiar to all. But the ones which you buy have probably clung in clusters to ropes hanging in or stakes planted in sea water in mussel 'farms'. Length up to 10 cm.

There is a smaller relation, *Modiolus barbatus* (Linnaeus), which is only 5 cm. long and very noticeably bearded. It therefore has names such as moule barbue (Fr.), cozza pelosa (It.) and mejillón barbada (Sp.).

French: Moule
Greek: Mýdi
Italian: Mitilo, Muscolo
Spanish: Mejillón
Tunisian: Tamr el bahr
Turkish: Midye
Other names: Peocio (Venice), Cozza (It.); Moule de Toulon (Fr., to distinguish it from Atlantic species); Muscle (Provence); Musclo(Cat.);Dagnja(S.C.)

CUISINE. Mussels may be eaten raw, with lemon juice. I recall eating some superb large ones, with flesh of a faintly coral colour, at Marseille and thinking that it would have been quite wrong to cook them. But ordinary mussels are best cooked, and there are scores of methods from which to choose. Try them fried; or grilled en brochette with cubes of bacon; or garnished in the open shell with breadcrumbs, chopped parsley and garlic, and a little olive oil and then gratinés; or in the well-known dish Moules Marinière.

RECIPES.

Moules Camarguaises, p. 313.
Moules Nautile, p. 314.
Zuppa di Cozze, p. 320.

Vermicelli alle Cozze, p. 329.
Cozze e Patate al Forno p. 349.
Midye Tavası Biralı, p. 370.

Note. The name 'mussel' is derived from the Latin (and Greek) word *mus* meaning mouse. I have not seen it explained why the mussel should have been thought of as the mouse of the sea. But Dr Richmond has pointed out to me that if a whisker, an eye and a tail are added to the illustration on this page the explanation is obvious.

Date-shell

Lithophaga lithophaga (Linnaeus)

FAO 547

REMARKS. Up to 10 cm., but slimmer than the mussel and coloured rather like dates. The datte de mer embeds itself in rocks and is therefore difficult to gather. The coast near La Spezia in Italy is one place where it is common.

French: Datte de mer
Greek: Solína
Italian: Dattero di mare
Spanish: Dátil de mar
Tunisian: Tamr el bahr
Other names: Prstac (S. C.)

CUISINE. Usually eaten raw. Quite good. Makes a better soup than mussels.

Fan mussel

Pinna nobilis (Linnaeus)
FAO 548

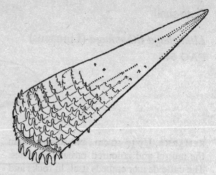

REMARKS. Shaped like a ham and up to 75 cm. long. The inside of the shell is a pearly yellow. A remarkable feature of the fan mussel is its byssus, or projecting tuft of silky fibres – like the 'beard' of the ordinary mussel but much finer. These were collected by fishermen in southern Italy (especially at Taranto) and spun and woven into a fabric from which gloves and stockings were made. They had a golden lustre, and sound to me highly desirable. But the practice has almost, if not entirely, died out.

French: Jambonneau
Greek: Pínna
Italian: Pinna
Spanish: Nácar
Turkish: Pines
Other names: Nacre (Cat.)
  Periska (S. C.)

CUISINE. Extract and cook the edible muscle, as with the coquille Saint-Jacques. It can be cooked under the grill, in the half-shell, with olive oil, salt, pepper and a sprinkling of parsley. Or it can be eaten raw.

Cockle

Cardium edule (Linnaeus)
FAO 549

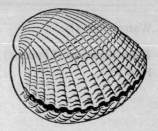

REMARKS. The diameter is about 5 cm. The cockle has some bigger relations, to wit *Cardium aculeatum* (Linnaeus) (spiny cockle and kindred names), *Cardium echinatum* (Linnaeus) (prickly cockle) and *Cardium tuberculatum* (Linnaeus) (the knotted cockle). The last, easy to identify by the fact that so long as the animal is alive it

French: Coque
Greek: Methýstra
Italian: Cuore edule, Cocciola
Spanish: Berberecho
Turkish: Acivades
Other names: Escopinya de
  gallet (Cat.); Čaša (S. C.)

is bright red in colour, with a red foot protruding from the shell, is the best. It is one of the species which the Neapolitans call fasolare, although its more official Italian names are cuore rosso and cocciola arena.

Cockles are common on sandy shores and in estuaries all round the British coast. They provide the most valuable mollusc fishery in Britain. The finest cockles in the world are Stiffkey (pronounced stookey) blues from the Norfolk coast. These belong to the species *Cardium edule* and owe their blueness to the anaerobic muddy sand which they inhabit.

CUISINE. Often eaten raw, although they may also be cooked in their shells until these open, in a court-bouillon. Whichever method you adopt, you will do well to let the cockles sit in clear sea water for a few hours first, so that they have an opportunity to disgorge sand, etc. before they are consumed.

Warty venus (!)

Venus verrucosa (Linnaeus)
FAO 555

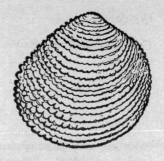

REMARKS. Not more than 6 cm. across. The strongly ridged shell is yellowish grey in colour. This and the smaller *Venus gallina* (Linnaeus) are called vongola in Italy, but cf. the next entry.

Salamis is one good hunting ground for this species. They are also quite common in British waters, yet unknown in British markets.

French: Praire
Greek: Kydóni
Italian : Tartufo di mare
Spanish: Verigüeto
Other names: Escopinya gravada (Cat.); Rigadelle, Praïro (Midi); Caparon, Caparozzolo (Venice), Tartufolo (Genoa)

CUISINE. As No. 549. Usually eaten raw. Good.

Carpet-shell

Venerupis decussata (Linnaeus)
FAO 557

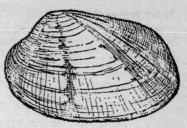

REMARKS. May be 8 cm. across. Light in colour (yellowish or greyish) but often with a darker mark in the middle of the shell. The shell is marked by fine lines in both directions, i.e. round the shell and also fanning out from the hinge.

CUISINE. The palourde is greatly esteemed by the French. It is good eaten raw with lemon juice, but may also be cooked. Be careful to sluice away any fine sand remaining inside the shell.

French: Palourde
Greek: Chávaro
Italian: Vongola nera, Vongola verace
Spanish: Almeja fina
Other names: Copinya llisa (Cat.); Beuda and variants (Languedoc); Clovisse (wrongly, see No. 558, in Provence)

Cavanna reported particular enthusiasm at Naples for this bivalve and commented on the excellence of the Vermicelli con le Vongole served at Posilippo.

Some palourdes are resident in Britain, notably those which have established themselves around the power station outfall at Poole Harbour.

RECIPES.
Zuppa di Vongole, p. 320.   Vermicelli alle Vongole, p. 329.

Tapes geographica (Gmelin)
FAO 558

REMARKS. This is half the size of the preceding species, and has only the concentric lines on the shell. Another variety, of the same small size, is *Tapes aurea* (Gmelin) (clovisse jaune, vongola gialla, etc.). The latter is present in British waters, and known as the golden carpet-shell.

French: Clovisse
Greek: Chávaro
Italian: Vongola grigia
Spanish: Amayuela
Tunisian: (the French name
  is always used)

CUISINE. As for the preceding. Although smaller, this is still good, and greatly enjoyed by the Tunisians. It may be eaten raw, but I believe that it is better cooked and commend the recipes listed below.

RECIPES.
Clovisses Farcies au Gratin, p. 312.   Clovisses à la Carthaginienne,
                                      p. 380.

Smooth venus

Callista chione (Linnaeus)
FAO 560

REMARKS. A larger bivalve, which runs up to 12 cm. The shell is smooth and coloured light brown, with broken bands of a darker (chestnut) colour radiating outwards. Known in English and Welsh waters.

CUISINE. Eaten raw, and very good.

Greek: Ghialisterí achiváda
Italian: Cappa liscia
Spanish: Almejón brillante
Other names: Petxinot de sang (Cat.)

Wedge shell

Donax trunculus (Linnaeus)
FAO 561

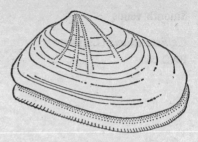

REMARKS. Maximum length 3·5 cm. A small neat bivalve, shaped rather like a wedge, which is plentiful in many parts of the Mediterranean, including the coast by the mouths of the Nile, where it is the bivalve most heavily fished and very popular with the local inhabitants.

French: Olive, Haricot de mer
Greek: Kochíli
Italian: Tellina
Spanish: Coquina
Other names: Arsella (Tuscany)

CUISINE. Eat raw. Prepare like clovisses (No. 558). Or make into a soup which, one eminent Italian authority has told me, is the best of the whole category of bivalve soups.

RECIPE.
Zuppa di Telline, p. 320.

Razor-shell

Solen vagina (Linnaeus)
FAO 562

REMARKS. The razor-shells are completely distinctive in appearance. This species attains a length of 13 cm. (i.e. the shell only – the head may protrude from one end and the 'feet' from the other). Another species which is slightly curved may be a little longer. There are several varieties of razor-shell to be found on the British coast, and they are very easy to catch. (Put a little salt on the holes in the sand which betray their presence, and the creatures will pop up out of them.) But at present they are used as bait instead of being made into a soup.

French: Couteau
Greek: Solína
Italian: Cannolicchio
Spanish: Navaja
Tunisian: Sandouq*
Turkish: Solinya
Other names: Capa longa (Venice); Longueiron (Sp.); Rasoir (Fr.); Ganivet (Cat.)

CUISINE. Eaten raw, or made into the soup listed below.

RECIPE.
Zuppa di Cannolicchi, p. 320.

*Meaning something hinged – the plural, snadiq, is used of the bivalves generally.

Cuttlefish, Squid and Octopus

This group of creatures lacks allure. They all look like bags with heads on top and eight or ten tentacles sprouting therefrom. But they can be very good eating if properly prepared, and the art of doing this is probably more advanced in the Mediterranean than anywhere else in the world.

Of all the molluscs these, I believe, are the only ones with a centralized nervous system: and the big heads cover real brains. Very interesting experiments are being conducted by British scientists at Naples on the ability of the octopus to learn and to remember. At the aquarium I was shown tanks in which 250 octopus can be housed for this purpose, and ingenious perspex constructions in which they can be taught to select rough rather than smooth, and so on.

I also learned at Naples that the octopus can change its colour as well as its shape at high speed. The colour change is effected by the expansion or contraction of pigment cells distributed all over its skin. A frightened octopus which has failed to escape the notice of a predator by melting into the background, both in shape and colour, has one more card to play – what is called a dymantic display, when it turns itself into a ghost-white figure, drained of colour and with only the dark eyes affording a sinister contrast. It would be a particularly intense experience to be confronted unexpectedly, under water, by a really large octopus switching on its dymantic display.

Species very similar to the little cuttlefish are very common in British waters. At times squid are quite common too, also the curled octopus, on our western coasts.

Cuttlefish

Sepia officinalis (Linnaeus)
FAO 568

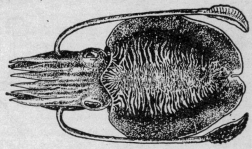

REMARKS. A more or less oval creature up to 25 cm. long, with eight short and two long tentacles. Colour variable, often with zebra-like markings on the back. Secretes an ink, which was formerly used to make the colour sepia. Contains a large internal shell or 'bone' familiar as a pecking object for pet birds. This species is fairly common off the south coast of England, for example in the Plymouth area.

French: Seiche
Greek: Soupiá
Italian: Seppia
Spanish: Jibia
Tunisian: Shoubia
Turkish: Supya*
Other names: Sepi, Sepia, Supi, etc. (Midi); Sipa (S. C.); Sípia, Sèpia (Cat.); Chocó (Sp.)

CUISINE. As for the octopus (No. 579), but this is more tender fare and need not be beaten before cooking.

RECIPES.
Seiches à l'Agathoise, p. 312.
Riso con le seppie, p. 326.
Spaghetti con le Seppie, p. 329.

Seppie alla Veneziana, p. 351.
Soupiá Yachní, p. 359.

*The more general name mürekkep balığı is used of both cuttlefish and squid, as is the corresponding English name inkfish.

Little cuttlefish

Sepiola rondeleti Leach
FAO 571

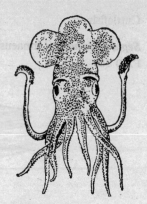

REMARKS. This smaller version of the cuttlefish has two 'ears' projecting towards the rear of its body. It reaches a length of 3 or 4 cm. only.

CUISINE. These are often sold ready to eat, after having been cleaned and fried. They are very good in Spanish rice and seafood dishes. If you are going to cook them your-

French: Sépiole
Greek: Soupítsa
Italian: Seppiola
Spanish: Globito, Chipirón
Other names: Supioun, Suppion and variants, Sépiou (Midi); Sipió (Cat.)

self ask the fishmonger to clean them, since it is rather finicky work extracting the small bone and the ink sac. The simplest procedure then is to wash and dry them and deep-fry them for rather less than ten minutes, taking care to cover the pan since drops of hot oil may be propelled out of the pan by the motions of the tiny creatures as they cook. The result is what the French call Suppions Frits, and is a delicious dish.

Squid

Loligo vulgaris (Lamarck)
FAO 573

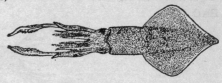

REMARKS. Length up to 50 cm. The projections at the rear of the body are swimming fins. These creatures swim near the surface, very gracefully. Since any attack would be likely to come from below they are normally almost transparent and thus invisible to potential predators. But they can blush a brownish colour. Small ones are calamaretti in Italian, chipirones in Spanish.

French: Encornet
Greek: Kalamári
Italian: Calamaro
Spanish: Calamar
Tunisian: Mettig
Turkish: Kalamar
Other names: Often called Calmar in French (cf. next entry); Taoutenno, Tautenne, etc., and variants, and Claougeou (Provence); Lignja (S. C.)

CUISINE. Squid are easy to stuff. Most stuffings incorporate the chopped up tentacles. The three recipes for stuffed squid listed below are all reasonably simple, but there are more complicated ones like the Provençal Tautennes Farcies, in which the stuffing includes mussels and spinach, and a version from Toulon which involves slices of sausage. Do not hesitate to invent your own stuffing.

RECIPES.
Calamares Rellenos con Jamón, p. 281.
Encornets (Calmars) à l'Étuvée, p. 311.

Calamari Ripieni, p. 349.
Kalamária Yemistá, p. 360.

Flying squid

Ommastrephes sagittatus (Lamarck)
FAO 577

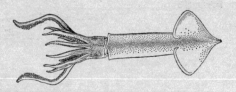

REMARKS. Twice the size of the preceding species (i.e. up to 100 cm.) and with broadened instead of elongated swimming fins at the rear. Violet in hue. Eight 'arms' and two much longer tentacles. The flying squid does not really fly, but can propel itself out of the water and glide through the air.

French: Calmar
Greek: Thrápsalo
Italian: Totano
Spanish: Pota
Tunisian: Totli?
Other names: Taouteno and variants (Provence); Canana (Cat.)

CUISINE. See No. 573, with which smaller specimens of this species are confused – not that it matters particularly. The biggest specimens are not the best.

Octopus

Octopus vulgaris (Linnaeus)
FAO 579

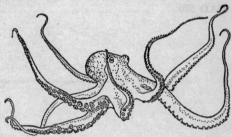

REMARKS. The octopus can measure up to 300 cm. As the name implies, it has eight tentacles. Each is lined with a twin row of suckers. The octopus passes the winter in deep water but approaches the coast in the early spring and passes the summer in inshore waters. It hunts by night, voraciously, but itself falls prey to the conger and moray eels.

French: Pieuvre, Poulpe
Greek: Octápous, Chtapódi
Italian: Polpo
Spanish: Pulpo
Tunisian: Qarnit kbir
Turkish: Ahtapot
Other names: Pourpre and variants (Provence); Hobotnica (S. C.); Pop (Cat.)

CUISINE. An octopus must be cleaned by removing the beak, eyes and interior organs; and beaten, e.g. against a stone, to make the flesh less tough. Cooking methods are numerous. For example, the octopus may be stewed in red wine, cooked en daube, or prepared à la provençale (simmered in the familiar olive oil/onion/tomato/garlic mixture). There are people who believe that placing a slice of cork in the pot with the octopus will make it tender.

The port of Sfax in Tunisia has long been conducting an important trade in dried octopus.

RECIPES.
Pulpos con Papas, p. 281.
Poulpe à la Niçoise, p. 311.
Polpetielli alla Luciana, p. 350.

Borthéto, p. 354.
Ochtapódi Krassáto, p. 360.

Octopus

Octopus macropus Risso
FAO 580

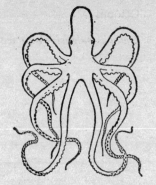

REMARKS. This smaller octopus has a maximum length of 120 cm., and its tentacles are relatively much longer and thinner than those of No. 579.

CUISINE. As for No. 579, but less good. It would be well to choose one of the simpler octopus recipes for this creature, perhaps that of the melodiously named Signora Sarina Serrano of Noci by Bari. She prepares octopus thus, and calls it Polipo al Raguncino. Heat olive oil and gently fry in it a medium onion, cut in fine slices. Add 2 tablespoonfuls of tomato purée and continue to cook slowly, adding a little water from time to time. Then add the prepared octopus (cut in pieces if large, whole if small). Season and add chopped parsley. Cook slowly until tender. The time could be as little as 30 minutes for small ones and as long as 2 to 3 hours for big ones.

French: Poulpe
Greek: Octápous, Chtapódi
Italian: Polpessa
Spanish: Pulpón, Pulpo patudo
Tunisian: Qarnit sghir
Turkish: Ahtapot
Other names: Poulpe rouge (Fr.); Poupresse (Antibes); Hobotnica (S. C.)

Curled octopus

Eledone cirrosa (Lamarck)

FAO 582

REMARKS. Smaller (maximum length 40 cm.) and lighter in colour than the two preceding species. Each tentacle is lined with a single row of suckers. There is a further species, ***Eledone moschata*** (Lamarck) which is smaller still and smells excessively of musk.

French: Eledone
Greek: Moschoctápodo
Italian: Moscardino bianco
Spanish: Pulpo blanco
Tunisian: Qarnit sghir
Turkish: Ahtapot
Other names: Pop blanc (Cat.)

CUISINE. As No. 579. Less highly esteemed, but I ate a delicious dish of small ones at Genoa, terracotta in colour, swimming in a sauce of tomato and basil, and perfectly tender.

(3) OTHER EDIBLE SEA CREATURES

To complete the catalogues I add notes on various creatures which fall outside the categories of fish, crustaceans and molluscs.

First, a creature from the family *Pyuridae* in the order *Stolidobranchiata*, which in turn is part of the class *Tunicata*.

Microcosmus sulcatus (Coquebert)
FAO 584

REMARKS. Up to about 8 cm. A knobbly creature with a leathery skin which lives anchored to rocks or the seabed and is so constructed as to permit the sea water to pass through it (in at one protuberance and out at the other).

French: Violet, Figue de mer
Greek: Eliá
Italian: Limone di mare, Uovo di mare
Spanish: Probecho
Other names: Mammello di vacca (Sicily); Bunyol, Ou de mar (Cat.)

CUISINE. The yellow part inside, which is what you eat, looks like scrambled egg and is considered to be a delicacy in Provence. The procedure is to cut the violet in half with a knife and to take from each half the edible part, which is eaten raw and is pleasant washed down with white wine. The small violets of Marseille, Toulon and Hyères are reputed to be the best. The ones which I ate in Marseille certainly tasted quite good, and were fairly small. I have never faced up to a big one.

Passing now to the class *Echinodermata*, the order *Diadematoida* and the family *Echinidae* we come to the sea-urchin, of whose sharp spines the bather and underwater fisherman must beware.

Sea-urchin

Paracentrotus lividus (Lamarck)
FAO 585

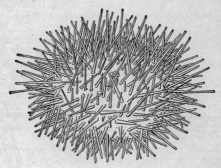

REMARKS. Up to 8 cm. in diameter. The decorative shell is often sold as a marine souvenir. Common on the south and west coasts of Ireland.

CUISINE. All that you eat of this creature (which is sold alive) consists of the five orange or rose ovaries, which are revealed

French: Oursin
Greek: Achinós
Italian: Riccio di mare
Spanish: Erizo de mar
Tunisian: Qanfoud bahr
Other names: Châtaigne de mer and Alisson (Midi)

by cutting the sea-urchin open (horizontally, across the middle with scissors if necessary, but better with the large special implement known as a coupe-oursins, the purchase of which I recommend). Tiny mouthfuls, but delicious. No cooking is needed, nor any accompaniment save a drop of lemon juice.

The three recipes listed below show how sea-urchins may be used to enhance fish dishes or omelettes. Ninette Lyon (*Le Guide Marabout du Poisson*) also suggests adding crushed sea-urchin corals to the egg mixture (one coral to one egg) when you are making scrambled eggs. One whole coral may then be placed on top of the cooked eggs as decoration.

RECIPES.
Oursinado, p. 288.
Omelette d'Oursins, p. 314.
Daurade à la Crème d'Oursins, p. 297.

Thirdly – and from this point onwards we are exploring territory outside the confines of the FAO catalogue – we note a pair of horti-cultural-sounding sea creatures, namely *Anemonia sulcata* (Pennant), the edible sea anemone and *Actinia equina* Linnaeus, the tomate de mer. Both are common on rocky shores on the British coast, where they are known respectively as the snake-locks anemone and the beadlet anemone.

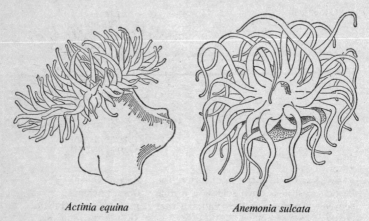

Actinia equina   *Anemonia sulcata*

The sea anemone (also known as ortie de mer in the South of France) is familiar to all who have played on beaches and paddled in rock-pools as children. One prepares them for consumption by rubbing them under running water to remove bits of grit, and (optionally) marinading them in vinegar. They can then be fried or used in an ome-lette or for beignets (*recipe*, p. 315).

The tomate de mer earns its name by being red in colour and as big as a tomato. Less edible, but some think it worth inclusion in a bouilla-baisse.

These creatures play, respectively, the eponymous and an important supporting role in Soupe d'Anémones de Mer, which is enjoyed by Frenchmen, but not often prepared anywhere else. (Euzière recommends heating in a large casserole, with a little olive oil, 36 sea anemones and 6 tomates de mer [all minus tentacles and scraped clean] and plenty of escargots de mer [Nos. 527 or 529], cleaned but in their shells. Add soon and brown a chopped onion, then 2 litres of water, 5 or 6 medium potatoes [peeled], salt and a bouquet garni. Bring to the boil. When the potatoes are cooked mash them. Add pasta, for example vermicelli, and serve when the pasta is ready, with grated cheese.)

Next, we turn to sea turtles. Of the three present in the Mediterranean only one is relatively common. This is the one illustrated above, *Caretta caretta* (Linnaeus), the French caouanne, Spanish caguama, Italian testuggine marina, tartaruga di mare, etc. In Britain and North America it is the loggerhead or common sea turtle. It is brown, and the Mediterranean specimens which I have seen were just under 1 metre long. The meat is good and it is this which is used for Maltese turtle stew (p. 387) and turtle soups.

The tortue de mer verte, *Chelonia mydas* (Linnaeus), a Red Sea species, is found along the southern shores of the Mediterranean as far as the Tunisian island of Djerba. It is olive green.

Thirdly there is the giant sea turtle, leathery turtle or tortue luth, *Dermochelys coriacea* (Linnaeus), which is about 2 metres long and is taken only very rarely. It lives on jellyfish and has special finger-like 'teeth' in its throat to help the food slide down. The back is shield-shaped and bears seven gold ridges running fore and aft. The epithet *coriacea*, incidentally, does not mean that the flesh is tough, but that the back is leathery. There is scope for culinary research here; but the reader should note that his first duty if witnessing or taking part in the capture of a tortue luth is to see that it is handed over in as good a state of preservation as possible to a natural historian, rather than to commence cutting it up and cooking pieces. A limited dispensation might be made for any of my readers so unfortunate as to suffer from dandruff, chronic toothache and shortness of breath. Such a one would command understanding and sympathy if, in accordance with the prescription of the elder Pliny, he first helped himself to a small quantity of the sea turtle's blood, smearing some on his scalp and some on his teeth and consuming the rest with barley to improve his breathing.

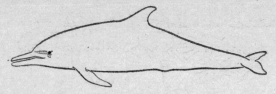

Finally I mention a mammal, the dolphin, **Delphinus delphis** Linnaeus. This large creature, which may be 2½ metres long, is the French dauphine, Italian delfin or dolfin and Spanish delfín. It is a familiar sight, gambolling in the sea, keeping pace with the swiftest ships and reminding us of the numerous legends of the dolphin-rider series (Depicted on the coin of Taras illustrated below).

In general, classical writers depicted the dolphin (Greek *delphis* and Latin *delphinus*) as the lord of the seas, a god-like creature beloved of Poseidon, the swiftest of living creatures, a lover of music, an affectionate parent and a willing helper of fishermen. (The elder Pliny explains how fishermen in the region of Nîmes could by a shout, if the wind was favourable, bring dolphins to their aid in trapping grey mullet, a task for which  they were rewarded by a feed of bread mash dipped in wine.) It is not surprising that it was considered sinful and displeasing to the gods to hunt the dolphin.

It would have been even more shocking to eat the dolphin. Even now the dolphin is not often thought of as food. Yet it is eaten, notably by Italian sailors from Genoa and Viareggio, who cut long strips of the flesh, dry them thoroughly in the sun, and keep and eat the results, which look from the outside like small charred logs. This product is known as musciame. It can be bought at certain shops on the waterfront at Genoa and elsewhere, and is certainly edible and of a distinctive flavour. Very thin slices are cut, rather as salami is sliced (but with more effort, since the musciame is quite hard) and dressed with olive oil and garlic before being eaten. The best which I have had was served with hot butter beans, laced with lightly cooked scraps of onion and olive oil, in the Trattoria Pacetti at Genoa. Being black, the slices of musciame have a dramatic decorative effect.

4. Note for Readers in Britain and North America

You will find that I have included in the introductory passages to the families in the catalogues a good deal of information about which Mediterranean fish or their equivalents occur in British and North American waters, and that there are some hints in the recipe section on possible substitutions. Here I sketch the general picture, so that you can see at a glance that a great deal of Mediterranean seafood is available in Britain by one means or another and that North American readers too have wider scope for using this book than might be thought.

BRITAIN

There are various families or other groups of fish of which it is enough to say that Britain, with her Atlantic and North Sea supplies, is better off than any purely Mediterranean country. This applies to the cod family, where we have hake and whiting in common and also enjoy fresh cod, whereas in the Mediterranean people must be content to make do with salt cod. It applies too to the whole range of flatfish. Our soles are better, we have plaice as well as flounder, and the splendid halibut is an excellent fish with which to perform feats of Mediterranean cuisine which are denied to our Mediterranean cousins. And we probably do rather better than they with regard to lobster, and the rays and skates, and dogfish and the like.

We are adequately provided with eels (although we have difficulty in obtaining lampreys) and can enjoy sea bass and John Dory. We have plenty of gurnards and mackerel. Grey mullet is obtainable, and red mullet too, in season and in the south. Our Dublin Bay prawns and shrimp are excellent, and we have abundant scallops, oysters, mussels and other bivalves. So far as sea bream are concerned our resources are less impressive but we muster enough to be able to use the appropriate Mediterranean recipes. Moreover, some bream are now being imported from the Mediterranean.

This importation of fish from the Mediterranean is a comparatively new development, which has been given impetus by the establishment in Britain of immigrants from the West Indies and elsewhere and by the growth of the popularity of Chinese restaurants. Immigrants look for fish like the fish which they cooked at home. If the demand is strong enough and nothing suitable is available from local supplies it will be obtained from elsewhere. The same applies to foreign restaurateurs. The Chinese are accustomed to cooking fish of the grouper family, and once you have enough Chinese restaurant keepers in Britain hankering for grouper someone will fill the need.

For some years now the firm of C. J. Newnes (at the Billingsgate Fish Market, London EC3) has been building up a specialized business in the importation of fish from the Mediterranean. My friend Jack Shiells is the partner who handles this side of the business. The last time I visited him he told me that he was now bringing in from Greece: barracuda (No. 100), bronze bream (No. 132), red bream (No. 133), black bream (No. 144), picarel (No. 146) and, greatest news of all, mérou (No. 116, etc.). These fish and others such as red mullet are now arriving regularly and in significant quantities, together with lavish supplies of squid (No. 573). They are mostly taken by fishmongers catering for immigrants or by the above-mentioned Chinese restaurateurs, but as British consumers come to realize that these fish are available and ask for them distribution will be more general. This is already happening to some extent. If you want to know where the nearest point of sale is to be found, telephone C. J. Newnes at 01-626 2032.

The growing import system is now also providing bonito from Turkey and frozen sardines from Greece, which both help to facilitate Mediterranean fish cookery in Britain. We do of course have some bonito ourselves, but it is not commonly sold. And the lack of fresh sardines has been a serious matter. We must hope that fresh anchovies will become available too before long, and that we will also enjoy supplies of fresh tunny and swordfish on a scale not known so far, and perhaps even a modest proportion of the Mediterranean catch of the rascasse, archetype of the fish required for Mediterranean fish soups and stews.

NORTH AMERICA

It is difficult to relate the Mediterranean species to those which are encountered in North America, with its three extensive coastlines and range of climate from the warmth of Florida to the Arctic ice. There is a bewilderingly large number of species in American waters, although disappointingly few in the markets. Yet the lists below will show that to a surprising extent the fish of the Mediterranean are found in North American waters in identical or closely related forms.

I list first those fish in North American waters which are similar to and sometimes the same as Mediterranean species, and which do not present any great problem in nomenclature. These include: anchovy, sardine, shad; barracuda and sea bass (of which the striped bass is a relation); dogfish and smoothhound; eel and conger eel; amberjack and bluefish; grey mullet; grouper and wreckfish; half-beak and John Dory; goby and sand-lance; mackerel (atlantic, chub, frigate and horse); pomfret and pompano; marlin and swordfish; many members of the tuna family, including bluefin tuna, albacore, skipjack, and bonito; sea lamprey; skate (or ray); sharks such as the porbeagle and the hammerhead; sturgeon; trigger-fish; crabs, lobster, oysters, scallops, hardshell clams of several kinds, mussels and sea urchins.

Some of these, such as the sea lamprey, are not marketed. Others, such as the wreckfish, goby, sand-lance and triggerfish, will only be found in certain local markets. Others again, notably the dogfish, smoothhound and skates, will be found in Chinese or other oriental markets. But they are all in North American waters.

Next I list species which correspond more or less closely, but whose correspondence is obscured by differences of name. Thus:

AMERICAN NAMES	FAMILY	MEDITERRANEAN NAMES IN ENGLISH
croakers, grunts, kingfish	*Sciaenidae*	meagre, corb
goatfish	*Mullidae*	red mullet
silver hake, pacific hake	*Gadidae*	whiting
gulf hake, and other hake	*Gadidae*	forkbeard
needle fish	*Belonidae*	gar fish
porgie	*Sparidae*	sea bream
ocean perch, redfish, rockfish, scorpionfish	*Scorpaenidae*	rascasse, blue-mouth
sea-robins	*Triglidae*	gurnards
silverside	*Atherinidae*	sand smelt *
shrimp	*Penaeidae, Pendalidae*	prawns

Finally, I must say something about flatfish. There is no practical problem here. There are plenty of flatfish in North American waters,

*'Smelt' in North America is the name for fish in the family *Osmeridae*, not represented in the Mediterranean.

and the Americans are in a position to follow any Mediterranean recipe for them. But there is a linguistic tangle. In Europe and the Mediterranean what we call soles all belong to the family *Soleidae* and have certain characteristics in common, like having their eyes on the right side. The same is not true of our use of the name flounder, which is muddling, but at least we are logical about 'sole'. In North America, however, the two names are applied in what seems like a haphazard manner across the whole range of flatfish, both right-eyed and left-eyed. So on seeing what we call a sole an American would be apt to describe it as a flounder. If served what we call a flounder he would probably wonder why it had been deprived of the more honorific title of sole. The situation is irremediable. I ask only that it should be borne in mind.

5. Note on Mediterranean Fish in Classical Times

A pleasant diversion for the student of Mediterranean fish is to examine what was written on the subject in classical times.

The fundamental work was that of Aristotle. His scientific studies in the field of biology, written during the fourth century B C, overshadowed and underlay just about everything else written on the subject in classical times and indeed until the emergence of the great European naturalists of the sixteenth and seventeenth centuries. The richest vein of ichthyology in the works of Aristotle is in Book IX of the *History of Animals*. Many of his observations, doubted by earlier scholars, have recently been vindicated by studies in the island of Lesbos where Aristotle did a lot of his own research on fish.

In Latin we have the *Natural History* of the Elder Pliny (first century A D), an encyclopaedist rather than a scientist, who enjoyed imparting knowledge without allowing scientific accuracy to spoil a good anecdote and without doing original research himself. Books IX and XXXII, especially the former, contain most of the material on fish. The other relevant major work is a Greek poem, the *Halieutica* by the Cilician poet Oppian. It was written around the end of the second century A D and is quite long – 3500 lines. It is all about fish and fishing and makes agreeable reading.

Although there is sundry other material, for example in the writings of Aelian, these are the main works. Several points stand out when we read them. First, there is the close observation of marine life which enabled Aristotle's work to stand supreme for some eighteen centuries and which is reflected also in Pliny and Oppian. Second, there is the contrast between the straightforward scientific approach of Aristotle and the rather moral, philosophical and romantic approach of Oppian, who treats many of the fish as characters in some sort of subaqueous classical tragedy and extracts from consideration of their failings, virtues, dooms, etc., many lessons for the human race. Third, we find, with a pleasurable feeling of sympathy, as much confusion in the nomenclature of fish in the ancient world as there is nowadays. Moreover there are some fascinating problems there for solving. What was the fish called anthias, for example? So far as we know, the same fish were present in the Mediterranean then as now. The numerous surviving mosaic floors which depict the various species of fish 2000 years ago bear this out.* But some of the ancient names still resist identification, although they have been worked over by classical scholars for centuries. For those who are interested in these mysteries I cite the principal sources and commentaries in the Bibliography.

Another interesting field of study is fish cookery in classical times. Here the principal source is the book *De Re Coquinaria* of Apicius (probably a later amalgam of the two main books which he actually wrote, with accretions of other material, but still essentially his work). Apicius was born about 25 A D. Contemporary references to him are unflattering. He was a wealthy man and spent enormous sums on culinary extravagances, inventing dishes composed of camel heels, peacocks' tongues and the like. On discovering that his fortune had dwindled to the point at which he could not continue his gastronomic whimsies and other expensive habits he committed suicide. All this was more than enough to draw upon him the disapproval of writers such as Seneca. I wonder, however, whether he was really so bad. Athenaeus relates that while Apicius was staying at Minturnae he heard someone vaunt the size of Libyan prawns and hired a ship on the spot to take him to Libya (where he was so disappointed by the prawns which were shown to him that he did not even go ashore). This is an endearing story. And his writings were a solid and lasting achievement, in which there are several interesting fish recipes, and a whole section is devoted to fish sauces. Apicius, I believe, deserves more praise than censure.

Readers who try to follow Apicius' recipes will find some baffling ingredients in them, such as garum. Garum was a strong essence of fish obtained (to put it in the simplest terms) by filling a barrel with fish entrails and salt, leaving it for quite a long time, and drawing off the liquid which formed. It had a strong smell and a strong taste, and

* Most of the fish in the mosaics can be identified easily. Others are puzzling. Since the craftsmen who made the mosaics mostly came from Asia Minor, some have suggested that they may have reproduced fish which they knew at home, for example Black Sea species as well as species common in Italian waters. My own conclusion is that after portraying the fish most common in the Mediterranean and most esteemed by their patrons the mosaicists took refuge in the addition of stylized or vague pictures in order to cover the required number of square metres, and that we rack our brains and tax our eyes in vain if we seek to identify every creature shown.

the Romans could not do without it. Others too have found a preparation of this kind useful. Something of the sort is made in South East Asia;* and in the Mediterranean itself the tradition has survived. The pei salat or pissalat of Provence (p. 292) is perhaps the best known descendant of garum, but it is not the only one. d'Arcy Thompson mentions a garum made from the salted livers of chub mackerel (No. 190) on islands in the Marmara: 'It looks like anchovy sauce, and has an evil but appetizing smell . . .'

The illustration is of one of the special fish plates (shallow pottery bowls on a low circular foot) produced in the south of Italy in the third century BC. This one shows a red mullet on the right, a cuttlefish below, and either a sheepshead bream or a comber on the left. The drawings are stylized, with some wrong details, but lively and pleasing.

*and known as nuoc-nam, nam-pla, etc.

6. Note on the Natural Historians

Rather more than 200 species are listed in the catalogues. The names of about forty natural historians, of many different nationalities, figure beside the names of the species. This shows up clearly the extent and the interlocking nature of the studies which have been conducted since 1758, when the two-name system of zoological nomenclature was introduced by the Swedish naturalist Linnaeus.

Carl Linnaeus (1707–78) scores a much larger number of entries than any other naturalist because, being the first user of this system, he laid down the rules of the game. Linnaeus, who is often referred to by the French version of his name, Linné, or abbreviated as Linn. or simply L., has been irreverently described as 'a queer old Swede who thought he could name everything'. He did indeed try to give a simple double-name in Latinized form to every animal and plant. The continued use of his system bespeaks its merit. Linnaeus was not himself particularly interested in fish, and most of his fish names were based on descriptions published by earlier naturalists, especially his fellow-Swede and friend from their days at Uppsala University, **Peter Artedi** (1705–35). Artedi had been obsessed with fishes from boyhood, and was a century ahead of his time in knowledge of their anatomy and in the accuracy of his descriptions. Unfortunately when still young he fell into a canal at Amsterdam and drowned.

Other earlier naturalists contributed to the foundations on which Artedi and Linnaeus built, amongst them **Ulisse Aldrovandi** (1522–1605), the Italian traveller and philosopher who published a huge tome on fish, and the French contemporaries **Guillaume Rondelet** and **Pierre Belon**. Rondelet, Professor of Anatomy at the University of Montpellier, led a quiet life; but Belon, a diplomat in those tempestuous Reformation years, journeyed in the service of François I to the Near East, to Spain and elsewhere in Europe, and was murdered by an unknown assailant in the Bois de Boulogne in 1564. These two laid the foundations of our knowledge of Mediterranean fish.

One of the scholars who came after Linnaeus was the lively and attractive **Constantine Samuel Rafinesque-Schmaltz** (1783–1840). Born of a French father and a German-Greek mother in Constantinople, Rafinesque (as he normally called himself) became a dominant figure in both European and North American fish literature. He lived for a time in Philadelphia, then spent ten years in Sicily, where he described the fish of the island with great thoroughness. In many ways he was ahead of his time. His attitude to nomenclature and to Mediterranean fish life differed from that of the zoological establishment, over which towered the august Parisian figure of Baron Cuvier, and much of his work was therefore treated with disdain. During the present century, however, many of his observations and names have been recognized as correct.

Rafinesque later returned to the United States, where he met the famous ornithologist John James Audubon, and accompanied him on some of his travels. It is related that the two fell out when Rafinesque, attempting to deal with a bat which had entered their cabin one evening, hit it with the most convenient weapon to hand, which was Audubon's favourite violin; and that Audubon took his revenge by presenting Rafinesque with a wholly spurious collection of drawings of fish from the Ohio River, which Rafinesque later described in good faith, to the detriment of his reputation.

One of the ablest of Rafinesque's Mediterranean contemporaries was an apothecary of Nice, **Antoine Risso,** who published in 1810 an account of the fish of Nice and later amplified it into the *Histoire Naturelle de l'Europe Méridionale* (1826). Another was **Bernard Germain de Lacépède** who during the years 1798 to 1803 brought out a series of five large volumes entitled *Histoire Naturelle des Poissons*. The troubled times in which he worked were reflected in the title page. Although he would properly have been styled Le Comte de la Cépède, his work appeared as '*par le Citoyen La Cépède*' and the style of dating was '*l'an VI de la République*'.

Paris continued to be the centre of ichthyological work, and **Cuvier** was recognized as the most eminent authority. From his study in the museum of the Jardin des Plantes a stream of correspondence went forth all over the world, and the museum was the focal point for international zoological inquiry. Cuvier's best-known work on fish, the twenty-two-volume *Histoire Naturelle des Poissons* was published by him jointly with his pupil and successor, **Achille Valenciennes.**

Two more Frenchmen of this period whose names are commemorated with the fish names which they proposed were the **Geoffroy Saint-Hilaires,** father (Étienne) and son (Isidore). They both accompanied Napoleon on his Egyptian campaign as part of the Emperor's scientific entourage, and were thus able to work on the Nile and in the

Red Sea, where an earlier Swedish naturalist, **Pehr Forskål,** had perished in the 1760s.

Another remarkable figure connected with the Emperor Napoleon was his nephew, **Charles Lucien Bonaparte,** who was educated in Italy, spent some time in the United States doing ornithological work and was active in Italian politics in the 1840s before settling in France. There he was Director of the Jardin des Plantes. Volume 3 (*Pesci*) of his *Iconografia della Fauna Italica* (1832–41) is a heavy folio with beautiful plates of Mediterranean fish.

As we approach the twentieth century the number of naturalists increases and there are fewer dominant figures to be compared with those I have mentioned. I therefore take these notes no further, hoping that what I have said will serve to remind my readers that the classification and naming of the fish in this book was carried out, often in conditions of excitement and danger, by a series of devoted and lively scholars; and that it is right to recall this when we take advantage of the work which they achieved.

(*Opposite*). An octopus on a jar from Knossos, Crete, of about 1450–1400 B.C., in the Ashmolean Museum at Oxford.

Recipes

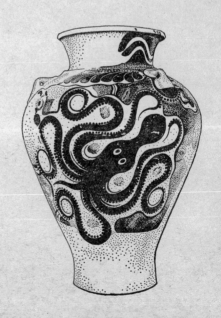

7. Keeping Fish Fresh

Fish is a highly perishable food which spoils rapidly at ordinary temperatures.

WHY AND HOW FISH SPOIL

The decomposition of fish, as of other flesh foods, is brought about in part by the enzymes which occur naturally in the flesh itself; and in part by the bacteria which attack the flesh from outside once the flesh is dead. For practical purposes we need not worry about the enzymes. The bacteria are by far the most important agents in spoilage.

A living fish carries a relatively small population of bacteria on its skin and in its gut. When the fish dies the bacteria penetrate the flesh, feed upon it, grow and multiply. Each bacterium divides into two when it has grown to a certain size. Under suitable conditions growth and division take only 30 minutes.

THE USE OF ICE AND SALT

Fortunately the rate of multiplication of bacteria can be greatly reduced by cooling. In a warm kitchen (75° F or 24° C) just over 500 bacteria grow to be several hundred million in 2 days; at the temperature of well-iced fish (32° F or 0° C) this process takes 2 weeks and at the temperature of frozen fish (below 19° F or −7° C) the growth of bacteria stops altogether. Be guided by this knowledge when buying and storing fish.

Salt halts the action of the bacteria. So gutted fish which are put into a barrel with lots of salt round them will keep for a considerable time.

HOW TO TELL THAT FISH IS FRESH

There are several useful indicators. The first at least cannot be counterfeited by the application of cosmetics or by any other means:

The eyes should be bright and should stand out properly. Dull, sunken eyes are a bad sign.

The gills should be moist and red, not grey.

The body should be firm to the touch and even rigid in some instances. It is a bad sign if you poke a fish and your finger leaves an indentation.

The scales should adhere firmly to the skin (although there are some fish with scales which more or less fall off even when the fish is fresh).

The smell should be fresh and salty.

8. Cooking Fish: A General Essay

It is proper to begin by answering two fundamental questions. What do we mean by cooking fish? And what happens when fish is cooked?

To cook fish is to prepare it for consumption by heating it until its internal temperature is raised to 145° F (63° C) or perhaps a few degrees less. One cannot be absolutely precise, since the temperature to be reached may vary slightly according to the nature of the fish being cooked, the chemical composition of any liquid in which it is being cooked, and other factors. There is, moreover, an interplay between time and temperature. The longer the cooking time, the lower the temperature which must be reached.* None the less it remains true that for any particular piece of fish in any particular set of circumstances there is one exact internal temperature which should be reached but not exceeded, and that this will be very close to 145° F (63° C). To keep this principle firmly in mind is the best safeguard against the sadly common fault of overcooking.

But the principle must be accompanied by another important piece of knowledge which bears on cooking times. This is that the time taken for heat to penetrate to the centre of a piece of fish (or indeed anything else) does not vary in simple proportion to the thickness of the fish, but in proportion to the square of the thickness. If the chosen method of cooking takes 15 minutes to raise to 145° F (63° C) the centremost point of a fish-steak 2 cm. thick, then the time required for a fish steak 4 cm. thick will be 1 hour, not 30 minutes. Remember this, and that most cooking times given in fish recipes, especially recipes for slices or steaks of undefined thickness, should be treated as approximate.

In answer to my second fundamental question Dr J. J. Connell of

*In experiments conducted in a special low-temperature oven at Brussels University I have shown that a fish raised to the temperature of only 125° F (52° C) but kept there for 6 hours will be cooked. The experiments illustrate in a striking way the point in the text. But I do not recommend this very slow low-temperature cooking for fish. And I must point out that while relatively few kinds of bacteria can survive normal cooking temperatures quite a lot will remain alive, although groggy, at the lower temperature.

the Torry Research Station has kindly explained that cooking has three main effects on fish. First, the protein in the flesh is coagulated, giving the flesh a dense, white, curdy appearance. Coagulation liberates about one quarter of the water in the flesh and, depending on the cooking process, this water and the flavouring substances in it separate. In oily fish coagulation may also bring about separation of some of the oil in the flesh. Secondly, the skin-like sheets of material which join the 'flakes' of flesh together are broken down. This allows the flakes to be separated easily from each other. Cooking also tends to soften any bone or skin adhering to the flesh. Finally, a number of chemical changes take place which produce the characteristic odour and flavour of the cooked fish.

These are the processes which it is the cook's task to carry so far but no further.

The basic methods of cooking fish are comparatively few. But cooking terms, like the names of fish, may cause confusion. Here then is my own account of these methods, with hints on their application.

TO GRILL (American BROIL). This is one of the simplest and best procedures. Certain rules are usually followed.* With few exceptions the fish should first be gutted. The sides of a fairly large fish (over 150 grammes) should be scored. The fish should be brushed with oil (some also dust with flour). The grill itself should be pre-heated and should also be brushed with oil. When grilling is under way you will find it necessary to baste the fish regularly. A good way of doing this is to take a quarter of a lemon (cut lengthwise), impale it on the end of a long fork and then dip it in e.g. melted butter or olive oil or a mixture of olive oil and lemon juice and use it to brush the fish. Finally, use a charcoal grill if possible. This really improves the flavour. It should be possible to obtain charcoal almost anywhere. But if you are in Provence, for example, you may achieve even better results by using Aleppo pine or wood from an old olive tree, well dried. Start such a fire well in advance and let it burn down to cinders before using it.

It is possible to buy various pieces of equipment for holding the fish in position while it is being grilled. One is a double metal rack, hinged at one side and with handles at the other, within which one can enclose small or flat fish. Another is a sort of fish-shaped metal basket on feet, which can be placed over the fire with the fish in it. This is suitable for bulkier fish.

TO BAKE. The word bake is used rather vaguely. I understand it to mean a method of cooking fish in an open dish in the oven, with a

*But I must draw attention to the rather different views of the late M. Brun (p. 283).

comparatively small amount of added fat or liquid, or even none. The amount will depend on whether the fish is naturally dry or has its own fat; also on whether anything being cooked with it, e.g. tomatoes, supplies moisture. Dry fish must be basted often. You will often find it useful to place a piece of aluminium foil underneath a fish which you are baking, so that it may later be transferred without damage to a serving dish. The foil is also handy if you are using a dish too big for the fish, since it can be arranged to make an inner lining of just the right size and shape.

We do not normally speak of roasting a fish in English. But the corresponding word in other languages, e.g. French, is used of fish. What is meant is more or less what is described above as baking, usually without added fat or liquid.

TO BRAISE. Braised fish is prepared as follows. Sauté lightly some thinly sliced carrots, shallots, onion, etc., in an oven dish. On this bed lay the fish (whole or a large piece of a big one), with thin strips of fat on top if necessary. Add liquid – usually white wine, perhaps combined with bouillon – up to about half the depth of the fish. Season, heat until the liquid comes just to the boil, and then put in the oven to continue cooking very slowly. Do not forget to baste the fish.

To cook fish EN PAPILLOTE. Place each fish or piece of fish on a sheet of aluminium foil or cooking parchment, add seasoning and herbs and dots of butter or brushings of olive oil, and then fold the foil or paper up on each side and crimp it together above the fish and at each end. If you have made a neat job you can put the result straight into the oven, not bothering with a dish.

TO FRY is to cook by immersion, complete (deep-frying) or partial (pan-frying), in hot oil or fat or butter. A higher heat produces better results, and oil has the advantage over fat or butter that it can be heated further without burning. Olive oil is the best oil to use, groundnut oil a satisfactory alternative. Whatever method or medium you choose, the fish or pieces of fish must always be prepared for frying. Stand them in, e.g., salted milk for a few minutes, pat them roughly dry and roll them in flour (shaking off the excess). The coating thus provided (which may be reinforced by further coatings of beaten egg and fine breadcrumbs) will, on contact with the hot oil, form a protective jacket capable of keeping the oil out and the juices in, while allowing the heat to pass.

Deep-frying is best done in a large frier with a fitted wire basket. The temperature of the oil should be nudging but not above 355° F (190° C). To check this, if you are not using a thermostatically controlled frier or a thermometer, put in a scrap of bread. It should rise to the surface and quickly turn golden-brown; if it turns black the oil is too hot. Be sure to strain your oil of impurities after each use, to store it in a cool place and to renew it completely before rather than after the need to do so becomes obvious.

For *Pan-frying* you will find it useful to have one of those iron oval-shaped pans which are used for fish in France. You may pan-fry with olive oil, or a mixture of olive oil and butter, or (as in the next paragraph) butter alone. The term to *sauté*, by the way, means to pan-fry things which you keep moving or tossing around while you fry them.

To cook fish *à la meunière* is to fry it in butter, good and hot (and preferably clarified). After the fish has been removed a little fresh butter is heated in the pan and then poured frothing over the fish.

TO POACH, usually in a COURT-BOUILLON. If you cook a sizeable fish by this method you will find a fish kettle very helpful – either a poissonière or a turbotière. The former is long and narrow, designed for a fish of conventional shape, while the other is shaped like a lozenge, to take turbot, brill, trigger-fish, John Dory, skate, etc. Each has a cover, and a removable grid inside which enables you to lift out the fish without damage once the cooking is completed. (See drawings.) After the enjoyable experience of buying these vessels you should feel sufficiently stimulated to master the technique of court-bouillon, if you have not already done so. The point of the technique is simply this. You can simmer a fish in plain water with satisfactory results; but the fish

will taste better if you use water with added flavours. Since fish cooks quickly, you will only receive the full benefit of the added flavours if you impart them to the water before you put the fish in. Court-bouillon is the flavoured water which you therefore prepare in advance. There are many recipes for preparing it. I suggest the following.

To 2 litres of water add 2 tablespoonfuls of wine vinegar, 50 grammes of salt, a few crushed peppercorns, a stick of celery, a carrot and an onion cut in slices, a couple of chopped shallots, a clove and a bouquet garni. (If you wish, add a clove of garlic and substitute white wine for some of the water.) Cook the whole gently for at least 30 minutes and allow to cool before using.

If you wish to give your fish a fishier as well as a better taste you should make something like a court-bouillon, but incorporating fish heads and trimmings. The French call such a concoction a fumet. After it has been used for poaching the fish it can be reduced and made into the basis of a sauce.

TO STEW. This is another term which has various shades of meaning. Like the poaching described above, it is a method of cooking things gently by immersion in a hot liquid. The difference, as I see it, is that when you stew you intend to consume the lot, fish and cooking liquid, together. The method, of which examples will be found on pp. 354 and 384, is particularly suitable for creatures like the octopus which require long, slow cooking.

TO BOIL. The only occasions for boiling sea-fish are in the preparation of bouillabaisse (p. 285) and related dishes.

TO STEAM. This procedure requires something like a double boiler, with a perforated bottom to the upper part. Water is boiled in the lower part, and the fish sits in a steam bath in the upper part until it is cooked. The method is comparatively slow.

Weights and Measures

In most of the recipes I have used the metric system. That is what is used in the Mediterranean, whence the recipes come, and what is coming into use in Britain.

But readers who use pounds and pints will need a conversion table. This I supply below. It is a very simple one. I have used as few units of measurement as possible in the recipes and drawn up the tables so as to provide equivalents for these few units only. I take account, where this is really necessary, of the notorious difference between British and American pints (and measuring cups). But when the amounts are small it is reasonable to disregard tiny differences. One should not, in cooking, be indiscriminately precise. Precision over temperatures is often necessary. But precision over quantities of ingredients is at best a virtue which need not be practised in the great majority of cooking operations and at worst a dangerous vice (if it distracts the cook's attention from other more important aspects of his work). I dare say that I should have to change my tune if I began to bake cakes. But I intend to continue leaving this to others, and I am confident that what I have said applies to the subject of this book, Mediterranean fish cookery.

WEIGHTS

In the recipes	British/American
2 kilos	$4\frac{1}{2}$ lb.
1 kilo	$2\frac{1}{4}$ lb.
$\frac{1}{2}$ kilo (500 grammes)	just over 1 lb.
$\frac{1}{4}$ kilo (250 grammes)	just over $\frac{1}{2}$ lb.
100 grammes	iust under $\frac{1}{4}$ lb.
50 grammes	just under 2 oz.

LIQUID MEASURES

In the recipes	British	American
1 litre	$1\frac{3}{4}$ pints	just over 2 pints
	$3\frac{1}{2}$ cups	just over 4 cups
$\frac{1}{2}$ litre (or 5 decilitres)	$\frac{7}{8}$ pint	just over 1 pint
	$1\frac{3}{4}$ cups	just over 2 cups
$\frac{1}{4}$ litre (or $2\frac{1}{2}$ decilitres)	just under $\frac{1}{2}$ pint	just over $\frac{1}{2}$ pint
	just under 1 cup	just over 1 cup
1 wineglassful ($1\frac{1}{2}$ decilitres)	$\frac{1}{2}$ cup	$\frac{5}{8}$ cup
1 decilitre	$3\frac{1}{2}$ fl. oz.	almost $3\frac{1}{2}$ fl. oz.
1 tablespoonful	1 tablespoonful	1 tablespoonful
1 teaspoonful	1 teaspoonful	1 teaspoonful

NOTE 3 teaspoonfuls = 1 tablespoonful
8 tablespoonfuls = 1 wineglassful

OVEN TEMPERATURES

Fahrenheit	Centigrade	General term and gas-regulo setting	
240	115	very slow	($\frac{1}{4}$)
290	145	slow	(1)
355	180	moderate	(4)
400	205	moderately hot	(6)
430	220	hot	(7)
470	245	very hot	(9)

9. Introduction to the Recipes

The recipes which follow are all from the Mediterranean area, and for seafood fished in the Mediterranean.* I have aimed to provide recipes from all parts of the Mediterranean, while favouring the parts which I know best, and to cover as wide a range of species as possible. I have been generous in including recipes which are easy and adaptable, calculating that this will excuse the inclusion of some which are difficult or of mainly local or academic interest. But perhaps no excuse is needed. The wholly practical and methodical cookery book has its place on every cook's shelf. Yet a place is reserved too for the cookery book which can be dipped into outside the kitchen as well as used within it. And variety of character and presentation is important in recipes, as it is in food.

ADAPTATION OF MEDITERRANEAN RECIPES

I spoke above of adaptable recipes. It is necessary to make a distinction here. There are some Mediterranean fish recipes which depend for their effect on the use of specified fish or other sea creatures which may not be found elsewhere and which have a distinctive flavour for which there is no adequate substitute. I am thinking of some of the fish which go into a Marseille soupe de roche, of the cigale and so on. Where a recipe depends on these, you can adapt it by using other ingredients, but you will produce something essentially different which people who know how the dish is supposed to taste are likely to regard as unsuccessful. It is not advisable to expend much effort in this direction. On the other hand there are many Mediterranean recipes which derive their effect not from the choice of fish but from the flavour imparted by the other ingredients and the method of cooking. Here you can adapt freely and successfully. If Mediterranean cooks had fresh cod and halibut and so on they would use these recipes for them. They don't. But if you are in Britain or North America you do, and you can.

*Hence the absence of recipes for dried cod (morue, bacalao, baccala, baccalyaros, etc.), even though these recipes are prominent in Mediterranean fish cookery.

GARLIC AND THE SOFFRITTO

Many Italian recipes include the instruction to make a soffritto, which is a mixture of chopped-up onion, garlic, parsley and probably tomato and other ingredients too, lightly cooked in olive oil. In France the corresponding instruction is so familiar as to be like an incantation: '*Faites revenir à l'huile un oignon haché, des tomates épluchées, épépinées et concassées, deux gousses d'ail écrasées . . .*' In Spain they talk of a sofrito. Chopped onion is coloured in olive oil. Tomato and paprika are often added, and sometimes garlic.

In all the variations of this common initial process there is one important rule to follow: apply the heat gently. Specifically:

(1) Do not burn the garlic, or it will turn bitter.

(2) Do not carry the cooking of the onion too far. It will become successively translucent, pale golden and brown. Stop at the right point.

(3) When paprika is used, as in Spain, take great care not to let it burn. It is best to add it at the last moment, away from the heat.

(4) If anchovy fillets are to be incorporated take care not to heat them too far or they will turn bitter.

TOMATOES

The housewife, especially in the Mediterranean, finds several kinds of tomato. One is red and of a uniform round shape. Another is small and shaped like a plum; it is often described as a cooking tomato. A third is irregular in shape, with bulges and ridges, and often marketed while still partly yellow or green. All three in fact belong to the one main species of tomato, *Lycopersicon esculentum*. But many maintain that the second kind is best for cooking and that the third has the most flavour and is best for salads.

Recipes often say that you may use either so many fresh tomatoes (peeled and seeded), or so much tomato paste (or purée or concentrate) diluted with water. The degree of concentration in tomato concentrates varies; but a rough guide is that 1 tablespoonful is the equivalent of 2 large tomatoes. It is often a good plan to use some fresh tomatoes and some tomato paste too. Fresh tomatoes have a surplus of liquid. This can of course be drained away to some extent beforehand, or cooked away; but even a touch of tomato paste is likely to be useful in thickening a soffritto or sauce quickly. Using tomato paste alone will save time, but then you miss the texture provided by the tomato flesh.

The Italians, incidentally, make particularly free use of tinned tomatoes, which they call pelati since they come peeled. These are often just as good as fresh ones, or better, in fish dishes. Drain them before use, saving the liquid for other purposes.

PARSLEY

Plain-leaved parsley is widely used in the Mediterranean area. In Britain the curly-leaved variety is preferred. Both belong to the same species (*Petroselinum crispum*) and the difference need not be regarded as significant for cooking purposes. Whichever you have, be generous with it.

PEPPER AND PEPPERS

Black and white, green and red and yellow, hot and sweet and mild, peppers, pimentoes and chillies – just how many different things are involved here? The answer is that we are concerned with only three plants.

First, there is *Capsicum annuum*. It bears fairly large fruit, of various shapes and of varying degrees of mildness, but always at the mild end of the hot/mild spectrum. The unripe fruit is green, and familiar as an ingredient of salads. The ripe fruit is yellow or red, and may be known as sweet or mild peppers or paprikas or (in Spain) pimientos. Paprika (the red powder) is made from them.

Secondly, there is *Capsicum frutescens*, the red pepper or chilli, which also covers a range of degrees of hotness but is very definitely at the hot end of the spectrum. The fruit are usually of a thin conical form. Unripe, they are green. They turn yellow and then red as they ripen. Some of them are very hot indeed. A paste made from them can be bought in tins. (This product is known as harissa in Tunisia, and the tiny tins which we bought there bore on the outside a picture of a volcano – very appropriate.) Hot red peppers are often dried, when they turn wrinkled and assume the colour of dried blood. Cayenne pepper is made from them.

Thirdly, there is *Piper nigrum*, a vine-like plant which produces peppercorns which are the source of both black and white pepper. If unripe peppercorns are dried in the sun the result is the little wrinkled black peppercorns which we are accustomed to putting in our pepper mills. White pepper is made by grinding the white seed contained within the ripe peppercorns.

End of note on peppers. But one word more: when a recipe calls for salt and pepper use freshly ground rock salt (or as it is sometimes called, sea salt) and freshly ground black pepper.

RICE

Rice is the grain of *Oryza sativa*. The main categories are long-, medium- and short-grain. Short-grain (and sometimes medium-grain) rice may also be called round-grain. Within these categories are many specific names which indicate strains and often show where they were originally produced (Patna, Carolina and so on). In Britain the rice most commonly sold, apart from the short-grain rice which we normally use for puddings, is long-grain Patna rice from the United States. (Much of it, e.g. Uncle Ben's and Sainsbury's Easy Cook, is parboiled before the brown cuticle is milled away from the white grain; the process transfers some of the goodness from the cuticle to the grain, tingeing it a pale brown and making it less apt to stick when cooked.) This American Patna rice is good for many purposes, but other kinds of rice are available and it is worth while seeking out the right kind for a particular dish when you can.

For Middle Eastern rice and fish dishes I recommend basmati rice, which is long-grain and has a relatively strong flavour. Patna will do instead, and is suitable for Turkish dishes. For Greek dishes I suggest either the medium-grain Carolina strain, or again Patna. An Italian risotto is made with the distinctive round-grain rice of Piedmont (ask for Arborio Superfino). For Provençal rice dishes, failing rice from the Camargue (which is mostly exported to franco-phone countries overseas), use Carolina or Patna. For Spanish dishes ask a Spanish grocer for Valencia rice. This is a small round-grain rice, so you could use Italian risotto rice instead, or indeed Carolina. I buy Carolina rice from Harrod's; Piedmont and basmati rice from Elizabeth David's shop at 46 Bourne Street, London S.W.1; and Valencia rice from A. Gomez Ortega of 74 Old Compton Street, London W.1.

WHAT I DON'T TELL YOU

This is a fish cookery book. I have not taken up space with explanations of all the general cookery operations to which I allude. There are lots of less specialized books which do this very well. Most readers will have their own favourites, to which they can turn for information about basic sauces, pastry and so on. I particularly recommend Len Deighton's *Où est le Garlic?* in the Penguin series.

10. Recipes from Spain

The regions of Spain differ considerably one from another in their cuisines as well as in other respects. Here we are concerned with five: Andalucia, Murcia, Valencia and Cataluña, which between them cover the Mediterranean coastline from the Strait of Gibraltar to the French frontier, and the Balearic Islands (Mallorca, Menorca and Ibiza).

In Andalucia, which also includes some of the Atlantic coastline and the port of Cadiz, we find interesting specialities at Málaga, the first of the great Spanish cities on the Mediterranean coast, and at Almería, the next. 'A la Andaluza', incidentally, normally indicates the presence of both tomato and red peppers.

Murcia offers a particularly interesting way of baking fish in a jacket of rock salt; and Valencia is famous for its rice and for combinations of rice and seafood, such as arroz a la marinera.

The first Spanish cookery book, published in 1477, was printed in Barcelona, and the literature of Catalan cookery has bloomed profusely ever since. There has been a certain neighbourly intermingling of cooking practices with the southern parts of France, especially the Roussillon and Languedoc; and the gastronomic frontier, like the linguistic one, is far less clear than the political one. But there are many Catalan fish dishes, such as Zarzuela de Pescado, which are quite distinctive, and a source of pride to the Catalan people. '*La cocina catalana no admite trampas en la cocina*', they say, meaning that they bar kitchen tricks such as would disguise inferior fish by masking it in a fancy sauce.

Finally, the Balearic Islands. In Mallorca there has appeared one of the most agreeable local cookery books to be found anywhere in the Mediterranean area. Entitled *Cocina Selecta Mallorquina*, it is the work of Señora Coloma Abrinas Vidal, who was born at Campos del Puerto in 1887, and went to work as a cook in Palma in 1901. Having passed the age of seventy, Señora Vidal agreed to commit her knowledge to paper, although she had never learned to read or write and her recipes had to be dictated. Every year thereafter the authoress dictated some more so that each successive annual edition of her book was larger. The seventh edition (1968) ends with the expression of religious sentiments and the following statement in bold type: 'In six years I have made six editions of my book and in each one I have added new dishes, and in this last one 86 new recipes; but it seems to me that these will be the last for now I feel myself very aged.' I salute this good and skilled lady, not least because she devotes so much attention in her book to Mallorcan fish dishes, which are more numerous than the tourist might suppose and of which a generous selection appears below.

Caldillo de Perro
' Dog soup' – a fish soup with juice of bitter oranges

This is an Andalucian soup. Its home port is El Puerto de Santa María, near to Cadiz and just round the corner out of the Mediterranean. The essential element of the recipe is small hake (pescadillas) which must be very very fresh, still shining with sea water. In his book *Guía del Buen Comer Español* Señor Dionisio Pérez described the scene at midnight on the quayside at Cadiz as the fishing boats came in. The dog-soup makers were waiting there in the dark, eager to secure their fish at the first possible instant.

The young hake are to be cut into slices 7 centimetres thick, and heavily seasoned with salt. They are left thus for an hour, stiffening.

The next step is to heat oil in a casserole and fry some cloves of garlic in it. When they are turning brown remove and discard them. Then put some finely chopped onion into the same oil, and before it can take colour add plenty of boiling water. Cover and cook until the onion is soft.

Now raise the heat considerably and add the pieces of hake, in such a way as not to arrest the boiling even for a moment. Continue to boil for 15 to 20 minutes, and at the last moment pour in a generous amount of the juice of bitter oranges. Some add bits of bread when the soup is served. The traditional way of serving it is in a 'cazuela de barro' or earthen plate, as is done at the restaurant 'El Resbaladero' at El Puerto de Santa María.

Sopa del Duelo
Mourning soup (serves six)

This Andalucian soup is also called Sopa de los Muertos (soup of the dead). The gloomy titles arise from its being served traditionally to mourners keeping watch on a dead body on the eve of the burial. It is a type of gazpachuelo, or soup made with the addition of mayonnaise. The following recipe, from El Rincón de Juan Pedro in Almería, produces a version which is pretty as well as delicious. You will need:

1½ litres fish broth (made by cooking fish heads, etc., in a court-bouillon and then straining the result)

2 slices smoked ham, cut into little squares

¼ kilo angler-fish (No. 249), cleaned and cut up

¼ kilo hake (No. 81), cleaned and cut up

6 prawns

a handful of green peas

1 sweet red pepper, chopped

sippets of fried bread

6 tablespoons mayonnaise made with lemon juice

Heat the fish broth to boiling point, and then simmer the pieces of fish, the prawns, the pepper and the peas in it for 20 minutes or until all are cooked. At the last moment add the mayonnaise, which should be very pale and lemony, and the sippets. You then have a milky lemony soup in which the pink of the ham and prawns and the red of the pepper and the green of the peas form a fresh colour scheme which is markedly unfunereal.

Sopa de Peix
Fish soup   (serves four)

This is the Mallorcan version. It is usually made with picarel (No. 145). Saddled bream (No. 143) is a common alternative. It may also be made with angler-fish (No. 249), when the fish would be eaten too.

Buy about 1 kilo of picarel, or other fish suitable for making soup. Gut them.

Prepare a sofrito by heating olive oil in an earthenware cooking dish (the kind called a 'greixonera'), frying tomatoes in this until you have a smooth mixture, and then adding chopped shallots, Swiss chard (optional) and parsley.

Add the fish to the sofrito and let them fry for a few minutes. Then add 1¼ to 1½ litres of water and boil the whole for half an hour.

Strain the soup, add a cup of rice, bring back to the boil and continue until the rice is almost cooked. At this point add a little very finely chopped (or pounded) garlic and parsley. Two minutes later remove from the heat and serve.

Suquillo (or Suquet)

A Spanish fish stew (serves four)

On some parts of the Spanish coast a dish with names like bulavesa is to be found, which is a Spanish variation or imitation of the French bouillabaisse. But there are also dishes of the same kind which are distinctively Spanish such as this one, of which the version below comes from San Carlos de la Rápita in the province of Tarragona.

Use if possible fish with fairly firm flesh, such as turbot or denté. Buy ¾ kilo. Clean the fish, cut it or them up if necessary, and apply a light sprinkling of salt.

Pound in a mortar 4 cloves of garlic with 1 small peeled tomato and a sprig of parsley. Meanwhile heat about 1½ wineglassfuls of olive oil in an earthenware casserole. When the oil is very hot fold into it the pounded mixture, stirring a little. Add a couple of pinches of paprika, stirring again but only a little. Next add the fish and enough hot water barely to cover them, bring the whole quickly to a fierce boil and keep it there for 5 minutes, after which let it boil more gently for a further 10 minutes or so until the fish is cooked through. Serve straight from the casserole.

Arroz a la Marinera

A dish of seafood and rice (serves eight)

Valencia is the great rice region of Spain, and the Valencian Paella is a justly famous rice dish. The paella includes a mixture of seafood, chicken, pork and maybe sausages. Arroz a la marinera is the name given to a paella-type dish in which the rice is accompanied by seafood alone. You will need:

⅓ litre olive oil
700–750 grammes rice (if possible Valencian–see p. 264)
plenty of paprika
2 onions, chopped
4 tomatoes, peeled and chopped

½ kilo in all of angler-fish (No. 249), squid (No. 573) and cuttlefish (No. 568), prepared and cut into chunks and strips
½ kilo in all of Norway lobster (No. 512), prawns (No. 503) and mussels (No. 545)
just over 2 litres of fish stock

Heat the olive oil and add the pieces of angler-fish, squid and cuttle-fish. When these are golden add the chopped onion and tomato and paprika. Continue to fry all this for a few minutes, taking care not to burn the paprika.

Next add the rice and twice the quantity by volume of fish stock. (This will work out at just over 2 litres or $3\frac{3}{4}$ British pints.) Three minutes later add the Norway lobster, prawns and mussels (cleaned but whole). Continue cooking for about 20 minutes until the rice has absorbed all the liquid.

This version has been formulated with expert advice from the Restaurant Blayet which is situated on the sea near Valencia and close to the Albufera. Arroz a la Banda is a related dish from Alicante, in which the rice is served separately from the fish, which is accompanied by potatoes. Fish and potatoes are dressed with a vinaigrette sauce.

Pastelillos de Pescado
Fish pasties

These are widely sold in the food shops in, for example, Valencia. They are semi-circular, not unlike Cornish pasties in appearance.

To make them, prepare whatever quantity you need of puff pastry. Lightly fry in hot olive oil some peeled and chopped tomatoes and chopped sweet red pepper, combine this with flaked tuna fish from a tin (the cheapest quality is suitable) and your filling is ready. Roll out the pastry thinly into six-inch rounds, place a good dollop of the filling close to the middle but just off centre, fold over into a half-moon shape and crimp the edges down all the way round. Brush with beaten egg and bake in a hot oven for 15 to 20 minutes until the pasties are cooked and golden in colour.

Peix en es Forn
Fish baked with chard, as in Mallorca (serves four)

3 large potatoes	800–900 grammes of slices or
1 large onion	fillets of a suitable fish (e.g.
large bunch parsley	hake)
large bunch Swiss chard	$1\frac{1}{2}$–2 wineglassfuls olive oil
2 tomatoes, peeled	$\frac{1}{2}$ wineglassful white wine
salt and pepper	

Peel and slice the potatoes. Oil the bottom of a baking dish and cover it with the slices of potato. Chop the onion, parsley and chard. Add half of this and half the peeled tomatoes. Season. Lay the slices or fillets of fish on top, cover them with the remaining onion, parsley, chard and tomato. Season again, pour the olive oil over all and bake for 1 hour in a moderate oven. Just before the cooking is completed add the white wine.

Pescado en Escabeche
Marinaded fish

Spaniards have various ways of preparing an escabeche or marinade which will impart flavour to fish and also help preserve it. Here is one.

Pound together in a mortar cloves of garlic, with saffron and a little ginger. Add vinegar and salt and water, sufficient to make the taste of the mixture palatable, and cover fried fish with this. Add slices of lemon and a couple of bay leaves, and leave overnight, or longer.

Similar marinades are in use in many parts of the Mediterranean, and the word 'escabeche' appears in a variety of forms (French escabèche, Algerian scabetch, Italian scapece, and so on).

Zarzuela de Pescado
A musical comedy of fish (serves twelve at least)

6 large tomatoes
4 to 6 cloves of garlic
4 tablespoonfuls chopped parsley
6 tablespoonfuls olive oil
½ teaspoonful paprika
½ teaspoonful saffron
salt, pepper
1 tablespoonful flour mixed with a little water
1 wineglassful wine (optional)

fish (quantities need not be too precise)
½ kilo squid (No. 573)
½ kilo hake (No. 81)
½ kilo angler-fish (No. 249)
2 or 3 sole (No. 238, etc.)
a few pieces of mero (No. 116, etc.)
300–400 grammes prawns
1 lobster (optional)

Clean all the fish and cut it into slices. Make a fish stock by boiling the heads, etc. in a little water with salt, pepper, herbs, sliced onion and reducing to a cupful. Strain and put aside. Chop the garlic and put it to cook slowly in the hot oil in a heavy pan. Peel, seed and chop the tomatoes and add them together with the parsley. Simmer for 10 minutes until all the ingredients are well blended.

Now add the fish – those that need long cooking first (i.e. anglerfish, squid, lobster, mero, prawns). Hake and sole can go in a little later. Cook for a few minutes, then add the paprika, saffron, stock and wine if used. Stir in the flour and water, taking care not to break up the fish. Cook for 15 to 20 minutes, season with salt and pepper and serve very hot.

Note: If you buy uncooked prawns they go in unshelled; but in England for example you may buy ready-cooked (and shelled) prawns, which would be put in for only a few minutes at the end.

All i Pebre

Eel stew (serves eight)

The Albufera, a lake near Valencia, is rich in eels, and this is a local method of cooking them. The title of the recipe is Valencian Catalan for garlic and pepper.

8 smallish eels (No. 66) about 18 ins. long	1 teaspoonful paprika
1 wineglassful olive oil	a piece of a hot red pepper (size according to taste)
3 or 4 cloves garlic ⎱ very finely	
12 blanched almonds ⎰ chopped	

Clean but do not skin the eels. Cut them into pieces. Heat the olive oil until it is very hot. Add the garlic and almonds, then the paprika (which must not be allowed to burn and turn black). Add next ½ litre water and the pieces of eel, and cook for 15 minutes, adding the piece of hot red pepper towards the end. Allow the dish to 'rest' for a few minutes before serving it.

Angulas

Larval eels cooked in boiling oil

This dish is popular in many parts of Spain. The particular version given here is recommended by Don Francisco Bauza, of the Restaurante Gina in Palma. It may be compared with Ce'e alla Salvia (p. 334).

Take individual earthenware dishes such as are used for frying in Mallorca. Put olive oil in each, enough to cover a helping of the tiny eels. Add hot red pepper, chopped but not too finely, and a whole clove of garlic to each, then heat them up until the oil is at boiling point. Toss in the tiny eels, which will be cooked in a moment. Serve them in the dishes in which they have been cooked, with the oil still bubbling.

Tradition insists that while the eels are being cooked they should be stirred with a wooden utensil, and they are eaten with little wooden forks.

Conchas de Atún
Tunny in scallop shells (serves six)

This is a pleasant and colourful way of serving tinned tuna fish. It is endorsed by Pamela Davidson, whose experience is reflected in the following instructions. Apart from the tuna fish you will need to have a hard-boiled egg, a sweet pimento (tinned or fresh, but if fresh take care to sear, peel and seed), some cooked peas, and the salsa escarlata described below.

To make the scarlet sauce you will need another 3 or 4 sweet red pimientos (again tinned or fresh), the yolks of 3 eggs, salt, olive oil and the juice of $1\frac{1}{2}$ lemons. The procedure is to pound the peeled pimentos and stir into them gradually the egg yolks, salt and olive oil until a fairly thick sauce is formed. Add the lemon juice to this.

Now take your scallop shells and put some tuna meat in each. Cover generously with the salsa escarlata, surround with peas, garnish with a slice of the hard-boiled egg on top of the sauce and small decorative pieces of pimento making a red tracery over the green peas.

Besugo con Almendras a la Castellana
Red bream with almonds (serves six)

1 large or 2 smaller red bream (No. 133) weighing $1\frac{1}{2}$ kilos, uncleaned	2 tablespoonfuls olive oil
	1 onion, finely chopped
1 lemon, cut in half slices	several sprigs parsley, finely chopped
100 grammes lightly toasted almonds	1 cup white sauce

Clean the fish and cut it (or them) into 6 large pieces. Slit each piece and insert a half slice of lemon. Blanch the almonds and heat them in the oven until they are just beginning to colour. Then stud the pieces of fish with them.

Coat the bottom of an oven dish with olive oil. Place the pieces of fish in this. Strew the chopped onion and most of the chopped parsley over them. Sprinkle a little more olive oil over all. Bake in a moderate oven for about 45 minutes. Meanwhile make a white sauce and pour this over the fish, with some more chopped parsley, just before serving.

Boquerones a la Malagueña
Fresh anchovy as prepared at Málaga

The Spanish coast around Málaga yields a rich harvest of anchovy, which are presented in an unusual way. Cleaned and dusted with flour, they are arranged in 'fans' of five in the left hand, with the tails held together between the thumb and forefinger and the bodies fanning out across the palm. If the tails are pressed firmly together, they can be held in place temporarily. The whole fan is then deep fried in very hot oil, which will cause the tails to stick permanently.

These fried fans of anchovy can be preserved for some time in an escabeche or marinade (see p. 270).

Cap-roig (o Dentón o Mero) con Salsa de Almendra
Rascasse rouge (or denté or mérou) with almond sauce   (serves four)

Don Nicolas Magraner Garcia of Palma recommends the following procedure, for which you will need 800 grammes or so (cleaned weight) of fish, cut into 8 pieces.

Dip the pieces of fish in seasoned flour, then brown them lightly in a frying-pan with olive oil. Grind up 100 or 150 grammes of toasted almonds. Peel, halve and grill 4 tomatoes (6 if they are small). Grill 2 chicken livers. Mix all this together, add $\frac{3}{4}$ of a wineglassful of sherry and mix some more. Place the pieces of fish, with the oil in which they were fried, in a greixonera (flameproof earthenware casserole) and pour the sauce over them. Cover and cook gently for about 30 minutes.

Chanquetes and Aladroch

Chanquetes are the tiny transparent gobies (No. 212). They are eaten whole – fried in batter, golden brown with the eyes standing out as tiny black dots, and served with lemon. This is a popular dish at Málaga.

The aladroch of Valencia may seem very similar, but are the fry of the anchovy (No. 61). Like the French poutine they are sold from buckets; and the French Omelette à la Poutine (p. 292) is matched by the Spanish Tortilla de Aladroch, both being made by adding these minute fish to the egg mixture before cooking it. Note, however, that aladroch, unlike poutine, is a name which can be applied to the anchovy when it is larger.

As in France, there is a good deal of confusion over these tiny fish. The name chanquetes is often used of anchovy fry, although it should properly be reserved for the transparent gobies.

Congrio o Musola con Pasas y Piñones
Conger eel – or smooth-hound or cuttlefish – with raisins and pine-nut kernels

A Mallorcan recipe which is most often used for cuttlefish, although it came to my attention through a household in Palma where children are given it in the smooth-hound version for their lunch, and are excited by the thought that they are eating a kind of shark.

Cut the fish into pieces and dust them with flour (leave out the flour if you are using cuttlefish). Fry the pieces in very hot oil, in an earthenware dish if you have a suitable one, until they are golden brown. Add a large onion, finely chopped, and let this brown too. Then add a large tomato, peeled, pipped and chopped. Lower the flame and continue cooking slowly. When the sauce seems to be ready add some raisins and pine-nut kernels, and shortly afterwards a 'picadillo' of chopped garlic and parsley mixed with black pepper and pimentón (ground sweet red pepper, or paprika).

Dentón al Horno
Baked denté   (serves six)

1 denté (No. 125), weighing just over 1 kilo, cleaned	6 cloves garlic, chopped
1½ kilos onions, sliced	several sprigs parsley, chopped
1 lemon, cut in half-slices	1½ tablespoonfuls dry bread-crumbs
salt and pepper	1 wineglassful olive oil

Put the sliced onions in the bottom of a baking dish, as the bed for the fish. Score the cleaned fish on both sides, insert the lemon half-slices into the score marks, and lay the fish on its bed.

Mix thoroughly the garlic, parsley and breadcrumbs and moisten the mixture with olive oil, then spread it over the fish. Sprinkle with freshly ground black pepper and rock salt. Pour the rest of the olive oil carefully over the fish and bake it in a medium oven until golden brown (about half an hour).

This robust Mallorcan recipe, from Sra Catalina Vera of Puerto de Andratx, has a milder counterpart on the mainland, which I have found very good also for other members of the bream family (e.g. pargo, breca, besugo, sargo, Nos. 129, 131, 133, 138). The fish is prepared in the same way, but with strips of red pimento as well as lemon half-slices in the score marks. No bed of onions; instead, a little melted butter and a bay leaf in the bottom of the dish. The fish is baked thus for 10 minutes; then a wineglassful of white wine is poured in; the fish is turned over and anointed with the olive oil/garlic (3 cloves only)/parsley/breadcrumbs mixture; and cooking is continued, with regular basting, for another 20 to 30 minutes.

Lubina en Salsa Verde
Sea bass in green sauce (serves four)

This recipe, which reflects the emphasis on colour which is so evident in Spanish cookery, can be used for many species of fish.

1 sea bass (No. 113), weighing about 1 kilo whole	1 small onion, chopped
	1 large bunch parsley
flour and salt	2 cloves garlic
1 wineglassful olive oil	freshly ground pepper
	juice of ½ lemon

Clean the fish and cut it into steaks. Salt these lightly, roll them in flour and fry them gently in the hot olive oil until they are golden-brown but not fully cooked. At this stage remove them to a baking dish and keep them hot. Using the same oil, which must not be too hot, let the onion cook slightly, adding a little flour to thicken the mixture, but not allowing it to become brown. Meanwhile, finely chop into a bowl the parsley and garlic. Pound it, add 3 or 4 tablespoonfuls of stock (if you have some) or water, add also the contents of the frying pan and some freshly ground pepper. Stir the lot together, pour it over the fish in the baking dish, add the lemon juice and bake in a moderate preheated oven for 15 to 20 minutes.

(Recipe of Mme de Bermejo)

Merluza Rellena
Stuffed hake

Hake is a favourite Spanish fish, and is served in many different ways. One of the most interesting methods, which should appeal to the British taste, is to stuff it with ham and egg.

The stuffing can be major or minor. For the minor stuffing it is only necessary to clean the fish, open it out from below, remove the backbone, fill up the space thus created with a mixture of chopped ham and hard-boiled egg (and stoned olives, if you like), sew the fish up again and cook it in simmering water to which you have added seasoning, a bay leaf and parsley.

The major stuffing is reminiscent of the Turkish recipe for Uskumru Dolması on p. 369, in that as much of the flesh of the fish as possible is taken out (without damage to the skin) and mixed with other ingredients before being put back as the stuffing. Chopped ham and hard-boiled egg would be among the other ingredients, also a sweet red pepper. The stuffed fish is sewn up and baked in the oven in an oiled oven dish with a bay leaf and chunks of tomato.

I came across traces of a similar recipe at Sfax in Tunisia, where the grey mullet was the fish chosen for a major stuffing operation. There the flesh was mixed with hard-boiled egg (no ham) and parsley. It would be interesting to know whether the Tunisian version derived from either the Turks or the Spaniards, or was itself the original dish which both the Turks and Spaniards, when ruling Tunisia, took over and adapted for use with their own favourite fish.

Mero a la Naranja

Mérou with orange sauce (serves six)

There is a saying in Valencia: '*De la mar el mero, y del monte el cordero*', which means that just as lamb is the best product of the mountains so the mérou is the finest fare to be had from the sea. The people of Almería also appreciate the mérou, and here is one attractive recipe for it which they have evolved.

The fish itself is easily prepared. Buy 6 steaks of mérou and either grill or fry them. The sauce is also easy, and only requires butter and flour, meat stock or bouillon, orange juice and seasoning. First make a thick roux with $1\frac{1}{2}$ ounces each of butter and flour, then blend in gradually up to $\frac{1}{2}$ pint of meat stock or bouillon with a touch of salt and $\frac{1}{4}$ pint of orange juice (the juice of two oranges), until you obtain the desired consistency – a moderately thick sauce. Pour this over the fish steaks and decorate them with very thin half-slices of orange.

I have myself always sensed an affinity between the mérou and oranges, and this sauce suits my taste very well. But some may prefer a sharper sauce, which they can achieve by replacing some of the orange juice with lemon juice, or using the juice of bitter oranges.

Mujol o Dorada a la Sal
Grey mullet or daurade baked in rock salt   (serves four)

This is an interesting method of fish cookery practised in Murcia.

A fairly large member of the bream or grey mullet clans is to be used. It should be washed but not scaled or gutted, and left absolutely whole.

Choose an oven dish large enough to take the fish, and of a reasonable depth. Pour in rock salt to form a fairly thick bed on which the fish is then placed. Pour more rock salt around and over the fish until it is completely enveloped. Pat it down. Put the dish in a medium oven and leave it for 50 to 60 minutes. When you take it out you will find that the salt has hardened into a kind of armour. Break it with a tap from something heavy, and prise it off. It should bring the skin of the fish away with it, exposing the succulent flesh inside, all ready to eat.

Raya a la Malagueña
Ray cooked in the Málaga style   (serves six)

1¼ kilos (cleaned weight) ray (preferably No. 31)
salt
½ wineglassful olive oil
1 thin slice of bread, crumbled
1 sprig parsley, chopped

12 almonds, peeled and blanched
1 kilo onions, sliced
1 or 2 cloves garlic
½ kilo tomatoes, peeled, seeded and chopped
pinch saffron

Cut the ray into manageable pieces. Arrange them in a baking dish. Sprinkle with salt. Preheat the oven to 'moderate'. Heat the olive oil in a frying-pan and fry in it the bread, parsley and almonds until the almonds are golden-brown. Remove these ingredients and mash them up together. Next fry, in the same oil, the onions with the garlic. When they are golden-brown add the tomatoes and saffron and set the whole to cook for another 10 minutes. At this point put the dish of fish into the oven.

After the contents of the frying-pan have completed their 10 minutes cooking strain them, return them to the frying-pan and add to them the bread-and-almond mixture. Then pour the whole lot over the fish (which will by now have had a good 10 minutes in the oven), add a little water, also salt and pepper, and leave cooking in the oven for another quarter of an hour. By then the fish should be cooked and there will be little sauce remaining.

Rape

Spanish ways with angler-fish

Spaniards are fond of angler-fish and inventive in cooking and presenting it. Rather than give a single detailed recipe, I offer a series of suggestions and one warning.

To take advantage of the resemblance between the flesh of angler-fish and of lobster, proceed as follows. Cut thick uniform steaks of angler-fish, salt them and bake them in the oven just as they are for about 20 minutes (depending on the thickness of the steaks). Cool, cut into pieces which will look like pieces of a lobster tail, mask with salsa escarlata (see p. 272) and serve cold with a salad.

Rape a la Marinera may be made in various ways. It is a dish which combines floured slices of angler-fish with, for example, whole mussels, carpet shells and shrimp. All are cooked together in a court-bouillon in a casserole with chopped sweet red peppers and seasoning. Sprinkle chopped hard-boiled egg, a favourite Spanish garnishing, over all before serving.

The region of Málaga, where they claim to make the best Sopa de Rape in Spain, is also the home of Rape con Patatas. Salted and floured slices of angler-fish are partly fried in hot oil, then removed to make way for chopped onion and tomato. When these have been lightly fried, rounds of potato are added with water to cover. Once the potato is half cooked the pieces of fish are put back in and the whole allowed to finish cooking very slowly, with a decoration of pimento strips on top.

Catalan cookery provides unexpected combinations of chocolate with meat and poultry and even with lobster or fish. A colleague tracked down for me in Barcelona a recipe for Rape con Chocolate, which I followed with some excitement. Slices of angler-fish are fried first and then cooked gently in a sauce made by pounding together (for $\frac{3}{4}$ kilo of fish) 75 grammes of cooking chocolate, 2 cloves of garlic and several sprigs of parsley, which are then combined with $1\frac{1}{2}$ tablespoonfuls of vinegar, 3 of olive oil and 6 of water, with $\frac{1}{2}$ a bay leaf and $\frac{1}{2}$ a teaspoonful of paprika added, and seasoning. Warning: to judge by family reactions this interesting dish is best prepared in small quantities, since everyone wants to taste it but few would like to make a meal of it.

Salmonetes con Salsa Romesco

Grilled red mullet with romesco sauce (serves four)

Romesco sauce is a speciality of Tarragona. It goes well with almost any grilled fish.

4 red mullet (Nos. 147 or 148) of about 200 grammes each
¾ wineglassful olive oil
juice of 1 lemon
parsley, chopped

for the sauce:

1 small onion, chopped
2 tablespoonfuls olive oil

4 tomatoes, peeled, seeded and chopped
6 cloves garlic
18 roasted almonds
a little more olive oil
2 teaspoonfuls vinegar or lemon juice
salt
2 teaspoonfuls paprika

Prepare the fish ahead of time, salt them lightly and let them marinade for a couple of hours in the olive oil and lemon juice.

To make the sauce, first fry the onion in olive oil. Then pound together onion, tomatoes, garlic and almonds, adding just enough olive oil to make a purée, into which you finally work the vinegar or lemon juice, salt and paprika. The result may be passed through a sieve to achieve a finer consistency.

Remove the fish from their marinade, drain and grill them. When they are ready, decorate them with the chopped parsley and serve the sauce separately.

Tortilla de Sardinas Frescas

A Spanish omelette with fresh sardines (serves four)

This is a Balearic recipe, for which you will need 4 fresh (or frozen) sardines and 6 eggs.

Clean, scale and debone the sardines, discarding the heads but leaving the tails intact. Separate the yolks from the whites of the eggs. Beat the yolks with a little salt and some chopped parsley. Beat the whites with a little salt, separately.

Heat olive oil in a large pan. Lightly fry a chopped clove of garlic in it. Combine the yolk and the white mixtures and add half of it to the pan, over a low heat. As this starts to cook, quickly lay out the sardines over it, opened out, and sprinkle over them some paprika and lemon juice. Then pour the rest of the egg mixture on top. Run a thread of olive oil round the edge of the pan, to prevent sticking.

Cook the tortilla very gently, and turn it over once so that both sides are browned. (Turning it over is tricky, and I prefer to finish off the top side under the grill – but this needs a large grill.) The sardines will be cooked satisfactorily inside the tortilla, and the dish is both unusual and good.

Sirviola con Salsa
Amberjack with a red sauce

Cut convenient pieces from an amberjack (No. 161) and fry them in olive oil. Place the pieces of fish in an earthenware cooking dish ('greixonera'). Set some carrots to cook in water. Sear, peel and cut into quarters some red pimentos. Fry them briefly in the same oil as the fish, then add them to the fish in the greixonera. Still using the same oil, fry some cloves of garlic lightly, and then add tomatoes. By now the carrots should be cooked. Cut them into rounds and add them to the garlic and tomato mixture. Pour all this over the fish. Serve with slices of bread which have been dipped in milk, then in beaten egg and fried.

(Sra Vidal, *Cocina Selecta Mallorquina*)

Langosta a la Catalana
Lobster in the Catalan style   (serves two)

More than one recipe corresponds to this title. One version involves making a sauce with a mixture of lobster blood and chocolate! The one which follows is simpler, and satisfactorily Spanish in flavour.

1 live lobster
1⅓ wineglassfuls olive oil
2 tablespoonfuls finely chopped onion
3 medium tomatoes, peeled, seeded and chopped
2 green peppers, seeded and cut into strips
a pinch of saffron
2 or 3 sprigs parsley, chopped
2 wineglassfuls white wine
1 tablespoonful cognac
½ teaspoonful cayenne pepper seasoning

Cut the lobster (which you will no doubt wish to kill first – see advice on p. 187) into equal-sized pieces of flesh and set these to fry in the olive oil over a reasonably high flame for a few minutes. Remove them and keep them hot.

In the same olive oil brown the onion. Then add tomatoes and the green peppers, and put the pieces of lobster back in, with the saffron, parsley and white wine. Cover and cook for 30 minutes or so.

Lift out the pieces of lobster, letting them drain, and keep them hot on the serving dish. Reduce the sauce over a vigorous flame, then add to it the cognac (flaming) and cayenne pepper. Pour it all over the lobster. You may decorate the dish with little squares of fried bread.

Calamares Rellenos con Jamón

Squid with a ham stuffing   (serves four)

4 squid of about ¼ kilo each	parsley
100 grammes smoked ham	1 large onion
2 or 3 ripe tomatoes, peeled	2 cloves garlic
salt, pepper	oil

Clean the squid, throwing away the intestines and the ink sacs since the ink is not needed in this recipe. Remove and chop the tentacles very finely together with the ham and 2 tomatoes. Add salt and pepper, and a little chopped parsley. The mixture should be quite thick. Stuff the squid with it, but not quite full, and fasten each with a toothpick.

Cook the chopped onion gently in oil with 2 cloves of garlic, whole. Add another tomato if you wish. When the ingredients have blended well together put the squid in and cook for 20 minutes over low heat. Add a little water (or wine) if the sauce is drying up towards the end of the cooking.

Pulpos con Papas

Octopus and potatoes   (serves four)

This recipe, which comes from Barcelona, where it is offered by the restaurant Los Caracoles, provides a good way of dealing with a fairly large octopus – of, say, 1 kilo.

Begin with the usual 'sofrito', by heating a wineglassful of olive oil and lightly browning in it 2 chopped cloves of garlic, 2 chopped onions and some chopped parsley. Add the octopus, cleaned and cut into pieces. It will sweat its own liquid as it begins to cook. But the amount so produced varies. It may be necessary to add a little water. Continue cooking gently for an hour or more, until the octopus is approaching a suitable degree of tenderness. At this point add a bay leaf, a little salt, and ½ kilo of potatoes, peeled and sliced. Simmer for another 20 or 30 minutes, until both potatoes and octopus are ready; add a pinch of saffron (blended with a tiny quantity of water or of the cooking juices, to ensure even distribution), stir and serve.

Almejas a la Marinera
Sailor's clams

(serves four)

1 kilo almejas (No. 557), not too big	½ wineglassful white wine
4 tablespoonfuls olive oil	½ bay leaf
1 onion, chopped	juice of ½ lemon
2 cloves garlic, chopped	black pepper
1 tablespoonful breadcrumbs	salt
	chopped parsley

Wash the clams and put them in a big frying pan with half a tumbler of cold water. Bring to the boil. As the clams start to open transfer them, still in their shells, to a suitable pot. When the process has been completed, strain and keep the water.

Heat the olive oil in a pan. Add the onion and the garlic. When they are golden-brown add the breadcrumbs and let them brown a little too. Next, add the cooking water from the first operation, the white wine, the half bay leaf, the lemon juice and a sprinkling of freshly milled black pepper. Let this mixture come to the boil, then pour it over the clams in their pot. Cook for 10 minutes. Add salt and chopped parsley. Serve.

The same recipe can be employed for Nos. 558 and 560.

11. Recipes from France

The Mediterranean coast of France runs in an arc round the Golfe des Lions from Perpignan near the Spanish frontier, through the Languedoc and the strange marshlands and lagoons of the Bouches du Rhône, to the great ports of Marseille and Toulon; and then in a wriggling line eastwards along the Côte d'Azur, through Cannes and Nice to the Italian border. In the west the influence of Spanish cookery is evident, to the east pasta and other signs of Italian influence begin to appear. But in the very centre of this coastline, from Aigues-Mortes to Marseille, we find one of the truly French regional cuisines, that of Provence. It is a cuisine of olive oil and garlic and tomatoes, of thyme, rosemary and fennel and the other herbs which grow wild on the limestone hills there. Of all the French regional cuisines this is perhaps the most interesting and distinctive in its treatment of seafood.

A sanctuary of traditional Provençal cooking exists at Marseille, on one side of the Vieux Port and looking across at the beautiful Hôtel de Ville on the other. This is the restaurant founded by the late M. Brun, where Mme Brun continues to serve – in a small and beautifully furnished Provençal dining room – dishes which follow the exacting specifications of her husband. M. Brun held strong views about fish, expressed in his book *Groumandugi* (price about £30, but Mme Brun lets her guests read a copy free). In this you learn that the three finest fish in the Mediterranean are, in order, the daurade, the rouget de roche and the loup. These are to be neither gutted or scaled, but grilled whole, provided of course that they are perfectly fresh. To score the fish before grilling it is to inflict wanton damage, which the useless practice of basting will do little to repair. Under the heat of the grill the scales will coalesce to form a natural armour within which the imprisoned juices will keep the flesh exquisitely succulent. The natural flavour is not to be qualified by any condiment or addition. The lemon (conceded to be good for other purposes such as making lemonade) is not to be used. Salt is banned.

The loup served to me by Mme Brun for a February meal, with the mistral blowing and masts tossing in the harbour outside, was indeed superbly good; and the experience almost convinced me that the commonly encountered hoo-ha with blazing fennel-stalks and so on is, as M. Brun averred, a banal solecism.

Mme Brun's set meal (with which, as with the choice of wines and the absence of condiments, her guests must all conform) includes several fish hors d'œuvres. I cite with enthusiasm her Tapenado (a mixture of black olives and capers and anchovy, all cut up very fine, with a touch of rum); the Melets au Poivre (prepared by putting melets, which are small sand smelt, in a saumure for forty days, then lifting the fillets and keeping them if possible for two years in a dressing of olive oil, fennel and coarsely ground white pepper); the Tartines de Poutargue de Martigues (preserved grey mullet roe shredded and mixed with a little water and olive oil and spread on croûtons); and the Pouprihoun aux Pommes d'Amour (baby octopus cooked with tomato and served hot). Here are important experiences for the student of French Mediterranean fish cookery.

But the recipes which follow are by no means exclusively Provençal. I have sought to illustrate the variety to be found along the 600 kilometres of French coast, including specialities of Sète and Agde, of the Camargue, of Toulon and of Nice. The two standard books on Provençal cookery, those by Escudier and Reboul, are cited in the Bibliography but deserve an additional mention here for covering the whole territory in such a thorough and serious manner – real œuvres de base, as the French would say and as their successive reprintings over many decades would suggest.

Aigo-Sau and Rouille

(serves four)

A Provençal fish soup. The recipe which I give is based on that in *La Cuisinière Provençale* by Reboul.

1 kilo mixed small white fish
4–6 potatoes, peeled and sliced
1 onion, finely sliced
2 tomatoes, peeled and chopped
2 cloves of garlic, crushed
1 bouquet garni (bay leaf, fennel, thyme, celery top, parsley)
salt and pepper
olive oil

for the rouille:
2 cloves garlic
2 sweet red peppers
chunk of bread, soaked and squeezed
2 tablespoonfuls olive oil
1½ wineglassfuls fish broth

Put the fish, cleaned as usual and cut up if they are at all large, into a casserole and add the other ingredients (except those for the rouille), using enough olive oil to moisten the mixture well, but no more. Cover with boiling water and cook over a vigorous flame until the fish is done. Serve it to each guest on one plate and the soup, poured over a slice of toast, on another.

The dish is accompanied by a sauce called rouille. Pound the garlic and peppers well in a mortar, add the chunk of damp bread and mix thoroughly together. Then add the olive oil and lastly the fish broth (of which you may not need quite as much as is indicated). This sauce, which has the consistency of a mayonnaise, is served separately. Reboul describes it, justly, as a '*sauce énergique au parfum sui generis*'.

The reader will notice that he has not been told precisely which fish to use. This is unnecessary, as people are much more relaxed about aigo-sau than about bouillabaisse. For those who would like suggestions I mention small specimens of sea bass, the bream family or grey mullet.

Bouillabaisse

Bouillabaisse is the most famous of the fish-soup-plus-fish dishes and a great number of recipes for it have been published, containing different and even contradictory injunctions on various points. Emotive expressions are used with relative frequency in this group of recipes.

The following points seem to be common ground:

(1) Marseille is top city for bouillabaisse.

(2) A wide variety of fish should be used, among which there must be a rascasse, several fish with firm flesh and some with delicate flesh.

(3) The liquid used consists of olive oil and water which must be boiled fast to ensure their amalgamation.

(4) Onions, garlic, tomatoes, parsley, saffron are always used.

(5) The fish is served separately from the broth. The broth is poured over pieces of toast or served with croûtons. The whole dish is accompanied by rouille (p. 284).

Points in dispute include whether you eat all the fish or let the delicate ones disintegrate in the cooking; whether any crustaceans or molluscs are essential, and if so which; whether white wine should be substituted for some of the water; whether the water must be brought to the boil before it is added; and questions about ingredients such as whether it is permissible to include potatoes, compulsory to put in a piece of orange peel, desirable to add fennel or a bay leaf, and so on.

The recipe I give for bouillabaisse is a simple and straightforward version which works well. I deliberately do not give a *de luxe* version – the sort which bids you include a langouste and goes on about the 'divine broth' and so on. Bouillabaisse is a simple dish and quite a good one. But it does not deserve or benefit from the mystique which has been built up around it or the costly ingredients which are sometimes put into it.

Buy fish as follows:

(*a*) a rascasse or two, depending on size (Nos. 216, 217)

(*b*) some other fish with firm flesh such as monkfish (No. 249), gurnard (Nos. 220 etc.) weever or star-gazer (Nos. 181 to 185), eel or moray or conger (Nos. 66 to 68)

(*c*) some delicate fish such as whiting (No. 77) or flatfish

(*d*) a few small wrasse (Nos. 170 to 177) or the like

(*e*) an inexpensive crustacean which might be squille (No. 525) or a petite cigale (No. 510)

Have 2 kilos in all. Gut and scale the fish, cut them in pieces where necessary and wash them.

Now heat a wineglassful of olive oil in a large cooking pot and brown in this a large onion, finely sliced, and 2 cloves of garlic. Add ½ kilo of peeled and chopped tomatoes (or a corresponding amount of tomato concentrate) followed by about 3 litres of water (preferably boiling) and the fish from groups (*a*) and (*b*) and (*d*) and (*e*). Those from group (*d*) are intended to disintegrate in the cooking, adding body to the soup. Season with salt and pepper. Add chopped parsley and a pinch of saffron. (Why not add also a piece of orange peel, a clove, a bay leaf and a sprig of thyme, thus appeasing four pressure groups who might otherwise complain?) Pour a wineglassful of olive oil over all. Bring to and keep at a vigorous boil for 15 to 20 minutes. Add the fish in group (*c*) towards the end of this period, allowing just enough time for them to cook.

When all is ready lift out the crustaceans and the fish which are still whole and serve them on one platter. Pour the broth over pieces of garlic-rubbed toast in soup plates (straining it in the process if you wish). Serve rouille (p. 284) alongside.

La Bourride

'*Bourride* is one of the great dishes of Provence. There are various different ways of presenting it but the essential characteristic is that *aïoli* or garlic-flavoured mayonnaise is added to the stock in which the fish has cooked to make a beautiful smooth pale yellow sauce – and of this there must be plenty, for it is the main point of the dish.

'M. Bérot, once *chef des cuisines* on the *Île de France* – a liner celebrated for its good cooking – served us his own version of this dish at the Escale, a hospitable and charming restaurant at Carry-le-Rouet, a little seaside place west of Marseille.

'The ingredients you need for four people are 4 fine thick fillets of a rather fleshy white fish. M. Bérot uses *baudroie* or angler-fish, but at home I have made the dish with fillets of John Dory, of turbot, of brill (*barbue*).

'In any case, whatever fish you choose, be sure to get the head and the carcase with your fillets. Apart from these you need a couple of leeks, a lemon, a tablespoon of wine vinegar, at least 4 cloves of garlic, 2 or 3 egg yolks, about one-third of a pint of olive oil, a couple of tablespoons of cream, and seasonings. To accompany the *bourride* you need plain boiled new potatoes and slices of French bread fried in oil.

'First make your stock by putting the head and carcase of the fish into a saucepan with a sliced leek, a few parsley stalks, a teaspoon of salt, a slice of lemon, the wine vinegar and about 1¼ pints of water. Let all this simmer gently for 25 to 30 minutes. Then strain it.

'While it is cooking make your *aïoli* with the egg yolks, 3 cloves of garlic and olive oil as explained . . . [below]

'Now put a tablespoon of olive oil and the white of the second leek, finely sliced, into the largest shallow metal or other fireproof pan you have; let it heat, add the spare clove of garlic, crushed; put in the lightly seasoned fillets; cover with the stock; let them gently poach for 15 to 25 minutes, according to how thick they are.

'Have ready warming a big serving dish; take the fillets from the pan with a fish slice and lay them in the dish; cover them and put them in a low oven to keep warm.

'Reduce the stock in your pan by letting it boil as fast as possible until there is only about a third of the original quantity left. Now stir in the cream and let it bubble a few seconds.

'Have your *aïoli* ready in a big bowl or a jug over which you can fit a conical or other sauce sieve. Through this pour your hot sauce; quickly stir and amalgamate it with the *aïoli*. It should all turn out about the consistency of thick cream. Pour it over your fish fillets. On top strew a little chopped parsley and the dish is ready . . .

'To make the *aïoli* sauce:

'Allow roughly 2 large cloves of garlic per person and, for eight people, the yolks of 3 eggs and nearly a pint of very good quality olive oil –

failing Provençal olive oil, the best Italian or Spanish will do. Crush the peeled garlic in a mortar until it is reduced absolutely to pulp. Add the yolks and a pinch of salt. Stir with a wooden spoon. When the eggs and garlic are well amalgamated, start adding the oil, very slowly at first, drop by drop, until the *aïoli* begins to thicken. This takes longer than with a straightforward mayonnaise because the garlic has thinned the yolks to a certain extent. When about half the oil has been used, the *aïoli* should be a very thick mass, and the oil can now be added in a slow but steady stream. The sauce gets thicker and thicker, and this is as it should be; a good *aïoli* is practically solid. Add a very little lemon juice at the end, and serve the sauce either in the kitchen mortar in which you have made it or piled up in a small salad bowl. Should the *aïoli* separate through the oil having been added too fast, put a fresh yolk into another bowl and gradually add the curdled mixture to it. The *aïoli* then comes back to life.'

(Elizabeth David, *French Provincial Cooking*)

Oursinado

Sea-urchins (serves six)

This is one of the best of the fish-plus-soup dishes, but it is not to be attempted unless you can obtain *lots* of sea-urchins (No. 585).

Buy 20 of them. Buy too 1 kilo of slices of angler-fish (No. 249), sea bass (No. 113), daurade (No. 128), sole (No. 238) or other good white fish. Take care as you go home to advertise your intentions, and indeed imply the prowess which you hope to display, by carrying the oursins in a fisherman's open basket, which is in any case the most practical method of transporting so many large and delicately spiked creatures.

The cleaned pieces of fish are put in a casserole with an onion and a carrot, both finely chopped, a little parsley and a bouquet garni or bay leaf. Pour over all this 1½ wineglassfuls of white wine and ½ litre of water. Season with salt and pepper. Bring to the boil, lower the heat, cover and cook gently for 10 to 15 minutes, depending on the size of the pieces of fish.

While the fish is cooking, cut open the oursins and remove the corals. They should fill a wineglass. In a second casserole mix 50 grammes of butter with 6 egg-yolks. By this time casserole No. 1 will be standing at the side of the stove, as the fish will be cooked. Remove from it about two-thirds of the broth and add this little by little to the butter and egg mixture in casserole No. 2. Place casserole No. 2 in a bain-marie (i.e. stand it in something bigger in which water is boiling) and beat the contents to a cream. To this cream add the oursin corals, and continue beating until you have a smooth mixture.

Cut some neat slices of bread of a good thickness (say 1 centimetre) and lay these in the bottom of a serving-dish of sufficient depth. Pour over them (through a strainer) the remaining fish broth from casserole No. 1, which they will soak up. Then pour over them the creamy oursin mixture. Serve the pieces of fish separately but simultaneously.

Soupes aux Crabes
Crab soups

All edible crabs can form the basis of a soup, but the common crab or crabe vert (No. 516) is perhaps the most suitable and is the choice of the Marseillais for soup-making purposes. The local name is favouille, and the soup is Soupe de Favouilles.

Finely chop the white part of a leek, and brown it in olive oil with a dozen crabes verts (washed but not dismembered). Add the flesh of a tomato and a clove of garlic and let all this cook for a few moments. Put in a litre of water, add a bouquet garni, salt and pepper, and bring to the boil, which is to be maintained for a quarter of an hour. Then strain the soup. Use the resulting bouillon to make a soup with pasta, and serve the crabs either separately with this, or in it after their legs have been removed.

The ériphie (No. 521) is the crab most highly prized for flavour in Provence, and is used to make Soupe de Pélous (which is its name at Nice and Monaco).

For this dish you begin by lightly colouring in olive oil a very finely chopped onion. Add two cloves of garlic and the chopped flesh of two tomatoes, and the crabs (six for each person). When the crabs are well coloured add a litre of water, salt and pepper and a bouquet garni, bring to the boil and keep boiling for 20 minutes. Take off the fire, add a pinch of saffron and then either pour the broth over slices of bread (as with bouillabaisse) or use it as the basis of a pasta soup; and in either event serve the crabs separately.

(Professor Jean Euzière, *Les Pêches d'Amateurs en Mediterranée*)

Soupe de Roche (or Soupe de Poissons de Marseille)
Marseille fish soup (serves six)

This is a real soup, not a soup plus fish-course combined. I prefer it to the more complicated dishes and give it very high marks indeed. It was our favourite fish soup when we were living in Tunis.

All the good ladies of Marseille, not to mention their husbands, have their own ideas about exactly how to prepare Soupe de Roche. But the general principles are clear enough. The main one is that you use a large variety of small rockfish, none of which survives to be served separately as happens with at least some of the fish used in making bouillabaisse. And apart from standard ingredients you will need leeks; and fennel and saffron. Provided that you have these last ingredients, and access to a fish market where small rockfish are deemed worth marketing, you can make this soup anywhere. (It is, by the way, not true as the Marseillais believe, that the right combination of rockfish is found only in the Golfe des Lions.)

Choice of fish Small specimens of any or all of the following: rascasses (especially Nos. 216 and 218, which are not much good for anything else), wrasses (Nos. 170 to 177 – these are mostly known as rouquiers or roucaou in Provence; No. 177, the girelle, should be included if possible) and conger eel (No. 68).

Procedure Heat a few tablespoonfuls of olive oil in a large fireproof soup pot. Add to this the white part of 2 leeks and 1 onion, finely chopped or sliced; allow to cook briefly; then add 2 large tomatoes (peeled and chopped) and stir the mixture around. Next add 2 crushed cloves of garlic, a sprig or two of fennel and of parsley and some thyme; a bay leaf and a piece of orange peel (these last items are optional); salt and pepper and almost 2 litres of water. The fish go in next (1½ kilos of them, gutted and washed as necessary), the water is brought to the boil and kept boiling vigorously for 15 minutes. Now pass the whole boiling through a fine sieve (lined with muslin to catch the tiny bones), rubbing it with a wooden spoon to extract every drop of juice from the fish. (An alternative is to sieve it twice, first roughly then finely.) Return the bouillon to the soup pot, bring it to the boil, add ½ kilo of pasta and a pinch of saffron and cook gently until the pasta is done. Serve with rouille (p. 284), croûtons and grated cheese.

Poutargue
How to use the dried roe of grey mullet

Poutargue (cf. p. 72) is a speciality of Martigues, where good grey mullet are to be had. It is often cut into very thin slices which are served with a simple dressing of olive oil, lemon juice and pepper. Alternatively it may be made into a paste and served with toast as an hors d'œuvre. Elizabeth David recorded some years ago, for the benefit of readers of the *Spectator*, the method followed by Charles Bérot, chef-patron of the Escale restaurant at Carry-le-Rouet near Marseille. This is to soften and partly desalt the roe (a piece weighing, say, 150–200 grammes) by leaving it overnight in a bowl with 4 or 5 tablespoonfuls of water. In the morning pound half a clove of garlic and combine it with the softened roe (which has of course been taken out of the water). Then add – a little of each in turn – 3 tablespoonfuls of olive oil, 2 tablespoonfuls of water and the juice of half a lemon; and lastly, a sprinkling of cayenne pepper. To be served 'with hot toast and cold white wine on the Escale's terrace, a shimmery view of the Mediterranean far below'.

This is a luxury. Poutargue is expensive nowadays. For some purposes smoked cod roe can be used instead, as explained, for example, on p. 361.

Poutine, Nonnat and Melet

I treat all these tiny fish together because they are often confused. I was not sure about them myself until I had authoritative advice from the Musée Océanographique at Monaco.

Sardines (No. 56) and anchovies (No. 61) in their larval state are known in Provence as poutine – poutine nue (or poutina nuda) so long as they remain without scales, and poutine habillée (or poutina vestida) when the scales appear. These minute fish (hundreds to the pound) are consumed in large quantities by the people of Nice and thereabouts when they appear in the early part of the year. In other parts of France it would be illegal to fish for them, but the Alpes-Maritimes is a region where the fishery regulations of Sardinia have continued to apply even after the Comté de Nice was reincorporated in France in 1860. The poutine which escape this fate are known as palailles or palaillettes in the next stage of their growth.

Nonnats are tiny transparent gobies (No. 212) which even in their adult life do not exceed a length of more than a few centimetres.

Melet is the name for small sand smelt (Nos. 102 to 104). The name is given to the garum-type preparation made from them – cf. p. 246. If very small they are melettu.

Poutine and nonnat are used in soups, beignets and omelettes. Fishermen in the area of Nice make a Soupe de Nonnat or a Soupe de Poutine as follows. They brown a little chopped onion and garlic in olive oil, then add water (say, a litre for five people), salt and a bouquet garni. Having brought all this to the boil they put in pasta of their choice, which will be a fine one such as that called cheveux d'ange. Once the pasta is cooked, they add the poutine or nonnat (50 grammes for each person). After a few minutes' more boiling they remove the pot from the fire, add a pinch of saffron and serve the soup with grated cheese.

To make an Omelette à la Poutine, simply add the poutine to the egg mixture with chopped garlic and parsley, and seasoning, and proceed as usual. This is very good, and a relatively inexpensive way of enjoying poutine. The dish is known in Spain too (cf. p. 273).

Poutine also serve to make a garum-type preparation known as pissalat (peï salat). If this is mixed with a purée of onions and spread on a thin disc of baker's dough, topped with black olives and baked in a very slow oven for half an hour, the result is pissaladiera (often sold ready made, and with fillets of tinned anchovy on top of the onion purée instead of pissalat mixed in with it).

Melets may be big enough for frying. Sprinkle them with vinegar, dredge them with flour and fry them in very hot oil just long enough to turn them golden-brown. This is a Friture de Melets.

Sartañado

This is the Provençal name for a dish of very small fish fried in hot olive oil. It may also be called sartagnade or crespeou. Sartan is the Provençal name for a frying-pan.

The fish to be used, with their catalogue numbers and local names, are the following:

small sardines, 56, 57, sardinettes
small anchovies, 61, petits anchois
sand smelts, 103, siouclet
small picarel, 145, 146, jarretons
shrimps, 506, petites crevettes grises, carambots

The fish are floured and salted, and when the oil in the pan is hot they are ranged in it close together, so that as they cook they will coalesce into a flat round mass like an omelette or pancake (the alternative name crespeou comes from *crêpe*). Set them off over a fierce flame. They must not stick to the bottom of the pan, and it may be necessary to shake the pan slightly over the flame to avoid this. But you must not stir or poke the fish, since this would prevent their adhering to each other. When the fish are well-coloured on the underside, take a spatula such as you would use for an omelette and turn the whole mass over. Brown the other side, then transfer your flat cake of cooked fish to a hot serving platter, put 2 tablespoonfuls of wine vinegar into the pan and let it boil for a moment, pour this over the fish, and start eating.

Salade Antiboise
A fish salad from Antibes

Escudier, whose recipe this is, explains that the fish may be what you have left over from another dish, or alternatively slices of whiting (No. 77) or conger eel (No. 68) bought especially for the salad. In either event the fish should have been cooked in a court-bouillon, not for too long, however, since it must be firm enough to be cut up into small cubes about the size of dice. I recommend the conger myself (or angler-fish, No. 249).

The cubes of fish are mixed with capers and with the following vegetables cut up into quarters or rounds: cornichons (pickled baby cucumbers), fresh cucumber, boiled potatoes, cooked beetroot. Add a few tinned anchovy fillets, roughly chopped. Dress with olive oil, either vinegar or lemon juice, salt and pepper.

Salade Niçoise
(serves eight as an hors d'œuvre, four as a main course)

This is a delicious summer dish and easy to prepare, so we eat it often, following this prescription:

12 lettuce leaves
½ onion, cut into thin rings
6 tomatoes, cut into quarters and then cut in half
1 green pepper, seeded and cut into thin strips
4 celery sticks, chopped roughly and including some leaves
12 black olives
12 green olives

4 hard-boiled eggs, cut into quarters
250 grammes tinned tuna fish, in small bits or chunks
12 fillets of anchovy, tinned

for the dressing:
3 tablespoonfuls wine vinegar
1½ teaspoonfuls Dijon or other French mustard
4 pinches of salt
1½ wineglassfuls (12 tablespoonfuls) olive oil

Method: Arrange the ingredients in a large bowl or platter (children are good at this, and enjoy the ritual of counting out the olives and so on, although of course the exact quantities are not really important), mix the dressing in a bowl and pour it over. Serve with crisp French bread.

Alose à l'Oseille
Shad with sorrel

The alose or shad (No. 55) is a bony fish, and various traditional ways of preparing it are supposed to result in some of the tiresome small bones melting away. Some believe that cognac will best perform this function. Others believe that sorrel does the trick. The matter is dubious, but what is certain is that sorrel goes very well with shad.

A possible procedure is to cook the shad whole in a court-bouillon with the addition of some strips of lemon peel, and then to serve it on a bed of sorrel purée. To make the purée you cook a generous quantity of sorrel in the same way as you cook spinach (hardly any water) and then put it through a sieve and combine it with 2 egg-yolks, a little French tarragon mustard, a pinch of nutmeg and (optional) a couple of tablespoonfuls of finely chopped raw sorrel and tarragon leaves.

l'Anchoïade

1. The basic recipe for anchoïade calls for salted anchovies (the kind which you buy from a barrel or a huge tin); the other main ingredient is stale bread – which of course one always has when it isn't wanted, whereas when the need arises the breadbin contains nothing but the freshest of loaves. Fortunately this recipe is so simple that you can use it at short notice when stale bread happens to be at hand. (Or you can do what is often done in Provence – leave out the bread altogether, using the anchovy mixture as a dip to be eaten with crudités such as carrot or celery sticks, for dunking cubes of boiled potato, or to go with hard-boiled eggs.)

De-salt the anchovies by rinsing them well or letting them steep for a while in changes of water; remove the tails and bones and mash them up with the backs of two strong forks, of which the prongs mesh together to produce a double action. Prepare a sauce of olive oil, a thread of vinegar, a pinch of pepper and a crushed clove of garlic. Cut the stale bread into rectangular crust-free slices and grill or toast these. Combine the sauce with the mashed anchovy and spread the mixture on the toasted bread, pressing it well in.

2. It is a matter for debate whether one should attempt to elaborate a dish which is at the same time so simple and so delicious. But for those who would like to try, here is a version, based on a recipe by Austin de Croze, which Madame Roland Ricard prepared for me at her home near Aix-en-Provence. Almost anything would be apt to taste good in her dining room, which commands a view, through Aleppo pines, across the valley to Cézanne's Mont Saint Victoire. But even with allowance made for the effect of this ambiance I can pronounce this anchoïade superlatively good. The ingredients are as follows:

12 anchois de Collioure à l'huile
  (tinned anchovy fillets)
12 salted anchovies (from the
  barrel)
12 fresh almonds, peeled
3 dried figs, minus stalks and
  chopped
2 cloves of garlic
1 small mild red pepper, seeded

4 tablespoonfuls olive oil (very
  fruity, author's stipulation)
1 small onion
50 grammes of fines herbes
1 stalk of fennel
juice of half a lemon
2 teaspoonfuls of orange-flower
  water
a dozen small bridge rolls

Chop finely the herbs, garlic, onion and fennel. Combine with the chopped figs. Pound together the red pepper, the almonds, the tinned anchovy fillets and the (de-salted) fillets of salted anchovy. Add 3 of the tablespoonfuls of olive oil in order to make a thick purée. Combine the first mixture with the second, adding a little lemon juice and, little by little, the orange-flower water. Cut the rolls in half. Spread the top halves with the mixture, and use the remaining olive oil to moisten the bottom halves. Put the halves together and leave them in a preheated hot oven for 5 minutes. When you serve this anchoïade de luxe you are expected to surround it with a profusion of fine black olives, 'en couronne d'un velours sombre et chatoyant'.

Terrine d'Anguille à la Martégale
Eel baked with leeks and black olives

'This was the traditional dish served at Martigues for the gros souper on Christmas Eve. This excellent recipe is worth recording – and cooking.

'Cover the bottom of a gratin dish with finely sliced leeks, so that they make a thick bed. Strew with chopped parsley and garlic. Add a good handful of black olives (stoned) and moisten with a good glass of dry white wine. On this bed lay a large skinned eel. Cover with bread-crumbs and cook in the oven for about 1½ hours, the precise time depending on the size of the eel.'

The above prescription is that of Escudier (*La Véritable Cuisine Provençale et Niçoise*). I would add that I have made this dish very successfully with small eels (about 1 foot long) instead of one big one. Cooking time then drops to half an hour or so. The dish looks unusual, with the eels convoluted on their bed and the black olives lodged be-tween them like obstacles in a maze.

Congre Braisé

Braised conger eel   (serves six)

You will need a single large piece of conger eel (No. 68) prepared for cooking, and weighing 1 kilo.

Take an oval casserole of suitable size, cover the bottom of it with olive oil, add enough thinly sliced carrot and onion to make a bed, and heat till very hot. Place the piece of conger on this bed, adding if you wish a dozen tiny onions. Season. Add a sprig of fennel, a little grated nutmeg and 1½ wineglassfuls of white wine. Heat until the liquid begins to bubble, then transfer to a moderate oven and continue cooking (and basting) for 40 to 50 minutes, until the conger is cooked through. Sprinkle it, before serving, with some finely chopped parsley. You may also turn the cooking juices into a sauce by working into them a knob of butter combined with a little flour.

Flan de Baudroie

A luncheon dish made with angler-fish   (serves four)

There is only one English fishmonger in Marseille, Kenneth Moss, and he has been there for twenty years. His wife Anna, whom he met when taking shore leave from a troopship and returned to marry not long afterwards, contributes this recipe. She points out that, for those to whom harmless deception appeals, this dish has a double interest since many will suppose it to be of lobster.

1 kilo tail of angler-fish (No. 249)	**olive oil**
1 kilo ripe tomatoes	**8 eggs**

Cut up the angler-fish into big slices and simmer them in barely boiling water for 20 to 30 minutes. Meanwhile peel and pip the tomatoes, and reduce them in a little olive oil.

Cut up the fish finely, and mix it with the tomato. Beat the eggs, yolk and white, into the mixture. Put it in a buttered mould and cook it in a bain-marie for 1 hour in the oven with the thermostat at 6 or 7. Unmould and serve cold.

Daurade à la Crème d'Oursins

Daurade with sea-urchin sauce (serves four)

a daurade (No. 128) of about 750 grammes
1 onion
1 carrot
sprig of thyme
bay leaf

salt and pepper
juice of two lemons
24 sea-urchins (yielding about ¾ cup corals)
olive oil
sauce hollandaise (about ¾ cup)

Clean the fish and place it in a poissonière. Cover with cold water and add vegetables, herbs, seasoning and lemon juice. Put it on a vigorous flame until it comes to the boil, then lower the heat and leave it to simmer gently for about 10 to 15 minutes, with the lid on.

For the sauce, take two dozen sea-urchins (No. 585), extract their corals and mash these up with a little olive oil. Mix this thoroughly with the sauce hollandaise before pouring over the fish and serving.

Daurade aux Tomates (à la Dugléré)

Daurade with a tomato sauce (serves six)

Dugléré was a Parisian maître d'hôtel, but this recipe is well known in Provence, where it is blessed with the happy name of Aurado i Poumo d'Amour – which I commend to readers who indulge in the useful habit of writing down menus for guests to read at the beginning of a meal (how otherwise can they gauge consumption of the earlier courses?).

Buy a daurade of 1½ kilos, or two smaller ones. Gut, scale, rinse and pat dry the fish, and cut it into 6 thick slices. Take an oven dish of suitable size and put into it 50 grammes of butter, an onion chopped finely, 3 tomatoes (peeled, seeded, and roughly chopped), a tablespoonful of chopped parsley, salt and pepper. Range the slices of fish on this, pour a wineglassful of white wine over all and put the dish in a medium oven. Cooking time will depend on the thickness of the pieces of fish, but allow 20 to 30 minutes, and turn the slices over at the halfway point. Remove the fish and keep warm.

While the fish is cooking prepare some sauce velouté. (Melt 25 grammes of butter in a saucepan; blend in 25 grammes of flour; allow this roux to cook for 2 minutes without colouring; remove from the heat and a few moments later pour in rather less than ½ litre of hot chicken or veal stock; blend vigorously; bring to the boil while continuing to stir; boil for 1 minute; and add seasoning if necessary after the pan has been removed from the heat.) Pour this into the pan in which the fish was cooked and in which the tomatoey cooking juices remain, and reduce the resulting mixture for 10 minutes, stirring it as it dwindles. Strain. You then have a sauce of a pleasing coral colour with which you cover the pieces of fish before serving them.

The recipe can of course be used for other white fish of good quality, such as sole, turbot, brill, John Dory, or even weever.

Daurade à la Niçoise

Daurade in the style of Nice   (serves four)

Buy a daurade weighing about 1 kilo. Gut, scale, rinse and pat dry. Season it, place a bouquet garni inside it, and put it in a gratin dish with a wineglassful of olive oil. Put thick slices of lemon on top, and dispose slices of tomato around it.

Cook the daurade in a hot oven for 20 minutes or so, basting with the olive oil from time to time. When it is just about cooked through add to the dish 8 black olives, each with a tinned anchovy-fillet wrapped neatly round it. Pour over the dish rather more than ½ wineglassful of dry white wine, and leave it for only another 2 or 3 minutes in the oven.

Denté Farci, Grillé et Flambé à la Farigoulette

Stuffed denté grilled and flamed with wild thyme   (serves four)

This is a recipe which calls for a certain amount of dexterity. It may be used also for sea bass (No. 113), grey mullet (Nos. 105, etc.) and daurade (No. 128).

Having acquired a denté (No. 125 or 126), gut, scale, wash and pat it dry. Season it in the ordinary way with salt and pepper. Then paint the inside with French tarragon mustard and some fresh tomato sauce, insert some thin slices of tomato and onion and fill up the rest of the cavity with a bouquet of farigoulette (wild thyme). Next make two deep slanting cuts along the sides of the fish (one on each side) from head to tail, reaching in as far as the backbone. Anoint these too with tarragon mustard, salt and pepper, and insert into them alternate slices of tomato and onion. (This is why they are slanting cuts. The slices would not otherwise be firmly lodged.) Place the fish, thus prepared, on a platter and sprinkle it copiously with olive oil, and with a thread of vinegar.

Grill the fish, on charcoal if possible, for only 4 minutes on each side. It will then be half cooked. At this point transfer it to an oven dish and pour over it the remains of the olive oil and vinegar from the platter on which the fish rested earlier.

Finish cooking the fish in the oven, basting often. When it is ready, transfer it to a heated metal platter, pour its juices over it and place on top another bouquet of wild thyme (dried and warmed in the oven), set this alight (with flaming brandy if you wish) and serve. The thyme as it burns gives off a strong scent and imparts a flavour to the dish.

Loup de Mer, Beurre de Montpellier
Sea bass with Montpellier butter (serves six)

Montpellier butter is best known as an accompaniment for salmon, but it is suitable for use with any grilled fish. As it bears the name of a famous city of the South of France I have thought it appropriate to suggest it for the sea bass which is so highly esteemed in that region.

Sea bass of a size suitable for grilling are often to be had (although of course this fish can grow too large for grilling whole). Buy two of about 700–800 grammes each and you will have plenty for six people. Prepare them and grill them in the usual way (see p. 256).

Recipes for Montpellier butter vary a good deal. This is the one selected by Elizabeth David to appear in *French Provincial Cooking*.

Weigh approximately 4 oz. altogether of the following herbs: leaves of watercress, tarragon, parsley, chervil and spinach, in about equal proportions. If chervil is unobtainable, substitute more parsley. Burnet (pimprenelle), a herb with a faint taste of cucumber, is mentioned in many recipes but is seldom to be found nowadays.

Plunge all the herbs into boiling water for half a minute. Drain and squeeze as dry as possible. Pound in a mortar, adding 6 anchovy fillets, 2 tablespoonfuls of capers, 4 miniature gherkins, the yolks of 1 raw and 3 hard-boiled eggs and lastly 4 oz. butter. Force all this through a fine wire sieve. To the thick pomade so obtained add, slowly, 5 to 6 tablespoonfuls of olive oil and a few drops of lemon juice. The sauce will keep some days in a covered jar in the refrigerator but should be removed some while before serving, or it will be too hard.

Petits Maquereaux
Baked small mackerel

Gut the fish and remove heads, tails and backbones. Cut some potatoes into slices about 1 centimetre thick. Put alternating layers of potato and fish in an oven dish, applying salt and thyme (or rosemary) to each layer. Then season the whole dish, adding a little cayenne pepper, and pour ½ wineglassful or so of olive oil over all, followed by water to cover. Cook in a moderate oven for about half an hour.

Mme Totte Feissel, who contributed this recipe, comments that it can well be used for fresh sardines, perhaps bought straight from the sea at l'Estaque, of a marvellous electric blue and silver.

Merlan en Raïto
Whiting in a Provençal red-wine sauce   (serves four)

Raïto is a sauce which according to tradition was brought to Marseille (the ancient Massilia) by the Phoenicians.

for the raïto:
1 onion, finely chopped
2 tablespoonfuls flour
2 tablespoonfuls olive oil
½ litre red wine
pepper and salt
2 cloves garlic
1 bay leaf
1 sprig each of thyme and parsley, tied together in a bouquet
1 tablespoonful tomato purée

1 large whiting (No. 77) of 1 kilo or more
flour
3 tablespoonfuls olive oil
capers

It is best to begin with the preparation of the raïto. Heat 2 tablespoonfuls of olive oil in a casserole, and then lightly colour the onion in this. Add the flour and work it in, then the red wine and an equal, or almost equal, quantity of boiling water. Bring the whole to the boil. Add the remaining ingredients and continue to cook until the raïto is thickening, by which time its volume will have reduced to about one third. Pass this sauce through a sieve and keep it hot.

Meanwhile, set the 3 tablespoonfuls of olive oil to warm in a pan, clean the whiting, cut it into slices about 2 centimetres thick, roll these in flour, put them in the hot olive oil and cook vigorously, turning once, until they are just done. Take them out, drain them, and add them to the raïto in which they should simmer gently for 10 minutes or so. Finally add some capers to the sauce, and serve.

Mérou au Bleu de Bresse

(serves six)

6 slices of mérou, each of between 150 and 200 grammes
1 baby Bleu de Bresse cheese
100 grammes butter

1 litre velouté de poisson
3 egg yolks
flour

The slices of mérou should be of even size and well trimmed. Flour them and cook them à la meunière. Set aside and keep warm. Grate the cheese and then work it into a paste, operating at the side of the stove and using a spatula. Add the egg yolks to the velouté. Add the cheese paste also. Season. The sauce should be quite thick. Butter a long oven-proof dish. Place the slices of mérou in it and cover them evenly with the sauce. Glaze in a hot oven for a few minutes.

Monsieur Max Maupuy of the Restaurant Max in Paris kindly gave me this recipe. He may be regarded as a specialist in the exploration of the results to be achieved by combining mérou and Bleu de Bresse: he also suggests serving mérou cold (after cooking it in a court-bouillon) with a choice of two sauces, one a Rougaille and the other made with Bleu de Bresse. Both are easily made. For the Rougaille, take the flesh of 1 kilo of tomatoes, drain, cool in the refrigerator, mix with a table-spoonful of strong Borsibus mustard and season to taste. For the other sauce, work together ½ litre of cream and half a baby Bleu de Bresse, preferably passing them through a fine sieve. Add a pinch of cayenne pepper and serve cold but not chilled.

Mulet à la Martégale
Grey mullet as prepared at Martigues

Gut, scale, wash and pat dry the grey mullet or mullets. Place them in an oiled oven dish on a bed of slices of tomato and rings of onion. Sprinkle a wineglassful of olive oil over all and season with salt and pepper. Place overlapping slices of lemon on top of the fish. Cook in a moderate oven for 25 to 35 minutes.

Pagre aux Moules
Sea bream with mussels (serves four to six)

This recipe has the smack of Toulon about it, although I am not certain
that it is used there in the form given. It is suitable for various members
of the bream family, and also for grey mullet.

1 sea bream (No. 129) of about 800–1200 grammes	1 leek
1 kilo mussels, preferably small ones	3 tomatoes, peeled and chopped
1 wineglassful white wine	4 tablespoonfuls chopped parsley
2–3 tablespoonfuls olive oil	fennel leaves
	1–2 cloves garlic, chopped
	salt and pepper

Clean and scrub the mussels, put them in a wide pan with the white
wine and let them open over a fairly fast flame. Remove them from the
pan as soon as they open, filter the stock left in the pan through a
muslin, and take the mussels from their shells. Heat the olive oil in a
small frying pan, and soften in it the finely sliced white part of the
leek. Then add the tomatoes roughly chopped, the parsley, garlic and
fennel, and seasoning. When the mixture begins to look like a purée,
thin it with a little of the strained mussel stock. Then, off the fire, add
the mussels.

Clean, scale, behead and gut the fish. Spread a sheet of aluminium
foil or greaseproof paper with a film of olive oil. Lay the fish on this.
Surround with the prepared sauce; wrap the foil or paper round,
twisting the edges so that no juice can run out. Put on a baking dish
and cook in a moderate oven for about 40 minutes. To serve, turn out
on to a heated dish with the sauce and juices all round. Add lemon
quarters.

Raie au Beurre Noir
Skate with black butter

'Supposing that you have a piece of wing of skate, weighing $1\frac{1}{4}$ to $1\frac{1}{2}$ lb.,
the other ingredients are an onion, a few sprigs of parsley, vinegar and
butter. You also need a pan sufficiently wide for the piece of skate to lie
flat while cooking. Into this pan you put the skate, cover it completely
with cold water, add a sliced onion, a couple of sprigs of parsley, a little
salt and 2 tablespoons of vinegar. Bring gently to the boil, with the pan
uncovered. Thereafter let it barely simmer for 15 to 20 minutes. Lift
it out and put it on a dish or board so that you can remove the skin and

the large cartilaginous pieces of bone and divide the fish into 2 or 3 portions. This has to be done with some care, or the appearance of the fish will be spoiled. Transfer it to a fireproof serving dish, sprinkle it with chopped parsley, and keep it hot over a low flame while the black butter is prepared.

'For this you put 2 oz. of fresh butter into a small frying-pan and heat it over a fast flame until it foams and begins to turn brown. At this precise moment, not sooner nor later, take the pan from the fire, for in a split second the butter will take on the deep hazel-nut colour which is *beurre noir*. (It should be only a little darker than *beurre noisette*, which is light hazel-nut colour.) Pour it instantly over the fish. Into the pan in which the butter has cooked, and which you have replaced on the fire, pour 2 tablespoons of wine vinegar, which will almost instantly boil and bubble. Pour this, too, over the fish, and bring at once to table; for, like all dishes in which *beurre noir* figures, the ideal is only attained when the dish is set before those who are to eat it with the sauce absolutely sizzling.'

(Elizabeth David, *French Provincial Cooking*)

Cassoulet de Rascasse à la Suffren
Conserve of rascasse (serves four)

I give this excellent recipe just as Dr Aronvald gives it, and as I have cooked it. The result has a very distinctive flavour, and it is good for breakfast. The dish is named after Admiral Suffren, of St Tropez, famed for his naval exploits against the English.

Readers who are not in the habit of making confit d'oie, and who are therefore not sure of having the right kind of terrine, need not be put off for that reason. If you can burn rum in it and squash the fish down in it it will do.

2 rascasses (No. 217) of 350–400 grammes each	pepper and salt
	cumin
2 onions, quartered	olive oil
3 cloves garlic	parsley
	rum

Gut the fish. Put fresh water into a poissonière, bring it to the boil, put in the onions and then, 3 minutes later, the fish. Cook them for exactly 10 minutes, then take them out, remove the skin and bone and allow the fillets to become completely cold.

Crush the garlic in a mortar, then add the flesh of the rascasses, crushing it to a moderate extent only, and sprinkling on a little salt and some pepper and cumin. When all is well mixed, put 3 soupspoonfuls of olive oil in a frying pan and place the pan on a hot fire. When the oil sings, fork out the fish mixture on to it, turning as necessary until it is golden brown.

Meanwhile take a shallow terrine (the kind used for confit d'oie) and burn a little rum in it. Place the fried fish mixture in the terrine and press it down firmly with a fork. Let it cool thoroughly, cover with ½ a centimetre of lard (to preserve it) and decorate with parsley.

This dish may be eaten with olives and red wine for breakfast, or served as the entrée for lunch.

(Dr J. Aronvald, *Le Trésor de la Cuisine du bassin Méditerranéen*)

Rougets à la Niçoise
Red mullet in the style of Nice (serves four)

In the Rue de la Préfecture in the Vieille Ville at Nice there is one restaurant, La Trappa, which is very long established and highly regarded by the Niçois. Monsieur Beltramo, the proprietor, comes of a fishing family. His grand-daughter, Madame Annie, was kind enough to discuss with me at length some of the fish dishes which I enjoyed from her kitchen, including the one given below, which is a speciality of Nice.

1 wineglassful olive oil	4 large rougets (No. 148) or 8
1 onion, chopped	small ones
2 cloves garlic, chopped	more olive oil
parsley, chopped	white wine
4 tomatoes, peeled and chopped	8 black olives
½ teaspoonful tomato purée	slices of lemon
a bouquet garni, salt and pepper	

Lightly brown the onion in the hot olive oil, also the garlic and parsley. Add the tomatoes, tomato purée, and bouquet; season with salt and pepper. Madame Annie insists on the importance of what she calls a 'point' of tomato purée in addition to the fresh tomatoes, since this addition helps to give the sauce body. Cook for 15 minutes. Meanwhile clean and scale the rougets and fry them lightly in olive oil, just enough to stiffen them, not to cook them through. When the sauce has cooked for 15 minutes add rather more than ½ wineglassful of white wine, the rougets and 8 black olives. Cook for 10 minutes, covered, over a low flame. Serve with slices of lemon on top.

Rougets en Papillote 'Baumanière'

The Baumanière is the famous hotel at Les Baux in Provence which scores the absolute maximum of points (five place-settings as well as three stars) in the Michelin guide. This refers with relish and respect to its '*demeures anciennes aménagées avec élégance; terrasses fleuries et piscine*'. I still have a recollection of seeing this place for the first time when I passed by on foot, on a summer day when the Alpilles were baking and shimmering in the sun, and of how as my eyes focused on this same piscine from half a mile away I wondered whether it could be a mirage. 'Some people have it pretty good, don't they?' was the epigrammatic and rhetorical question which did not flash across my mind, the heat being too great, but sulkily bubbled from it like a puff of marsh gas while I took the weight off my dusty legs and lowered to the ground the bag of books and old socks and stale bread which I was carrying from Avignon to Arles. In fact I did not realize just how good those little blobs flickering on the edge of the piscine had been having it. It was 3 p.m. and they had probably eaten for lunch M. Thuilier's creation of which a version is given below.

Buy for each person a fine rouget de roche (No. 148) of about 175 grammes. Scale but do not gut them. Make ready for each rouget a well-oiled piece of aluminium foil sufficiently large to receive it en papillote. Put a bay leaf on each, a rouget on the bay leaf and on the rouget a very thin slice of lightly smoked pork tenderloin or fillet (failing which I suggest, e.g., Ayrshire bacon). Wrap the fish up in their covers, twist the ends, place the packages in a well-oiled oven dish and cook in a moderate oven for 20 minutes, turning the packages several times. Serve the rougets in their coverings, with an anchovy-flavoured hollandaise sauce and rice cooked in mussel broth.

This, by the way, is not the only recipe to bring together pig and red mullet. At Ancona in Italy red mullet which have been marinaded in lemon juice and chopped rosemary, and then coated with chopped parsley and breadcrumbs, are wrapped each in a slice of Parma ham before being baked with the strained marinade poured over them.

Rougets au Safran
Cold red mullet with saffron   (serves four)

This dish can be served hot, but is generally preferred cold. You will need to have 8 smallish rougets, which are not to be gutted but should be scaled, washed and patted dry. Lay them in an oven dish, ready to receive the battery of aromatic flavourings which this recipe demands. First they are sprinkled generously with olive oil. Then add ½ kilo of tomatoes, peeled, pipped and chopped, sprigs of fennel and thyme, and 2 bay leaves. Next sprinkle on ground coriander, 3 pinches of saffron and salt and pepper. Pour over a wineglassful of white wine, place the dish in a hot oven and cook for 10 minutes from the time when the liquid starts to bubble. Then cool and decorate with lemon slices.

Rougets aux Feuilles de Vigne
Red mullet cooked in vine leaves

Auguste Escoffier recommended this pleasing recipe, which is an easy one provided that you have both red mullet and vine leaves. Buy one red mullet (preferably No. 148) of about 150–175 grammes for each person. Gather the same number of vine leaves. Gut, scale, wash and pat dry the fish. But in gutting them take care to leave the livers inside. Make cuts along the back of each, so that the fish have been opened up above as well as below. Season them with salt and pepper and brush them freely with olive oil. Dip the vine leaves in boiling water for a minute or so, to make them supple. Then wrap each prepared fish inside a vine leaf. Range the wrapped fish in an oven dish. Sprinkle with olive oil. Cook in a moderate oven for 20 minutes.

Saint Pierre à la Parmentier
John Dory baked with potatoes   (serves two)

Buy a John Dory of medium size and have it cleaned. As usual with this fish there will be surprisingly little left by the time this process is completed. Remember, however, that the trimmings, if you care to take them away, will make a good fish bouillon.

Select a gratin dish of about the right size for the fish. Cover the bottom of this with a bed of sliced potatoes. Wash the fish and pat it dry, then place it on this bed, season it and pour a little melted butter over it. Next cover the fish with half a dozen slices of lemon, followed by a layer of sliced potatoes. Repeat the seasoning and melted butter. Pour a wineglassful of white wine over all.

Put the dish into a preheated moderately hot oven and let it cook for 30 to 35 minutes, basting every 5 minutes or so and making sure that the liquid remains sufficient. Sprinkle with chopped parsley before serving.

This dish, or something very like it, may also appear under the names Saint Pierre à la Ménagère or (with onion as well as potato) Saint Pierre des Pêcheurs.

Sar ou Dorade au Fenouil et au Vin Blanc
Bream cooked with fresh fennel and white wine (serves four)

Mme Totte Feissel demonstrated this dish for me in the kitchen of her house on a Marseille hill-top. She pointed out that she used an oven tray which held the juices and had a grill fitted over it which kept the fish just above them. In the absence of this piece of equipment it would be well to use a large shallow oven dish with a grid of some kind fitted into it.

Select and clean a large sar (No. 138) or red bream (No. 133) weighing about 1 kilo, or several smaller ones. Make deep incisions in the back of the fish. Insert feathery sprigs of fresh fennel in the incisions, and put some sprigs of fresh thyme in the fish's belly together with a knob of butter and salt and pepper.

Place the fish on its grid (see above), pour over it 1½ wineglassfuls of dry white wine and 1 tablespoonful of olive oil, which will then collect below. Add a few slices of tomato to the liquid, and place thin slices of lemon on top of the fish (also a few slices of onion if you wish). Cook in a moderate oven for 15 to 25 minutes (less for the sar than for the dorade), basting from time to time although this is not essential. Serve with the cooking juices strained off and used as a sauce.

Beignets de Sardines
Sardine fritters

First prepare some fritter batter by mixing 200 grammes of flour with salt, pepper and whatever you like to use in the way of baking powder or yeast. Beat into this mixture the yolk of an egg, the beaten white of an egg, and a generous tablespoonful of warm water. Leave to stand for 1 hour.

Behead and gut fresh sardines. Remove their backbones from below, but leave them joined at the tail. You may then either close each sardine up again, or take a pair opened out and press them lightly together, inside to inside.

Prepare the apparatus for deep frying. When the oil is hot enough dip the sardines, single or double, into the batter, holding them by the tails. Then cook them in the hot oil briefly.

Sole à la Provençale
Fried sole with aubergine

Wash and pat dry fillets of sole, then fry them in olive oil. Fry in the same way thin slices of aubergines, cut lengthways, one for each fillet. (Or you could use courgettes instead.) Have ready some chopped tomato flesh. Place a slice of aubergine on top of each fillet of sole, and a couple of teaspoonfuls of tomato on top of each aubergine slice. Keep all this hot in the oven. Melt a little butter and let it turn brown. Pour this over the dish, sprinkle some chopped fines herbes over all and serve.

Petits Pâtés au Thon
Tunny in pastry (serves two)

For this recipe you may use either pâte brisée or pâte feuilletée. I suggest the latter, as it is lighter and tunny is a substantial food. Conversely, if you choose to make a filling of anchovy instead of tunny you will probably do better to encase the strong anchovy taste in pâte brisée.

Start by soaking 50 grammes of breadcrumbs in milk and then squeezing them thoroughly to expel the excess liquid. Mix this (with pestle and mortar or in a blender) with 200 grammes of tinned tuna fish, 50 grammes of butter, the yolk of an egg and seasoning.

Cut out rounds from your dough by means of a water tumbler pressed upside down on it – this will give you rounds of something like 7½ centimetres in diameter, but the exact size does not matter. Be sure, however, to make an even number of rounds. On half the rounds place a spoonful of the tunny mixture. Cap each with the second round, moisten the edges of both and crimp them together so that the tunny mixture is sealed inside. Brush with egg yolk and cook in a hot oven for 20 minutes.

The anchovy version is made in the same way, but substituting mashed anchovy fillets for the tunny.

Thon en Chartreuse
Tunny cooked in a 'chartreuse' (serves four)

A 'chartreuse' is a dish of mixed vegetables, and there are various ways of combining tunny with such a mixture. For the version below you will need:

a steak of tunny 1 inch thick and just over ½ kilo	2 onions
lemon juice	6 carrots
4 fillets of anchovy	4 to 8 lettuce hearts
3 tablespoonfuls olive oil	a handful of fresh sorrel
salt and pepper	1½ wineglassfuls white wine

First select a heavy covered pan, preferably what the French call a casserole à sauter, or sauteuse, big enough for the piece of tunny. Blanch the tunny in water to which has been added salt and lemon juice, take off its skin, and lard it with the fillets of anchovy.

Put the olive oil in the sauteuse and set it to warm. Slice thinly the onions and carrots and add them. Place the tunny on top, cover, and leave over a moderate flame for a short time while you blanch the lettuce hearts. This done, turn the piece of tunny over, arrange the lettuce hearts on top of it in a circle and place the sorrel over the lot, adding salt and pepper. Cover once more and leave cooking for another 3 or 4 minutes. By this time the liquid which has been 'sweated' out will have more or less evaporated and the vegetables will begin to stick to the bottom of the pan. Having thus got rid of the water, supply the necessary liquid by adding the white wine. Continue to cook for another 40 minutes, still over a moderate flame, turning the lettuce hearts over several times, but leaving the tunny undisturbed.

When all is ready the tunny is placed in the middle of a heated serving dish, the vegetables around it, and the juices poured over.

Langouste comme chez Nenette

This is a variation of Langouste à la Sètoise, in its turn a variation of Homard à l'Américaine. It is an expensive dish, but the langouste is among the most costly and delicious of Mediterranean sea creatures and can appropriately be treated in a lavish manner.

'Cut a live crawfish* into not too large pieces; put them at once into a wide and shallow pan containing a little smoking olive oil, add salt and pepper and cook until the shell turns red. Add some finely chopped shallots and a clove or two of garlic, crushed and first cooked separately in a little oil.

'Pour in a small glass of good cognac and set light to it; when the flames have gone out, add a half bottle of still champagne or chablis, and a spoonful of tomato purée. Cover the pan and cook over a steady fire for about 20 minutes. Remove the pieces of crawfish, which are now cooked, and keep them hot.

'Press the sauce through a very fine sieve, let it boil up again, season with a scrap of cayenne and, at the last minute, add 3 good spoonfuls of aïoli (p. 287).

'Pour the sauce over the crawfish and sprinkle a little finely chopped parsley over the dish.'

(Elizabeth David, *French Provincial Cooking*)

Riz aux Favouilles

Crabs with rice   (serves four)

Buy 8 or 12 crabs (No. 516) and remove their legs. Give each a sharp blow on the carapace (to 'unseal' them), and set them to cook in a wineglassful of olive oil. Once they are cooking add some water and a bouquet garni and let them continue cooking thus for 20 minutes. Remove them and keep warm, and strain the cooking liquid.

Heat another wineglassful of olive oil, and add a chopped onion and the chopped flesh of 2 tomatoes. Pour in 1 measuring cup of the strained cooking liquid, season, and add a pinch of saffron. When this mixture comes to the boil add half the quantity, by volume, of rice (i.e. about ¾ of a measuring cup). You may have to add a little more strained cooking liquid while the rice is cooking.

When the rice is ready pile it up on a heated platter, sprinkle it with grated cheese, arrange the crabs on it and serve.

*Author's footnote. Or kill the creature first – see page 187. Note also that the names crawfish (for the langouste) and crayfish (for the fresh-water crustacean) are confusing because often treated, and with authority from lexicographers, as interchangeable. So, if you are shopping in English and thus exposing yourself to the risk of this confusion, make clear that it is the langouste which you want.

Encornets (Calmars) à l'Étuvée
Stewed squid (serves six)

4 squid (No. 573), weighing rather less than 1 kilo in all	salt and pepper
$\frac{3}{4}$ wineglassful olive oil	a bouquet garni, to include a sprig of fennel
3 onions, sliced	6 tomatoes
2 cloves garlic, chopped	$\frac{1}{4}$ wineglassful olive oil
1 wineglassful red wine	

Cut the body of the cleaned squid into rings about $\frac{1}{4}''$ wide and the tentacles into slices. Heat $\frac{3}{4}$ wineglassful olive oil in a stewpan and add the onion and garlic. Cook these gently until they take colour, then put in the squid, followed a couple of minutes later by the wine. Once the wine has begun to bubble for a minute or two reduce the heat and add the seasoning and bouquet. Continue to cook slowly, covered, for up to an hour and a half. Towards the end of the cooking, peel and chop the tomatoes and add them to the $\frac{1}{4}$ wineglassful olive oil which you have heated in another pan. When the tomatoes are almost reduced to a purée season them and add them to the squid, which should be served a few minutes later.

Poulpe à la Niçoise
Octopus in the style of Nice (serves six or more)

Buy the octopus the day before, and let it hang overnight, tentacles down, to help make it tender.

Prepare the octopus in the usual way (see p. 233) and cut it into strips. Put these in a casserole by themselves and heat the casserole for 5 minutes or so while the excess water sweats out of the octopus. Drain.

Lightly brown a chopped onion in olive oil, with 2 chopped cloves of garlic and chopped parsley. Add a bouquet garni and the strips of octopus and go on cooking for 5 minutes until the octopus is well coloured. (It is a nuisance that the English language has no exact equivalent for 'doré' – 'browned' is a bit too strong.)

Next pour a generous wineglassful of cognac over the dish and set it alight. When the flames have died down add a tablespoonful of flour, stir, then add 5 or 6 chopped tomatoes and a very little (say, a teaspoonful) tomato purée and a wineglassful of white wine. If necessary in order to cover the octopus add a little water too. Also salt and pepper. Cook gently, covered, for 3 hours or so until the octopus is tender.

(Directions given by Mme Annie, Restaurant La Trappa, the Old Town, Nice)

Seiches à l'Agathoise
Cuttlefish as prepared at Agde (serves six)

The little town of Agde, close to the sea and about halfway between Narbonne and Montpellier, is to be congratulated on the formation of such a charming adjective from its name. Like the people of Sète, not far away, the Agathois have their own traditional recipes. This one, for cuttlefish (No. 568), may also be applied to squid (Nos. 573, 577).

1 cuttlefish, cleaned, of about 1 kilo	*for the stuffing:*
1 wineglassful olive oil	150 grammes minced veal
1 onion, chopped	150 grammes minced pork
3 carrots, cut into rounds	1 onion, finely chopped
	parsley, finely chopped
	1 egg yolk
	salt and pepper

Rinse the cleaned cuttlefish thoroughly under cold running water. It should be of a spooky white colour, which the rinsing will improve. Prepare a stuffing from the veal, pork, finely chopped onion and parsley. Bind with the egg yolk and season with salt and pepper. Place the stuffing inside the cuttlefish and sew it up.

Heat the olive oil in a casserole, let the other chopped onion take colour in it, and add enough water so that the cuttlefish will be covered when you put it in. Bring to the boil. Then put in the cuttlefish and the carrots, cover, and cook gently for 3 hours or more until the cuttlefish is tender.

Clovisses Farcies au Gratin
'Stuffed' clams (serves two)

This recipe can be used for many of the bivalves, for example mussels (No. 545) and praires (No. 555), but I think that it is best as a treatment of clovisses (No. 558), provided that you can get reasonably large ones. It is too finicky if they are very small.

Wash several dozen clovisses and set them to open in a large casserole with a glass of white wine. After a few minutes over a moderate flame they will all have opened. Take them from their shells, preserving the half shells only, and strain the liquid.

Chop an onion finely. Heat some olive oil and colour the chopped onion in this, then add a dozen or more button mushrooms chopped up, a small amount of breadcrumbs soaked in milk and then squeezed, the flesh of 2 tomatoes, 2 sprigs of parsley, black pepper and (if you wish) a little grated nutmeg. All this should be mashed together to make a fairly thick 'stuffiing', bound with some of the strained cooking liquid from the first operation.

Put one clovisse in each half shell, cover it with the 'stuffing', and lay them all out in a gratin dish. Sprinkle with dry breadcrumbs. Let a drop of hot olive oil fall on each clovisse. Then gratiner them until they are well browned on top. Sprinkle with lemon juice and serve.

Coquilles Saint-Jacques à la Provençale
Fried scallops with garlic and parsley

'The scallops which come from the Mediterranean are very much smaller than those from the Atlantic, but this method of cooking them can be applied just as well to the large variety. Slice the cleaned white part of the scallops into two rounds, season them with salt, pepper and lemon juice; immediately before cooking them, sprinkle them very lightly with flour, fry them pale golden on each side in a mixture of butter and olive oil. Put in the red parts, add a generous sprinkling of finely chopped garlic and parsley and shake the pan so that the mixture spreads evenly amongst the scallops. Five minutes' cooking altogether will be enough.'

(Elizabeth David, *French Provincial Cooking*)

Moules Camarguaises
Mussels with a special mayonnaise   (serves two or three)

This is simple and decorative.

Clean and beard 1 kilo of mussels. Set them to heat and open in a large pot with 2 wineglassfuls of white wine. Let them cook for 5–10 minutes. Then remove them and discard the surplus half shells. (If the mussels are on the small side arrange them two to a half shell, but if they are of a good size leave them one in each.)

Make a mayonnaise using lemon juice, not vinegar. Blend with it 2 tablespoonfuls of the strained mussel broth. Spoon the result over the mussels and sprinkle with parsley.

(Recipe of Mme Ricard, Aix-en-Provence)

Moules Nautile
A mussel recipe from Toulon

For those who like myself were overwhelmed with excitement by their first boyhood reading of *20,000 Leagues Under the Sea*, an agreeable and evocative experience is available at Toulon. This is to go and stay at Jules Verne's old house, now the Hotel Nautilus, in a favoured position overlooking the tiny harbour of Mourillon at Toulon. Monsieur Chabot, the proprietor, is an expert on seafood. Sitting below a large oil painting of Jules Verne, he explained to me his favourite methods of preparing the mussels for which Toulon is famous.

For Moules Nautile he opens the cleaned and bearded mussels by heating them in a large pot with white wine and chopped shallots. They are then taken out and ranged in their half shells on a platter. The broth is strained and reserved. Meanwhile the sauce is made ready. First colour a chopped onion in hot olive oil, then add a sprinkling of flour, several peeled and chopped tomatoes, a bouquet garni, and equal quantities of white wine and mussel broth. Cook all this gently for 7 or 8 minutes, certainly not more than 10, and add at the last moment a sprinkling of black pepper and a pinch of saffron (but no salt). Pour the sauce over the mussels, and add a sprinkling of chopped parsley. The sauce is not a thick one. Its orange colour contrasts well with the blue-black mussel shells. The bits of onion remain quite distinct, giving texture to the sauce. I noted that M. Chabot counts about fifteen mussels to a helping.

Omelette d'Oursins
Omelette with sea-urchin corals   (serves two)

3 eggs	salt and pepper
18 oursins	butter

Cut open the oursins and extract from each the quintet of corals. Collect these together. Break the eggs into a bowl, add 2 tablespoonfuls of water and salt and pepper and mix all this up roughly with a fork (or beat it if you prefer to do so) and add the corals to the mixture. Meanwhile heat butter or oil in an omelette pan. Slip the mixture into the pan carefully and then proceed as if you were making an ordinary omelette.

Beignets de Pastègues
Sea anemone fritters

Charles Giorgi is a devoted and accomplished French under-water fisherman who takes as close an interest in the preparation or cooking of his prey as in shooting or catching it. He has shot some enormous mérous, but will discuss with equal passion such apparently trivial questions as how to make sea anemone fritters. He prefaces his direction by a warning that the sea anemones (French orties de mer, Provençale pastègues) must be kept well away from the eyes when they are being gathered.

Having gathered your sea anemones with due precaution, put your thumb up each from the rock side, so to speak, so that it comes out between the tentacles, thus extruding whatever the creature may have been eating and any grit.

Prepare a fritter batter (p. 307). Warm some groundnut oil in a pan. (Monsieur Giorgi's somewhat unorthodox view is that the use of olive oil is excluded for anything but salads.) Dip the sea anemones in the batter, put them in the pan and fry them for 10 minutes. The cooking should be done over a low flame. The result, according to this connoisseur, is 'exquisite'.

12. Recipes from Italy

The geography of Italy is such that almost every region of the country has its share of coastline; and the Adriatic Sea and the waters around Sicily are two of the richest parts of the Mediterranean. It is therefore not surprising that fish and other seafood dishes feature prominently in the regional cuisines.

Indeed there are so many Italian recipes for fish that it is difficult to make a selection which will seem reasonably compact and yet do some sort of justice to all the rival claims. In the field of fish soups alone it would be possible to cite dozens of good recipes. Caminiti, Pasquini and Quondamatteo, in their book *Mangiari di Romagna*, observe that if one takes the Marche alone one finds that there are seven towns – San Benedetto, Porto S. Giorgio, Porto Recanati, Numana, Ancona, Falconara and Senigallia – which claim, and claim with passion, the best brodetto of that particular stretch of coastline.

It is true that the variations between local versions are often small; true too that the number of dishes is certainly not as great as the number of recipe titles to be found on menus. My friend Giorgio Bini, in a series of analytical articles written for the magazine *Mondo Sommerso*, has classified seafood dishes in a way which shows how few basic ones there really are.

None the less, there is a wealth of material here, and the most which I can say for the selection which I have made is that it is at least illustrative of this wealth; it has something from each of the great gastronomic regions, it has some typical less-known dishes alongside famous ones, and it gives space to two groups of dishes which belong uniquely to Italy – those which combine pasta with seafood, and the seafood pizza dishes. I find both particularly satisfying and harmonious (provided that they are not over-elaborated) and believe that Vermicelli alle Vongole, for example, achieves a smoother fusion between seafood and other food than can ever be managed by the fish and two vegetables formula.

Brodetto di Pesce Veneziano
Venetian fish soup (serves eight)

Venetians are justly proud of this soup, and point out that its flavour is a true fish flavour, unadulterated by strong spices. (The innuendo is not lost on the men of Marseille and Genoa.) The preparation is clearly divided into two phases. In the first, flavourful but bony or uncouth fish yield a strained broth and then disappear into it via the sieve. In the second, choice bone-free morsels of superior fish are made ready for combination with the broth.

PHASE I

1 kilo of gobies ('go' in Venice, Nos. 213, etc.)
1 kilo of rascasses ('scarpene', Nos. 216, etc.)
1 kilo of shrimp ('schile', No. 506)
1 lemon   4 tomatoes

Clean the fish and remove the heads from the rascasses. Set the heads to boil in water, with the halved lemon and the quartered tomatoes, for an hour. For the last 20 minutes add the rascasse bodies, the gobies and the shrimp. Then strain off the fish and debris, put it on one side and reserve the liquid on another. Next, pass the fish and debris through a sieve, thus obtaining a fishy cream. Add this to the reserved broth.

PHASE 2 (which can be started while PHASE I is in progress)

$2\frac{1}{2}$ kilos in all of grey mullet ('bosega', Nos. 105, etc.) tail of angler-fish ('coda di rospo', No. 249), and if you wish choice gobbets of octopus head ('testa di polpo', Nos. 579, 580)
100 grammes each of olive oil and butter
2 cloves of garlic   parsley   salt

Clean and prepare the fish, and simmer it in water until it is cooked. The morsels of octopus and the angler-fish will take longer than the grey mullet, so they should be started sooner. Meanwhile prepare a soffritto by heating the olive oil and butter and letting the garlic and parsley, chopped, take colour in it.

Remove the fish. Behead and debone the grey mullet and cut it up. The angler-fish tails may be cut up too, but the octopus morsels should already be the right size. Put all the pieces of fish into the soffritto and let them take colour. Next, pour over the pieces of fish the broth (including of course the fishy cream) from PHASE I, add a little salt and let the whole boil gently for a few minutes. Then serve in deep roomy soup plates with slices of 'casada' bread fried in oil.

Zuppa di Pesce alla Barese

A fish stew from Bari (serves four)

This recipe comes from Signora Delia (Lennie) Conenna, a native of Bari. She emphasizes that it is a main course.

4 large thin steaks of smooth hound (Nos. 13, 14) or dogfish (Nos. 10, 11) or mérou (Nos. 116, etc.) or other large fish	$\frac{3}{4}$ kilo tomatoes (or a slightly smaller quantity of tinned ones)
2 cloves garlic, finely chopped	150–200 grammes black olives (preferably the small Bari ones)
	1 wineglassful olive oil
	parsley

Heat a wineglassful of olive oil in a wide low flameproof dish (what the Italians call a teglia) and lightly fry the garlic in it, adding as soon as the oil begins to sing the tomatoes, roughly chopped, the chopped parsley and salt and pepper. Cook all this for a few minutes, then add the olives. Put in the fish steaks, and let them cook until they turn fully white, no longer. They should be ready in 5 to 10 minutes.

Cacciucco Livornese

Leghorn fish stew

This is a real fish stew, in which the fish, molluscs and crustaceans loom larger than the broth. There are many ways of preparing it – all the more since the domain of Cacciucco extends some way north and south of Livorno. The variety of recipes was personified for me by a group of Tuscan ladies who, playing bridge with their husbands in a villa not far from Livorno, found me suddenly in their midst, fish recipe notebook in hand. With remarkable courtesy they abandoned their husbands to continue the game alone and formed an advisory committee on Cacciucco which sat for an hour over tea and gave me much conflicting guidance from which I was ultimately able to distil what follows.

The first principle to be grasped is that the dish is by origin both simple and cheap. Expensive ingredients are therefore out of place. So is any complicated and prolonged method of preparation. On the other hand it is worth a little extra effort to ensure that the result is not spoiled by the presence of little bones. The second point is that hot red peppers are essential for any version of the dish. (The Italian name is peperoncino, but in Tuscany it is zenzero.)

The fish should include rascasse (Nos. 216, etc.), gurnard (Nos. 220, etc.) and perhaps small dogfish (Nos. 13 and 14 or 10 and 11) and some non-bony pieces of conger or moray eel (No. 68 and No. 67). Small cuttlefish (No. 568) and small octopus (Nos. 579 or 580) are essential. It is usual to include crustaceans, which could be squilles (No. 525); and mussels (No. 545) may be added as well. As a general principle you can include any seafood which is to hand and not too costly.

The first step, as in so many Italian recipes, is to prepare a soffritto. Heat olive oil and add plenty of chopped garlic and chopped hot red pepper. When this has started to colour add either fresh tomatoes (peeled and seeded) or tomato paste diluted with water; also salt, black peppercorns, and chopped parsley. Cook this for a while.

The next step is to put in the small and bony fish. Cook them in the sauce until they begin to disintegrate, then rub the entire panful through a sieve so as to eliminate the fish bones and other debris while retaining in the broth the full flavour of the rascasses and gurnard. Cook the remaining seafood in this broth, adding the various kinds in order in accordance with how long each will take to cook. They should of course be cleaned and cut up as necessary before being added. When all is ready place a piece of toast, which has been rubbed with garlic, in the tureen, set the pieces of fish on it and pour the broth (of which there will not be a great deal) over all.

Burrida alla Genovese

A Genoese fish soup (serves ten or more)

I give here a recipe for this splendid dish as it is made in Genoa. It can be adapted for use where not all the right kinds of seafood are available; but bear in mind that for the Genoese the essential items in the list which follows are angler-fish, octopus and squid.

You will need 2 kilos of seafood altogether. 1¾ kilos should be selected from angler-fish (No. 249), rascasses (Nos. 216, etc.), gurnards (Nos. 220, etc.), weevers or a stargazer (Nos. 181, etc.), dogfish (Nos. 10, 11), octopus (Nos. 579, 580) and squid (No. 573). The remaining ¼ kilo or so should include some or all of mussels (No. 545), shrimp (No. 506) and razor clams (No. 562). The other ingredients are:

3 tablespoonfuls olive oil
50 grammes streaky bacon (lardo), chopped
1 small onion, chopped
1 small carrot
½ stick celery
1 clove garlic
1 head parsley, chopped fine

3 anchovy fillets, chopped
½ kilo tomatoes, peeled and chopped
fresh basil, chopped
salt and pepper
1 wineglassful white wine
about the same amount of warm water

Heat the olive oil and bacon in a pan, add the chopped onion and let it take colour. Then add the carrot, celery, garlic, parsley and anchovy fillets. Five minutes later add the tomatoes, basil, seasoning and liquids, and the octopus and squid (cleaned, prepared and cut up). Let it all simmer gently for half an hour.

Then add the fish (which you have cleaned and where necessary cut up into large pieces) and the comparatively small quantity of mussels (in their shells but very carefully washed and bearded), shrimp and razor clams (in their shells but carefully washed). Let the whole simmer somewhat more vigorously for a further 20 minutes. Have ready slices of fried or oven-crisped bread. Set the fish on these and pour the broth over all.

Zuppa di Granchi o di Favolli
Crab soup

These instructions are for making a soup from either the common shore crabs (No. 516) or the ériphie (No. 521).

First put the crabs in a bath of milk and leave them for 2 hours. Simmer together in salted water some peeled and chopped tomatoes, a few shallots, a carrot and a leek, some cloves of garlic, a couple of bay leaves and a few cloves and peppercorns. Sieve the result and combine the purée with two parts of olive oil to one of white wine. Place the crabs in the mixture and cook them for half an hour, adding a little more liquid if it is needed.

Zuppa di Telline/Vongole/Cozze/Cannolicchi
Soup made with bivalves such as the mussel

Of the four bivalves listed in the title of this recipe the best for the purpose are probably telline (No. 561); but all will make an excellent soup in accordance with the same basic instructions. The principle is simple. Prepare a well-flavoured liquid or sauce (in which olive oil, garlic, tomatoes and herbs should figure) in the bottom of a large pan; put the bivalves in on top of this and continue heating until they open, releasing their own juices into the cooking liquid; and serve the bivalves with the liquid poured as a soup over pieces of toast.

Here are two versions, offered as illustrations of the countless ways in which the technique described above can be applied. For convenience I refer to mussels in both, but the other bivalves could be substituted – with the proviso that in dealing with the smaller ones you should be particularly careful not to go on cooking them for long after they have opened.

(1) Heat ½ wineglassful of olive oil in a large, deep pan, let a clove of garlic take colour in it, then discard the garlic. Add 2 tablespoonfuls of tomato purée, diluted with water, or some tinned cooking tomatoes (pelati). If you wish, add also a teaspoonful of finely chopped hot red pepper or a sprinkling of cayenne pepper. Cook for about 5 minutes, then add chopped parsley and 2 kilos of mussels, which you have carefully washed and bearded beforehand. Wait for the mussels to open, moving them around as necessary so that the ones on top do not take too long. Make toast. Soon after all the mussels are open pour them and the soup over the pieces of toast.

(2) Heat ½ wineglassful of olive oil in a large, deep pan. Add a finely sliced medium onion. Once this has taken colour add 2 sliced cloves of garlic and half a stick of celery, chopped. Put in at the same time some fresh marjoram (or basil, or thyme) and ground black pepper (but no salt). A couple of minutes later add ¾ kilo tomatoes (either pelati which you have first drained, or fresh tomatoes which have been peeled and roughly chopped). Let the mixture go on cooking for 4 or 5 minutes.

Add next rather less than a wineglassful of dry white wine. Turn up the heat and let it bubble briefly, then lower the heat again, cover the pan and continue to cook gently until the tomatoes are turning into a pulp. At this stage you have to add about 1½ wineglassfuls of hot liquid, which can either be hot water or, for pelati-users, a heated mixture of water and the juices which were drained from the pelati earlier. Simmer for a few minutes longer, giving a good stir, and check that you have the desired result which is a sort of thick soup. This can be left and heated up again when you are ready for the final stage.

Begin the final operation 15 minutes before serving. Add the carefully washed and bearded mussels to the hot soup and keep the pan over a fairly brisk flame until all the mussels have opened. Then turn off the heat, sprinkle chopped parsley and a very little grated lemon peel over the mussels, and serve, pouring each person's helping over pieces of toast and providing a bowl on the table for the empty shells.

Cappon Magro
A unique but imitable Genoese construction of fish and vegetables

This is a lavish dish. Mr Alexander Moll, who explored for me in
Genoa the niceties of the recipe and subsequently kept me company
when I ate the dish for the first time, stresses that one principle should
be followed, namely to spare no expense. You will need quite a bit of
time too. The recipe is split up into sections so that the whole complicated process will seem more manageable. I should add that the recipe
is subject to many variations even in Genoa and that there is no reason
why successful versions should not be devised anywhere where fish
crustaceans and vegetables of top quality can be bought.

The Vegetables

You will need 1 celery plant (washed), 1 beetroot (cooked), 6 artichoke
hearts (tinned) and some pickled gherkins. In addition, you must cook
(by steaming or boiling) 200 grammes cauliflower, ¼ kilo potatoes (the
very best), 150 grammes runner beans and 6 young carrots. Take great
care not to overcook these; they must remain firm. When all the vegetables are ready, dice them or cut them into slices or strips and leave
them to cool, seasoned with salt and dressed with olive oil.

The Fish

This is not the occasion for bargain-hunting. Buy 1 kilo of very fine
fish, which may be sea bass (No. 113), daurade (No. 128), denté (No. 125)
or a good gurnard (say No. 221). Buy too some lobster or spiny lobster,
prawns and perhaps some shellfish as well. Finally, you should acquire
a few slices of musciame, which is dried dolphin (p. 240). Cook the fish
in a court-bouillon, and prepare the crustaceans in the usual way.
Bone the fish and cut it into manageable pieces. Remove the flesh from
the crustaceans and cut it into pieces. Season with salt and olive oil and
leave to cool.

The Sauce

Remove the thick stalks from one bunch of parsley. Wash it, put it
into a mortar with a little salt and half a clove of garlic, and pound
until it is beginning to turn to a paste. Then add 1 tablespoonful of
capers, 2 filleted anchovies and 6 stoned olives. Continue pounding,
and add a handful of the soft part of a loaf which should have been
softened in a little vinegar and pressed dry. By this time there should be
a thick sauce. Next, pound in the yolks of 2 hard-boiled eggs. Now

start to add 2 wineglassfuls of olive oil, drop by drop, stirring vigorously with a wooden spoon as if making mayonnaise, until the sauce has the consistency of thick cream.

Final Construction

The object is to build a pyramid from the ingredients which you now have ready, and to make it as decorative as possible. The base of the pyramid should be ship's biscuit, which has previously been rubbed with garlic and then soaked in a mixture of olive oil and water. On this base spread a little of the sauce. Then place a layer of vegetables, followed by a slice of musciame and a layer of fish and more sauce. Repeat, narrowing the width as you work upwards. When you come to a point, at the top of the pyramid, pour the remaining sauce over the structure. Then set to work on the final decorations, which may consist of the coral of the lobster, the prawns, slices or eighths of lemon, and olives. Serve at one, while everything is fresh and glowing.

Fritto Misto Mare
Mixed fried fish

This is one of the most common fish dishes in restaurants on the Italian coast. The composition varies according to what is available, and there are scores of possible combinations.

In Venice a typical mixture would be from the following range: ink-fish or squid; soft-shell crabs; prawns or shrimp; eel; sardines.

In Naples the list would be shorter, as Signora Caròla explains:

'If you taste a fritto di pesce in a Neapolitan trattoria, with a view of the sea, you feel the sea itself in your mouth with all its exciting perfumes and that light and not displeasing flavour of iodine. Our fritto di pesce, the ultra-classical one, is not too varied: red mullet and squid only. The former will be the triglie di scoglio and therefore more flavourful. The bodies of the little squid will be cut into rings, after the tufts of tentacles have been chopped off. These tentacles – small, slender and crisp – will make a pleasing contrast with the tender 'rings' which melt in the mouth. Naturally even with the classical fritto we do not fail to allow ourselves some licence, often adding small prawns, which do very well, and sometimes anchovies and at other times garfish. But these are exceptions to the rules: for the true fritto of Naples the contrasting flavours of the red mullet and the small squid are sufficient.'

The general principles to be followed are that the fish should be cleaned and lightly dusted with flour and fried in very hot oil. Prawns should be fried raw and unpeeled. Inkfish or squid should be cooked ahead of time if they are large, and then cut up into rings for frying; but the very small ones do not need to be pre-cooked.

Pesce in Saor
Sardines or other fish tastily preserved   (serves six)

This is a Venetian recipe which can be applied to many fish. 'Saor' means 'sapore' or 'flavour'. The procedure followed is essentially one of marinading the fish, and the original purpose of the procedure was no doubt to preserve the fish. In his learned *Il Veneto in Cucina* Signor Ranieri da Mosto recalls that Venetians used to say that the various social classes in the city could be distinguished by their choice of fish for this preparation. Poor people used the sardine, the better off chose flounder, and the wealthy made the conventional rich man's choice of sole. Since the introduction of refrigerators the use of the 'in saor' technique has dwindled and it is now reserved almost entirely for the sardine.

1 kilo sardines (fresh; if buying them in Venice ask for sardele)	3 wineglassfuls olive oil
	2 to 3 wineglassfuls wine vinegar
1¼ kilos white onions	flour and salt

Scale, gut, behead, wash and dry the sardines, then flour them and fry them in olive oil. Take them out, drain them, salt them and keep them aside. Next use the same oil to fry the onions (sliced) to a golden colour. Then pour the vinegar in and keep it on the fire for a few minutes to effect some reduction. Tradition calls for the addition at this stage of pine-nut kernels and sultanas and bits of lemon peel.

Fill an earthenware pot with alternating layers of fried sardine and onion, adding the liquor and taking care to finish up with onions on top and vinegar up to their level. After this has stood in a cool place for a day or two, eat it. Signor da Mosto advises having cold polenta with it. It will keep for quite a few days.

Pesce alla Pizzaiola

This recipe can be used for just about any fish, but is best applied in situations where you have fish steaks (of about 150 grammes for each person) which are not so marvellously fresh as to demand simple grilling or which belong to one of the less well-flavoured species, such as dogfish.

First rinse and dry your fish steaks, then leave them for 1 or if possible 2 hours in a marinade of olive oil with chopped parsley and a bay leaf or two and pepper.

Cover the bottom of a pan with olive oil, of which you may be able to salvage enough from the marinade, and set it to heat. Meanwhile drain the fish. When the oil is hot brown the fish on both sides and then let them go on cooking until done (10 to 15 minutes, depending on the kind of fish and the thickness of the steaks).

Meanwhile warm a little more olive oil in a pan with some chopped garlic (or a couple of cloves of garlic, which you can remove once heated, if you prefer a more discreet flavour). Add the flesh of some tomatoes (one per person); salt and pepper; and as many anchovy fillets as tomatoes (or washed, cleaned and boned fresh anchovy if you have some). Cook vigorously until this mixture is reduced to a sauce-like consistency (I find it useful to add a little tomato purée to promote this process). When it is ready, sprinkle with chopped oregano and parsley. Finally, remove the fish to a heated dish and pour the sauce over it.

Pizza with Fish

(1 large pizza each for six people)

The classic Pizza alla Napoletana does not include any element of seafood; but there are several pizzas which do, and which are very good.

There are three stages in the preparation of a pizza: the making of the dough, the provision of the filling, and the baking. I deal with each in turn.

(1) To make the dough take 800 grammes of flour, 40 grammes of yeast, a little salt and some warm water. Dilute the yeast in a cup with a little warm water, add 2 pinches of flour, mix well and leave to rise for half an hour. Next put the rest of the flour on to a pastry board, make a well in the middle and put the yeast mixture and the salt in that. Work it all together for 10 minutes, adding a little warm water from time to time, enough to produce a stiff dough. Divide the result into 6 balls, cover with a clean cloth and leave it to rise for 2 hours or so, in a warm place. Then roll each ball out into a round which should be 20 cm. across and ½ centimetre thick (but very slightly thicker round the edge than in the centre).

(2) Here are seafood fillings which may be added. They should be spread on or arranged uniformly but leaving the outer 2 cm. of the pizza uncovered. (Note, by the way, that Pizza alla Marinara, at least in its traditional form, does not include seafood despite its name.)

for Pizza alle Cozze

1½ kilos mussels, opened in the usual way and the shells discarded
6 cloves garlic, finely chopped

oregano – enough to sprinkle over all (or parsley)
black pepper
12 tablespoonfuls olive oil

for Pizza alle Alici Fresche

900 grammes fresh anchovies
6 cloves garlic, chopped
oregano – enough to sprinkle over all

12 tablespoonfuls olive oil
black pepper and salt

for Pizza ai Cecinielli

750 grammes cecinielli (tiny larval anchovies and sardines)
6 cloves garlic, chopped

oregano – enough to sprinkle over all
12 tablespoonfuls olive oil
black pepper and salt

(3) A pizza should be baked, after the filling has been added as described above, in a very hot oven for from 5 to 10 minutes, not so long as to let it brown.

Riso con le Seppie

Cuttlefish risotto

In pasta seafood dishes the pasta is cooked separately and then dressed with a seafood sauce. In an Italian seafood risotto the seafood is cooked with the rice.

Good seafood risottos may be made with many different ingredients. Those with prawns are popular nowadays. But the traditional one is made with either cuttlefish or mussels. This is because they are comparatively cheap as well as being suited to the purpose.

One of the traditional Venetian dishes is called Riso co' i Peoci. This is the version with mussels. The mussels should be opened in a pan in which garlic has been coloured in hot olive oil with a little salt, and the rice cooked (with the mussels) in the resulting mussel broth.

The recipe which I will give in full is a Roman one, for the version with cuttlefish (Riso con le Seppie).

Take a cuttlefish (No. 568) of good size; skin and gut it. Remove and discard the 'bone' and the eyes. Take care not to break either of the two sacs inside, of which the lower contains the ink and the upper one a thick yellowish substance. Discard the former, but keep the other in order to add flavour to the sauce later. Wash what you have left of the cuttlefish, then cut it into strips and dry them.

Prepare a soffritto in the usual way with olive oil, a finely chopped onion, a clove of garlic and (once these have taken colour) a tablespoonful of tomato paste diluted with a little water. After all this has cooked for a few minutes add the strips of cuttlefish, the liquid from the second sac, and salt and pepper. Continue to cook, stirring every now and then. As the sauce thickens dilute it with a wineglassful of red wine. When the wine has evaporated completely put in about the same amount or a little more of boiling water and let that evaporate too, over a gentle flame. Then put in the rice and let it cook in the sauce for 20 minutes, adding a little more boiling water occasionally and stirring to keep the consistency right and to prevent the rice from sticking.

Pasta e Broccoli col Brodo d'Arzilla

A Roman soup involving ray (skate), pasta and broccoli   (serves six)
Professor Giorgio Bini, an eminent ichthyologist and a leading Italian gastronome, has contributed this recipe for a well-known Roman dish.

1½ kilos ray (skate)	½ kilo broccoli
3 or 4 cloves of garlic	salt and pepper
1 salted anchovy	300 grammes pasta (trenette or
2 sprigs parsley	fettuccine spezzate are
2 more cloves garlic	suitable or cannolicchi which
½ wineglassful olive oil	Romans call 'strozzapreti')
2 tablespoonfuls tomato paste	

Arzilla is the name used by Rome and many places near by for various rays. The best for this dish is the thornback ray (No. 31), but others will do provided that they are fresh. Ray is the chosen fish because its cartilaginous 'bones' partly dissolve after prolonged cooking and make the broth thicker and richer. The ray should be set in cold water with 3 or 4 whole cloves of garlic, brought to the boil and cooked for a long time (say, 2 hours) so that all its goodness is yielded to the broth (the ray itself does not survive to be eaten separately).

When the broth is almost ready prepare separately a soffritto. First take the salted anchovy, wash it free of salt and debone it. Pound it with the parsley to produce a pesto. Take a large pan (big enough to accommodate later the broth and the broccoli), heat the olive oil in it, add two cloves of garlic and gently brown them. Then add the pesto of anchovy and parsley, keeping the pan over a very low flame since the anchovy will turn bitter if heated too hard. Add the tomato paste, diluted in a little water.

The next step is to add the flowerets of the broccoli, salt and pepper. Once the broccoli is cooked pour in the fish broth, which will now be ready, straining it as you do so to keep back the debris of the ray. Bring back to the boil and add the pasta, which should be cooked only until it is 'al dente', i.e. still firm enough to offer some resistance to the biting tooth.

Pasta con le Sarde

A Sicilian macaroni and sardine pie   (serves six)

500 grammes fennel bulbs (if in
   Sicily use the mountain kind,
   called finocchielli)
50 grammes sultanas
500 grammes fresh sardines
   (about a dozen)
2 wineglassfuls olive oil
a few shallots
3 salted anchovies

pinch of saffron
100 grammes pine-nut kernels
salt and pepper
500 grammes maccheroncini
   (a kind of pasta which is a
   little thicker than vermicelli,
   and may also be found under
   the names bucatini or perciatelli
   grossi)

Clean the fennel bulbs, trimming off bits which are too tough. Boil them for 10 minutes in water. Take them out, drain them, and cut them into very small pieces. Save the cooking liquid. Soak the sultanas for 15 minutes in warm water. Drain them. Remove the heads and backbones from the sardines. Take one third of them and cut them up very small to go in the sauce. The remaining two thirds are to be floured and then fried in olive oil.

Heat some more olive oil and let the shallots take colour in this. Add the chopped up sardines and crush them in the pan with a spoon. Add the chopped fennel and let the whole cook for a little, adding if necessary a small amount of the fennel cooking liquid.

Wash and bone the salted anchovies. Heat some more olive oil, then add the anchovies – but at the side of the stove, not over the flame. Help the anchovies to 'melt' by using a fork.

Now add to the shallot/sardine/fennel mixture the melted anchovies, the saffron (mixed with a very little water), the sultanas, the pine-nut kernels and salt and pepper, and let it all go on cooking for a few minutes.

Meanwhile cook the pasta: bring the fennel cooking liquid to the boil, supplement it if necessary with water, and cook the pasta in this with a little salt. Drain. Combine with the sauce.

Finally, place a layer of the pasta in an oven dish, with fried sardines on top and more pasta on top of them and so on. Bake this dish in a hot oven for 15 minutes or so. This is the practice at Trapani. At Palermo you would be more likely to find that all the sardines had gone into the sauce, and that this last stage would therefore be omitted.

Spaghetti con le Seppie
Spaghetti with cuttlefish

Prepare a soffritto of olive oil, onion, a very little garlic, a small quantity of chopped parsley, salt and pepper. Put the cuttlefish, cut into pieces (indeed very small pieces), into this and when it is half cooked add a generous amount of tomato juice or tinned tomatoes. Leave it to finish cooking on a moderate flame, and use the delicious result as a sauce to put over the spaghetti, which you have already cooked and drained. 300 grammes of cuttlefish can suffice for a ½ kilo of spaghetti. If the ink sacs are not removed from the cuttlefish the spaghetti turns blackish and unattractive in appearance but also assumes a musky flavour which is pleasing to many.

(G. Cavanna, *Doni di Nettuno*)

Vermicelli alle Vongole con i Pelati
Four recipes in one for vermicelli with vongole or mussels

The basic recipe below covers a range of Neapolitan specialities, which involve dressing vermicelli, or a similar form of pasta, with a vongole sauce or a mussel sauce. If the sauce is made with tomatoes it is 'con i pelati'; if not the epithet is 'in bianco'.

For Vermicelli alle Vongole con i Pelati you will need:

1 wineglassful olive oil	600 grammes tinned tomatoes
2 cloves garlic	(pelati)
1¼ kilos vongole (Nos. 557–8),	lots of parsley, chopped finely
well washed and purged in	black pepper and salt
clean sea water	600 grammes vermicelli

Heat the olive oil in a large pan and let the cloves of garlic take colour in it. Add the vongole and a sprinkling of black pepper and the tomatoes (drained beforehand). As the vongole open, remove them from the pan, take them from their shells and keep them aside. Continue to cook the sauce until it is almost sufficiently reduced. At this point put the vongole back in, with the chopped parsley, and let it all cook for another 2 or 3 minutes only.

Meanwhile cook the vermicelli in lightly salted water. Strain it and dress it with part of the sauce. Serve the rest of the sauce with the vongole in a sauceboat.

To make Vermicelli alle Cozze in Bianco you would proceed in the same way. You might, however, prefer to use linguine (a pasta which comes in slightly thicker strips than vermicelli). You would halve the amount of olive oil and leave out the tomatoes. And you would use 1½ kilos (not 1¼) of mussels (No. 545) which had been well washed and bearded. The sauce would probably need to cook for rather longer, since quite a lot of mussel juice would be in it and would need reduction.

You should be able to work out for yourself how to make the remaining two versions – Vermicelli alle Vongole in Bianco and Vermicelli alle Cozze con i Pelati.

Acciughe Tartufate
Piedmont truffled anchovies

The white truffles of Piedmont are a lure for many travellers, but of course it is not necessary to make a journey to the truffle district, around the city of Alba, in order to taste them. I, however, went to Alba in order to buy a truffle-cutter, having long desired to possess such a refined and specialized implement, and stayed to eat truffled dishes at the bustling Hotel Savona.

Having filled this gap in our batterie de cuisine, I was pleased to learn of a delicacy which marries the white truffle to the anchovy. Salted anchovies (not tinned ones) are to be washed thoroughly, patted dry and filleted. The fillets are then arranged in layers in an earthenware dish, alternating with layers of very thinly sliced white truffle. Enough olive oil to cover is added. The dish is covered and left in a cool place; and the contents may be eaten two or three days later.

Alici Ammollicate
Fresh anchovies au gratin (serves six)

Buy a kilo of fresh anchovies (No. 61). Wash and gut them, removing heads, tails and backbones. Arrange them in a shallow oiled oven dish and pour over them most of a wineglassful of olive oil. Sprinkle them with 2 or 3 finely chopped cloves of garlic, and salt and pepper. Mix 2 chopped sprigs of parsley with about 4 tablespoonfuls of breadcrumbs, moisten the result with the remainder of the wineglassful of olive oil and distribute the mixture evenly over the fish. Bake in a hot oven for 15 minutes.

For a different flavour try Alici Areganate, another Neapolitan favourite. The fish are sprinkled with chopped garlic and parsley, salt and pepper, and oregano, but no breadcrumbs.

Both recipes can also be used for fresh sardines, or outside the Mediterranean for small herring.

Alici Ripiene
A Sardinian recipe for stuffed anchovies (serves four)

800 grammes large fresh anchovies (No. 61)	5 salted anchovies
130 grammes fresh cheese (dolce Tirso or dolce Sardo)	2 eggs flour, breadcrumbs, olive oil

Clean the fresh anchovies, opening them along their bellies and removing the backbones. Wash, debone and fillet the salted anchovies. Inside each fresh anchovy lay one fillet of salted anchovy and a thin strip of cheese. Close the fresh anchovies over again so that they resume their natural shape. Flour them, dip them in beaten egg and then in breadcrumbs. Heat plenty of olive oil in the frying-pan and once this is really hot deep-fry the stuffed anchovies in it, handling them delicately to avoid breaking them. When they are cooked and golden-brown in colour take them out and serve them at once.

The same recipe can be used for fresh sardines.

Anchovies as an Antipasto

The anchovy is a star performer in the antipasto league. Here are two simple and delicious ways of using it. I verified their excellence in the Trattoria Oswaldo at Boccadasse, a tiny fishing village formerly close to but now engulfed by Genoa.

First, Acciughe al Limone, or anchovies marinaded in lemon juice. All you have to do is to clean and behead fresh anchovies, split them open as far as the tail and leave them thus opened out in a bath of lemon juice for 24 hours. When I exclaimed at the simplicity of this recipe the congregation of Oswaldo family and waiters who were observing me as I tasted showed pleasure at my shared recognition of the principle that what tastes best is not necessarily what requires most effort.

Second, Peperoni con Bagna Cauda. Roast some large mild red peppers just long enough to sear the skin. Then cut from them squares or circles about an inch across. Keep these ready. Next chop 1 or 2 cloves of garlic very finely, and combine them in a pan with some olive oil and fillets of salted anchovy (previously washed). Keep this mixture over a low flame while you mash it in the pan with a fork. When all is well mashed spread the mixture on to the pieces of red pepper, and let these dramatic-looking titbits wait for an hour or two in a flat dish of which the bottom is covered with olive oil, before being eaten.

Anguilla or Capitone Arrosto

Spit-roasted eel

The flesh of eel is rich, and spit-roasting is a good way of cooking it. A typical Italian method is to cut sections 8–10 cm. thick from a large eel and impale them on the spit, with sage, bay leaves or sprigs of rosemary in between. The skin is left on, since it forms a protective crust which prevents the flesh itself from hardening during the cooking – and it can easily be peeled off afterwards. While the eel is being spit-roasted it is basted with its own fat drippings and plenty of salt. Towards the end the fire should be very hot. The dish is often accompanied in northern Italy by mostarda di Cremona, the famous fruit mustard from Cremona, which can be bought in Italian food speciality shops abroad. It is made of whole fruits – tiny pears and oranges, apricots and cherries – and slices of melon, preserved in sugar syrup and flavoured with mustard oil and garlic. I recommend the combination.

A dish which is well-known in southern Italy (and traditional there on Christmas Eve as is a similar dish in the South of France) is Capitone Arrosto. A capitone is a specimen of the common eel (No. 66) which has grown uncommonly large and fat.

For six people buy rather more than 1 kilo of cleaned capitone, and cut it into pieces about 10 cm. long. Wash them, dry them and rub them with garlic. Then thread them on to skewers, alternating them with bay leaves, souse them with a mixture of 2 tablespoonfuls of olive oil and 1 of vinegar, with pepper added, and let them marinade for an hour.

Spit-roast the fish on a grill of medium heat, turning them and basting them frequently with a sprig of parsley dipped into the marinade. They will take about half an hour to cook.

Bisato in Tecia and Bisato sull'Ara

Two eel dishes from Venice   (each serves eight)

Bisato is the Venetian name for eel, and Bisato in Tecia is a favourite Venetian recipe for it. You will need:

1½ kilos eel (No. 66) of moderate size	2 or 3 sage leaves
¾ wineglassful olive oil	1 wineglassful Marsala
100 grammes butter	½ kilo tomatoes, peeled, seeded and chopped
2 cloves garlic, chopped	salt and pepper
several sprigs parsley, chopped	

Skin and clean the eels. Remove the heads if you wish. Cut the bodies into pieces 5 cm. long. (You may marinade these for a few hours in wine vinegar with bay leaves, but this is not essential.)

When you are ready to cook them, the pieces of eel may be coated with breadcrumbs. Put them into a pan with the olive oil and butter over a strong heat, and let them turn golden-brown. Add the garlic and parsley. A minute or two later add the sage leaves and then the Marsala; and after another short pause the tomatoes (or a corresponding amount of tomato purée) and the seasoning. Continue cooking for 20 minutes, during which the red tomato colour will change to brown and the sauce will thicken. Serve with polenta (see p. 351).

Polenta also accompanies the second dish, Bisato sull'Ara, which is an interesting and ancient by-product of the glass industry in the island of Murano near Venice. The ara is the enclosed space above the old-fashioned wood-fired kiln, where red-hot glass would be put to cool gradually. The Muranese discovered that the space would serve equally well for cooking eels, and have for long practised the following method.

Skin and gut 1½ kilos eel of moderate size. Make incisions round them at intervals of 5 cm. or so, as though you were going to cut them into sections but without actually doing so. Lay the eels, thus prepared, on a bed of fresh bay leaves in a big dish. Sprinkle them with salt and pepper and a little water. Cover them with a second layer of bay leaves. Put the dish in a slow oven and cook until the eel is tender.

Strictly speaking, this recipe might have begun: 'You will need . . . one disused but operational wood-fired glass-making kiln . . .' It seems, however, that the 'ara' was used simply as a convenience and for economy, not because it imparted to the eel any subtle taste of molten glass or the like. So all but the most severe purists may feel free to make this dish in an ordinary oven.

Ce'e alla Salvia (Cieche alla Pisana)
Baby eels cooked in the Pisan fashion

The tiny transparent eels (see p. 48) which fetch up at the mouths of European rivers in the winter are nowhere awaited more eagerly than in the vicinity of Pisa, where they are regarded as a great delicacy. Cavanna gives a fascinating account of how these ce'e or cieche, as they are known in Tuscany, were fished at the beginning of the century. The cieche fishermen were mostly porters or other workmen, who stationed themselves at night, when the flood tide was due, at chosen spots along the river banks close to the sea. They were clad in thick overcoats of red wool cloth, with fur caps on their heads, and armed with large sieves and lanterns. Dipping the sieves like spoons into the water, against the incoming tide, they would hope to land masses of the tiny eels. 'At the mouth of the Callambrone,' wrote Cavanna 'on certain not too cold February nights I have seen quintals of cieche fished in a few hours, while on other nights which were colder and less lucky for the fishermen not a baby eel was found, and the fishermen abandoning their enterprise, sad and chilled and empty-handed, took the road back to the city. At the hour of their return an acute observer could foretell the result of the fishing from the speed or slowness of the twinkling lanterns crossing the countryside.'

The instructions below for cooking ce'e may also be used for cooking the tiny transparent goby (No. 212) which is rossetto in Italian.

The recipe is as follows. Heat ½ wineglassful of olive oil in a large pan (choosing one with a cover). Let a couple of cloves of garlic take colour in this, and add a few leaves of sage. Be careful that the garlic does not cook too much. Meanwhile wash the ce'e in running water, lay them out on a towel and pat them dry – gently for they are still alive and must remain so until they enter the pan. Next, put them into the hot oil, which should be very hot, and quickly cover the pan to prevent them from jumping out. Let them cook for 5 minutes, during which seasoning should be added. Then put in a teaspoonful of tomato concentrate diluted in ½ wineglassful water. Cook for another 15 minutes or so until the water has evaporated.

This completes the essential cooking. You may then sprinkle grated parmesan over the ce'e, leave them for another 3 minutes, and serve. This is the prescription of Signora Lina d'Ascanio, to which I revert below. But there is an alternative, recommended by Signora Bianca Berlendi. This is to sprinkle breadcrumbs over the ce'e and put the dish in a hot oven until a little crust forms on top. Either way, the product is eaten like spaghetti, with a fork.

I should explain that these ladies live in Pisa and are experienced in dealing with ce'e. Signora d'Ascanio impressed on me, however, that the price of ce'e has for some time been rather high, and that the practical Pisan housewife therefore finds ways of making a small quantity go a long way, for example by incorporating into an omelette ce'e which have been prepared as described above and finished off with the parmesan treatment.

Capone Apparecchiato
A Sicilian way of preparing dolphin fish   (serves four to six)

Signor A. La Porta of Palermo contributes this recipe, for which the ingredients are:

1 kilo dolphin fish (No. 166)	1 small (100 gramme) tin of
1 bunch celery	tomato purée
50 grammes capers	salt and pepper
100 grammes green olives	1 tablespoonful sugar
1 onion	3 tablespoonfuls wine vinegar
1¾ wineglassfuls olive oil	

Clean the fish, wash it under running water and cut it into slices. Clean the celery and cook it in gently boiling water. Wash the capers. Wash and stone the olives.

Chop the onion finely and let it take colour in 4 tablespoonfuls of olive oil, heated in a suitable pan. Add the tomato purée, previously diluted with some of the water in which you have cooked the celery. Chop the celery and add it too, with seasoning. Cook all this over a medium flame until you have a fairly thick sauce. Meanwhile flour the slices of fish and fry them in a wineglassful of olive oil, which should be hot, until they are lightly browned all over.

Now back to the sauce, to which the olives, capers, sugar, wine vinegar and 2 tablespoonfuls of olive oil are to be added. Let it cook for a few more minutes after these additions. Then put in the fried slices of fish and cook for 5 minutes more. Let it become cold before serving.

Cernia Ripiena

Stuffed mérou   (serves four)

a mérou (or other suitable fish, e.g. a denté) of about 1 kilo

the stuffing:

bread soaked in milk
6 small prawns, shelled and pounded
1 small onion, finely chopped
dried mushrooms, previously soaked, chopped
finely chopped parsley
a little butter

2 tablespoonfuls of grated Parmesan
nutmeg
salt and pepper
2 eggs, beaten

for the cooking:

some more butter
half a dozen tiny onions
more dried mushrooms, previously soaked
½ glass white wine

Open the mérou, clean it and remove the backbone, without breaking the fillets. Make the stuffing with the ingredients listed, and put it in the fish, which should then be sewn up.

For the cooking, melt butter in the bottom of a casserole and fry in it the tiny onions and dried mushrooms until the former turn golden. Add the mérou and the half glass of white wine. Cook in a fairly hot oven until done – allowing not less than an hour.

Dentice Farcito

Stuffed denté

This recipe (like the following one) is adapted from Maria Nencioli's charming book *Cacciucco*. It requires a fine denté (No. 125) of about

1 kilo. Clean it, remove the backbone and marinade for half an hour in a mixture of olive oil, lemon juice and herbs.

Meanwhile prepare a stuffing with the following ingredients: soft breadcrumbs soaked in white wine; 100 grammes of cooked rice; half a sweet pear passed through a sieve; a mixture of onion, celery and parsley chopped very finely and lightly fried; a chopped hard-boiled egg and a raw egg beaten stiff; salt and pepper and spices.

After having worked this all together and made it of the right consistency stuff the fish with it and fasten it together again with toothpicks. Lay the fish in an oiled baking-dish, pour melted butter over it, sprinkle it with breadcrumbs and put it for 18 to 24 minutes in a very hot oven, basting it occasionally with some good fish broth.

Lampreda al Vino Bianco, *which can be turned into* Pasticcio di Lampreda

First select a fireproof dish with a tight-fitting lid, in which you fry lightly, in plenty of butter, some finely chopped shallots and a little thyme.

Meanwhile skin the lamprey and cut it into chunks, which should be lightly floured. Add the pieces of lamprey to the shallot mixture, together with some good bouillon and salt and pepper, then put the lid on and cook for about a quarter of an hour. Towards the end of this period add a glass of vernaccia (Sardinian wine). Bring the dish piping hot to table. End of basic recipe.

If you wish to make a Pasticcio di Lampreda do not bring the dish piping hot to table. Instead postpone the meal, let the dish cool, take out the pieces of lamprey and pass them through a sieve. Turn the result into a paste by adding butter. See to it that the paste is fairly stiff, and form it into the shape, e.g. oval, of the mould in which you are to present the pasticcio.

Meanwhile, in fact some time ago if you do it properly,* you have got ready some aspic and set it to cool. When it begins to set pour enough into the mould to cover the bottom, then put the lamprey paste, all ready and shaped, on top, and finally add another layer of aspic on top of that. Cool in the refrigerator.

*To make the approved aspic you need a collection of miscellaneous fish and crustaceans and a calf's foot. Simmer these together for three or four hours in water to cover, with onions stuck with cloves, bay leaves, lemon peel, salt and black peppercorns. Skim, strain, add some leaves of isinglass (a very pure form of gelatin) and cool.

Muggine al Sugo di Melagrana

Grey mullet with pomegranate juice

This is a recipe from the vicinity of Comacchio, where the grey mullet are especially good in the autumn and winter.

Clean the fish, but do not gut them, since like the red mullet (to which the grey mullet is not related) this fish gains added flavour by being cooked with gut in place. Marinade the fish for a while, then grill them on both sides, taking care to salt and pepper them and to baste them sufficiently with olive oil. When they are done put them between two soup plates at the side of the fire so that they will soak up instead of losing the juices which will continue to be exuded. Finally, and this is the distinctive feature of the dish, sprinkle them generously with pomegranate juice instead of the usual lemon juice.

Naselli alla Marchigiana

A recipe from the Marche for small hake (serves four)

Buy 4 small hake (No. 81) of about 200–250 grammes each. Gut, scale and wash them. Lay them side by side in a bowl which is just big enough for the purpose; sprinkle them with salt and pepper, 2 finely chopped shallots and a finely chopped clove of garlic; pour a wine-glassful of olive oil over them and leave them to marinade for an hour. Then remove them from the marinade, coat them with breadcrumbs, sprinkle them with olive oil, and grill them on both sides over a strong heat.

While the fish are being grilled, melt 50 grammes of butter in a pan and add a salted anchovy which you have previously washed free of salt, deboned and chopped up. Add also a good pinch of potato flour, a tablespoonful of red-wine vinegar and a little salt and pepper. Let all this cook over a low flame, mashing the pieces of anchovy with a fork until they 'melt'. Pour this sauce over the grilled fish when you serve them.

These instructions closely match those given in *Le Ricette Regionali Italiane*, an encyclopaedic volume on Italian regional cooking edited by Anna Gosetti della Salda.

Orata alla Pugliese
Daurade cooked in the Apulian style (serves six)

Buy a fine daurade (No. 128) of 1½ kilos. Clean, wash and pat dry.
You will also need:

1 wineglassful olive oil	100 grammes grated pecorino
lots of chopped parsley	cheese
6 to 8 potatoes, peeled and	salt and pepper
sliced thinly	

Pour most of the olive oil into an oven dish which will accommodate
the fish. Add half the chopped parsley, half the potato and half the
grated cheese. Then the fish. Then the other half of the parsley, potato
and cheese. Finally the small remaining amount of olive oil. Season.
Cook in a hot oven for 25 minutes or so.

Trancie di Pagro col Pesto
Sea bream with pesto (serves four)

Pesto is the pride of Genoa, but the combination suggested here is not
specifically Genoese. Provided that you like pesto you will find the
recipe an excellent one for general use.

To make the pesto, pound 2 cloves of garlic in a mortar with a handful each of fresh basil leaves and pine-nut kernels and a pinch of salt.
Add gradually, while you pound, 100 grammes of grated Parmesan
cheese (or better still if you can get it Sardo cheese from Sardinia) and
then, gradually, 2 tablespoonfuls of olive oil, obtaining eventually the
consistency of a very thick cream.

Next, start grilling 4 steaks of bream (No. 129). Peel, pip and chop
2 tomatoes, and set them to cook gently with 4 chopped anchovy
fillets and salt and pepper in olive oil in a large pan. Turn over the
fish. After the tomato and anchovy mixture has cooked for 5 minutes
stir the pesto into it and make sure that it is all thoroughly hot. Remove
the fish from the grill (the steaks will have had 5 minutes on each side,
which should be ample), pour the sauce over them and start eating.

Filetti di Pesce Gallo al Marsala
Fillets of John Dory cooked with Marsala (serves two)

The John Dory, or pesce San Pietro, is known in Sicily as the pesce
gallo (an echo of the Catalan gall and French poule de mer). My

colleague George Evans, who has served both in Venice and Palermo, finds that the pesce gallo is not as popular as one would expect in Sicily, and therefore fairly cheap. On the other hand, he says, it is difficult to find a fishmonger who will fillet it properly in the Venetian manner of slicing the fillet nearly through its thickness and then opening it up like a butterfly. The fillet therefore remains rather thick and is best cooked in the manner of Scallopine alla Marsala, a wine much used in Sicilian cookery. The instructions which follow are also suitable for fillets of sole or other good flatfish.

Make some fish stock from the bones and head of a John Dory of 1 kilo or more. Wash and dry the fillets and coat them lightly with flour. Fry them gently in butter until they take colour. Add 2 wineglassfuls each of Marsala and fish stock. Cook gently until the liquid is reduced by half. Serve the fillets in their sauce.

Impanata di Pesce Spada
Sicilian swordfish pie (serves eight)

½ kilo swordfish (No. 199)
olive oil
2 medium onions
2 tablespoonfuls tomato paste
2 celery stalks
100 grammes green olives
2 tablespoonfuls capers
4 or 5 courgettes (zucchini)
1 egg and a little flour

for the pastry:
400 grammes flour
200 grammes butter
175 grammes castor sugar
4–5 egg yolks
grated peel of 1 lemon
pinch of salt

Mix beforehand a short pastry dough (pasta frolla) with the ingredients shown above. If it remains too crumbly add a very little water. Make it into a ball, wrap it in greaseproof paper and leave it in the refrigerator for an hour.

Finely chop the onions and brown them in olive oil. Add the tomato paste (diluted with water), celery (finely chopped), olives (stoned and chopped) and capers. Cut the swordfish into tiny pieces and add it too, with seasoning. Cook gently, until well reduced.

Cut the courgettes into strips of about 5 cm., coat them with beaten egg and flour, fry them in hot oil and drain them on absorbent paper.

Butter and flour a pie dish 7½″ or 8″ across and 2½″ deep, preferably of the kind which can be unclasped and taken apart. Divide the pastry into three. Gently roll the first piece into a disc slightly larger than the dish and put it therein, to cover the bottom and come partly up the side.

Lay half the swordfish mixture and half the courgettes in this bed. Repeat. Top off with a third layer of pastry, making sure that it reaches the side of the dish all round. Brush it with egg yolk. Cook it in a moderate oven for about 50 (perhaps 55) minutes. Undo the pie dish and serve. If you foresaw disaster for the centre layer of pastry your prophecies will now be confounded. The combination of tastes in the pie is unusual – and the recipe may be adapted for use with other suitable fish, e.g. halibut.

Coda di Rospo
Tail of angler-fish

The angler-fish is fairly common in the Adriatic and regarded as a delicacy by the Venetians – so much so that supplies are imported from distant waters. Even Atlantic specimens of this huge-headed and easily caught creature are likely to finish up on slabs near the Rialto. What you eat is the 'tail', which provides very firm white flesh, not unlike crab or lobster meat. My own inquiries in Venice led to the conclusion that you cannot do much better than split the tail lengthwise, open it out and grill it well on both sides (20 minutes). But it is also very good fried in fillets; or simmered for half an hour (i.e. longer than other fish would need). In the last instance, serve it with boiled potatoes, big sprigs of parsley, and mayonnaise or other dressing.

Scapece alla Vastese
Skate fried and marinaded   (serves six)

For this recipe, which comes from the port of Vasto halfway down the east coast of Italy, you will need:

just over 1 kilo of pieces of skate	**a generous pinch saffron**
flour, and olive oil for deep-frying	**8 wineglassfuls or 2 English pints**
salt	**white-wine vinegar**

Directions are given thus by Ada Boni in *Italian Regional Cooking*:

'Lightly coat the fish steaks with flour and deep-fry in hot oil until golden brown. Take from the pan with a perforated spoon, drain on absorbent paper and sprinkle with salt.

'Dissolve the saffron in a little of the vinegar and stir it into the rest of the vinegar. Pour into a non-metallic pan, bring just to boiling point, then immediately remove the pan from the heat.

'Cover the bottom of a shallow earthenware or porcelain dish with a layer of fish steaks and sprinkle with some of the hot vinegar. Cover the dish and leave to marinade in a cool place for 24 hours. Serve the fish thoroughly drained of vinegar.'

Sarde a Beccaficcu

A Sicilian way of stuffing and baking sardines   (serves six)

The experience and skill of several Sicilian ladies, notably Signora Maria Bianca Cutolo, are reflected in the following recipe, which is for a well-known Sicilian speciality. The beccaficco (beccaficcu in Sicily) is a tiny bird, and the recipe takes its name from the circumstance that the sardines are arranged in the dish so as to look rather like these birds. The same treatment can be applied to fresh anchovies.

You will need just over 1 kilo of fresh sardines (about two dozen, or 4 for each person) and the following ingredients for the stuffing:

100 grammes soft breadcrumbs	60 grammes capers
1 tablespoonful olive oil	60 grammes black olives
2 cloves garlic	(preferably of Gaeta)
chopped parsley	40 grammes sultanas
2 or 3 shallots chopped	40 grammes pine-nut
salt and pepper	kernels
1 teaspoonful lemon juice	

all finely chopped

But note that the choice and proportions of the ingredients for the stuffing are not invariable. Some would use grated pecorino cheese; salted anchovy; a pinch of nutmeg, etc.

The procedure is as follows. First mix well together the ingredients of the stuffing. Next clean and behead the sardines, splitting them open underneath almost to the tail and removing their backbones. Lay them out flat on their backs and spread each thinly with the stuffing. Then roll them up, working towards the tail, and place them in rows in an oven dish, well packed against each other and with the tails sticking up. Bay leaves can be inserted between them here and there if you wish. Pour a little olive oil over all and bake the dish in a hot oven for 10 minutes or so.

Sarde alla Napoletana

Sardines in the Neapolitan fashion   (serves six)

Buy a kilo of fresh sardines (No. 56). Slit them open underneath from the head almost to the tail. Remove heads, gut and backbones, but leave the tails undisturbed so that you can open the fish out without their coming completely apart. Rinse them and pat them dry.

Choose an oven dish large enough to take all the sardines, opened out, in at most two layers. Put in enough olive oil to cover the bottom of the dish, then the sardines. Add plenty of salt and pepper and chopped parsley, a finely chopped clove of garlic, a good pinch of oregano, and dotted here and there chunks of peeled and seeded tomato. Finish off with a thread of olive oil over all, and cook in a hot oven for 15 to 20 minutes.

Filetti di Sfoglia, Veri e Falsi
A way of cooking fillets of sole, with an explanation of how to fake fillets of sole

Cavanna (in *Doni di Nettuno*) gives the following curious instructions for cooking fillets of sole, and explains also how to prepare bogus ones (by a technique which even the most unscrupulous are unlikely to follow nowadays when the price of oysters is so high and packets of frozen fillets of sole are available in every town). I have used the recipe, and found it good; but have not even attempted the deception.

'From soles which weigh about 200 grammes, skinned, cut the four fillets, leave them immersed in beaten egg for two or three hours with salt and pepper, then coat them in breadcrumbs and fry them in olive oil. After that, put them in another pan with olive oil and butter, sprinkle them with more salt and coarsely ground pepper, and when they have become thoroughly hot pour dry white wine over them. The cooking completed, sprinkle over them, before serving, some chopped parsley and surround them with lemon slices.

'There exist men with the ability to bring to table fillets of sole which have never been the flesh of any sole! They take fillets of tench (the freshwater fish), flatten them a little and smear them with a paste made of oysters (very little is enough), salt, pepper and lemon juice, then fry them golden and proceed as above. For discovery of this trick a keen connoisseur is required, and one in whom suspicion is already at work.'

Sogliole alla Parmigiana
Sole with Parmesan cheese

'Have medium-sized soles, one for each person, skinned on both sides. Lay them in a buttered flame-proof dish, well seasoned with salt and pepper, and with more butter on the top. Let them brown gently, and turn them over so that they brown on the other side. Spread a thin layer of grated Parmesan over the top of each and add 1 tablespoonful of chicken or fish broth for each sole. Cover the pan, and simmer slowly for 5 minutes, until the soles are cooked through and the cheese melted. Serve in the dish in which they have cooked, with halves of lemon and a green salad. The cooking can be done in the oven instead of on top of the stove.'

(Elizabeth David, *Italian Food*)

Spigola al Forno
Sea bass cooked in the oven   (serves six)

A dish which I ate cooked to perfection in a private kitchen in Naples. Success depends on having in the first place a really fresh fish. The ingredients are:

a sea bass (No. 113) of 1½ kilos
1 clove garlic, chopped
lots of fresh herbs (rosemary, thyme, marjoram are all suitable), roughly chopped

lots of parsley, roughly chopped
1 tablespoonful dry breadcrumbs
1 wineglassful olive oil
1 teaspoonful lemon juice

Scale, wash and gut the fish. Put the chopped garlic and herbs and parsley into the gut cavity and the gills. Place the fish in a shallow oiled oven dish, salt it lightly, sprinkle it with the breadcrumbs and pour over it the olive oil into which you have previously beaten the lemon juice. Cook for 25 to 30 minutes in a preheated hot oven.

Spigola in Agrodolce
Sea bass sweet and sour

This recipe can be used for other fish too, although especially suited to the sea bass (No. 113). Buy one whole fish, allowing 250 grammes un-cleaned weight per person. Prepare the fish, and cut it up into slices.

Set some chopped onion to cook gently in olive oil, with a few strips of bacon. Add the pieces of fish, season them and brown them on both sides, and leave them cooking.

Meanwhile prepare a sauce as follows. Dissolve in a pan a tablespoon-ful of sugar. Add a tablespoonful of flour and a knob of butter, stirring to prevent the mixture from browning. Squeeze into it, little by little, the juice of a lemon, and let the sauce thicken.

Next, pour the sauce over the fish, and let it finish cooking thus.

Ragù di Tonno

Tunny fish stew   (serves six)

Sicilians prefer to use a piece of tunny cut from the tail for this dish. They call the cut tarantello. The ingredients are:

1 kilo tunny (No. 192), cut from the tail in one piece	½ kilo ripe tomatoes, peeled, chopped and sieved
fresh mint	2 wineglassfuls olive oil
2 cloves garlic	1 wineglassful dry white wine
salt and pepper	2 onions, sliced
flour	

Chop one of the garlic cloves finely. Make some cuts in the sides of the pieces of fish. Into each cut put a leaf of mint and some chopped garlic, also salt and pepper. Sprinkle salt and pepper over the fish generally as well, and flour too.

Heat the oil in a pan, and brown the fish on all sides. Sprinkle the wine over the fish and continue cooking until the wine has evaporated. Then remove the fish to a warm casserole. Add the second garlic clove (crushed) and the onions to the pan and let them turn golden. Add this mixture to the fish in the casserole, put it over a medium flame and cook it for another 5 minutes, turning the fish once. Then add the tomatoes, followed a few minutes later by 2 wineglassfuls of hot water. Simmer the whole for 20 minutes, by which time the tuna should be cooked through and tender. Remove it and cut into thick slices. Pour some of the sauce over the slices and serve the rest with the noodles or rice which accompany the dish.

Tonno alla Genovese

Fresh tunny in the Genoese style   (serves four)

4 slices of fresh tunny (No. 192), weighing about 600–700 grammes in all	2 cloves garlic
	1 wineglassful olive oil
	1 tablespoonful flour
20 grammes dried mushrooms, soaked in a little warm water beforehand	2 wineglassfuls white wine
	salt, pepper and spices
	juice of a lemon
3 salted anchovies	50 grammes butter
parsley	

Drain the mushrooms. Debone the anchovies, wash them well and pat them dry. Then pound the mushrooms and anchovies with a couple of sprigs of parsley and the 2 cloves of garlic. Add the result to the olive oil in a wide pan, and add the flour too. Fry the mixture lightly, stirring it. Then add the wine and let it come to the boil. At this point put in the slices of tunny, in a single layer. Season them, and add a pinch of the spices. Cover and continue to cook for 5 minutes. Then turn the slices over and transfer the dish to a preheated oven to continue cooking. It will need about 20 to 25 minutes.

When the tunny slices are cooked through and tender remove them to the serving platter and keep them hot. To the cooking juices add the lemon juice and butter. Pour the resulting sauce over the fish and serve at once.

Triglie alla Ligure
Red mullet poached in a wine and tomato sauce (serves six)

This is a recipe which can well be used if you have red mullet which are for any reason not suitable for the more usual methods of cooking them, such as grilling. Since they are delicate fish and easily damaged it is convenient to have one good method of preparation which does not require a perfect set of fish.

Carefully clean and scale, wash and pat dry half a dozen red mullet of about 200 grammes each. Heat a wineglassful of olive oil in a large pan and cook lightly in this 1 clove of garlic and 3 sprigs of parsley, all chopped fine. Add a wineglassful of white wine. Meanwhile peel 4 tomatoes and chop them roughly, and chop up finely a couple of tinned or salted anchovy fillets. When the wine mixture is slightly reduced add the tomatoes and chopped anchovy. Continue cooking for 15 to 20 minutes, gently. Then add the fish, season and cook the whole for another quarter of an hour. Just before you extinguish the flame add a dozen pitted black olives, cut into halves or quarters, and a tablespoonful of capers. And a moment after you have extinguished the flame add a squeeze of lemon juice.

Triglie alla Livornese
Red mullet in the style of Leghorn

Select red mullet of about 200 grammes each, or nearly as much. Whether or not you gut them, clean, rinse and dry them.

Set some olive oil to heat in a broad pan, suitable for taking all the fish side by side. When the oil is hot, flour the fish and put them in. Turn them carefully when they have barely begun to cook and sprinkle over them:

some *very* finely chopped parsley	and (say some)
tiny pieces of bay leaf	a *minute* amount of onion
practically *no* pepper	or (say others)
the merest *sliver* of garlic	a *discreet* quantity of fennel

The flavour of the red mullet is very delicate. Perhaps I exaggerate the delicacy with which you must therefore administer additional flavours, but this dish is a subtle affair.

Meanwhile you have prepared with fresh tomatoes a tomato sauce of moderate thickness. This you pour over the fish (in moderation) when they are just about cooked; and the dish is ready to serve a few minutes later.

Triglie Fredde con Salsa di Menta

Cold red mullet with a mint sauce

Good summer fare. The red mullet, cleaned and scaled, are to be gently fried and then put aside to cool while the sauce is prepared. The sauce, incidentally, comes from the family recipe book, built up over five generations in Palermo, of the Baronessa Pucci in Moore.

Soak 300 grammes of soft breadcrumbs in a mixture of water and wine vinegar, then squeeze it well to expel the excess moisture. Finely chop a bunch of parsley and a bunch of fresh mint, discarding the stalks. Pound the result in a mortar with the bread, 2 teaspoonfuls of capers, a raw egg, 2 teaspoonfuls of sugar, a generous squeeze of anchovy paste and a little salt. Keep on pounding for some time, then pass the result through a sieve and make it into a sauce by adding olive oil gradually as you would for a mayonnaise. Serve the red mullet and the sauce separately.

Schile Agio e Ogio

A traditional Venetian way of cooking shrimps.

Put the fresh shrimps in a pot with water to cover and salt. Heat until there is a good froth. Then remove and drain the shrimps and place them in a casserole with plenty of olive oil, garlic and chopped parsley. Cook over a fierce flame for a few moments.

Moleche alla Muranese (Granchi Molli alla Muranese)

Soft-shell crabs cooked in the Murano way   (serves six)

First you must buy live crabs which have recently shed their hard shells. You will need 1½ kilos, probably 2½ or 3 dozen of the creatures. Remove their claws and legs (but see p. 187 for advice on killing them first).

In a pan beat up 2 whole eggs. Add the crab bodies. You will find that they absorb the beaten-egg mixture within a few minutes. When this has happened coat them at once with flour and fry them in very hot oil.

Cape Sante in Tecia (Cappe Sante in Tegame)

A Venetian recipe for scallops   (serves four)

16 large scallops (No. 541)	1 clove garlic
fine breadcrumbs	3 sprigs parsley
2 tablespoonfuls olive oil	salt
30 grammes butter	juice of half a big lemon
	3 tablespoonfuls white wine

Open the scallops. Remove, wash and pat dry the edible white muscles, and coat them with breadcrumbs. Reserve the 8 best half-shells and clean them well.

Heat the olive oil and butter in a pan with the clove of garlic and a chopped sprig of parsley. After a few minutes remove the garlic and put in the scallops with a very little salt. They will take about 12 to 15 minutes to cook. Make sure that they colour evenly all over. Sprinkle the lemon juice and the wine over them towards the end of the cooking. Serve them in pairs in the half-shells which you have kept for the purpose, pouring the cooking juices over them and using the remaining parsley for decoration.

Cozze e Patate al Forno

Mussels baked with potatoes (serves six)

The prescription for this dish comes from Signora Teresa Turco of Rutigliano, Bari, who has been making it regularly since the first year of the century, when Queen Victoria was still on the British throne and King Victor Emmanuel III had just succeeded his father, slain by a New Jersey anarchist, in Italy.

1 kilo potatoes	parsley, chopped
1½–2 kilos mussels (No. 545)	olive oil
¼ kilo tomatoes	breadcrumbs
salt and pepper	2 cloves garlic, finely chopped

This dish is to be made in a wide baking tin, about 2" deep. Oil this with olive oil, then cover the bottom with the potatoes (peeled, sliced and seasoned). Strew chopped parsley generously among the potatoes and pour a couple of tablespoonfuls of olive oil over them. The tomatoes are to be of the pear-shaped cooking variety. Better to use tinned ones of the right kind than fresh ones of the wrong kind. Cut half of them in slices, and lay these on top of the potatoes.

The mussels are to be carefully washed and bearded, and opened in the usual way by being steamed in a large pan. Leave each mussel in the half-shell, discarding the other half. Do your best to retain some of the mussel juices with the mussels. Lay them out, side by side, on the bed of potato and tomato.

Next sprinkle breadcrumbs over all. Moisten these with a thread of olive oil. Add salt and pepper and more chopped parsley, the finely chopped garlic and the remaining tomatoes (peeled, seeded and cut into small chunks or pezzetti). Bake in a slow oven for 1 hour.

Calamari Ripieni

Stuffed squid

This is an excellent dish, popular in many parts of Italy and found with interesting regional variations. The version which I offer is from Naples, where Assunta Viscardi, for many years the cook at H.M. Consulate-General, gives the following instructions.

Clean and prepare the squid as usual; chop up the head and tentacles. Heat a little olive oil in a frying pan and add successively a chopped clove of garlic, the chopped head and tentacles of the squid, half a dozen stoned and halved black olives, 1 tablespoonful of capers and 2 of chopped parsley, 2 peeled and chopped tomatoes, some small pieces of hot red pepper (or a little tabasco sauce) and, when all these ingredients have browned, a tablespoonful of breadcrumbs. Stuff this mixture into the body of the squid and sew it up. Next heat some more olive oil in a pan, let a chopped clove of garlic take colour in it, and add a couple of peeled and chopped tomatoes, some oregano and salt and pepper. Put the stuffed squid into this sauce, cover and cook slowly for about 30 minutes.

Polpetielli alla Luciana
A Neapolitan way of cooking octopus (serves six)

In introducing the section on octopus in her book *La Cucina Napoletana* Signora Caròla warns her readers to be sure to buy the true octopus, the one with a double row of suckers along each tentacle, i.e. No. 579 or No. 580, and not to be satisfied with the inferior 'sinisco' (diminutive 'sinischiello') which is the local name for the kinds with a single row of suckers, i.e. No. 582. 'The differences between the two species is even to be seen in the methods of capture. The "sinisco", which lives further out to sea, is normally taken by boats with nets; while the "true" octopus, which is especially attracted by the colour white, is lured by a white feather or by a rag of the same colour, placed in the centre of a tiny anchor with five arms (called a "filatiello"). It is also fished with a pottery amphora (called a "mummarella") which is likewise painted white and contains white stones; this is lowered to the bottom on the end of a rope, near a rock. The "true" octopus, if he sees it, will empty the pebbles out and instal himself inside as though in a nest. The fisherman, alerted by seeing the white pebbles scattered outside the amphora, pulls it up and thus catches the octopus.'

The recipe calls for the following ingredients:

1¼ kilos small 'true' octopus (No. 579 or 580)	lots of chopped parsley
1 wineglassful olive oil	2 tablespoonfuls lemon juice
2 cloves garlic	pepper and salt

Clean the octopus, turning the bodies inside out and gutting them, removing the eyes (not to be confused with the suckers on the tentacles) and the little bone which the octopus have at the bottom of their bodies, and washing them.

Cook the octopus in a little salted boiling water (or better still a mixture of three parts sea water to one part ordinary water with no salt added) for from 20 to 45 minutes; the time will depend on the size of the octopus.

Drain the octopus, cut it up into small pieces, season it with the garlic (chopped or whole), the olive oil, the lemon juice, lots of parsley, and pepper. Do this well before the meal so that the seasoning will have time to permeate beforehand and make them tender. And I would add as my own gloss that I have eaten the same dish made without olive oil in the dressing and with only a trace of garlic, and found it very good thus and particularly light.

Seppie alla Veneziana con Polenta
Cuttlefish cooked in the Venetian way, with polenta (serves four)

This substantial dish is well known in the whole region of the Veneto. Be sure to buy fairly small young cuttlefish. You will need 800 grammes. Prepare them by removing the guts, eyes and beaks. Keep aside at least one ink sac. Give the creatures a good wash.

Next put the cuttlefish in a pot with a little olive oil (say $\frac{1}{2}$ wineglassful) and a clove of garlic which should be removed when it has taken colour. Sprinkle salt and pepper, and cook slowly for 20 minutes. Then add $\frac{1}{2}$ wineglassful of white wine and the contents of an ink sac (or two if the first does not produce a sufficiently inky effect). Cook for another few minutes, then serve with polenta (the yellow maize flour of the Veneto which is cooked by being gently boiled and stirred for 20 minutes in plenty of salted water – $2\frac{1}{2}$ litres for 500 grammes).

I should mention here the corresponding Tuscan dish, which is Seppie* al Nero con Spinaci. A Tuscan friend recalls having to eat this every Friday without fail when she was a child. As a result of this experience she is now quite incapable of enjoying the dish, and never makes it, although the method is indelibly imprinted in her brain and she may fairly claim to be one of the foremost authorities on it. Her summary directions are for 1 kilo each of seppie and of spinach. Clean the former as usual, reserving the ink sacs. Colour a finely chopped clove of garlic in seasoned olive oil, add the seppie and cook, covered, until they are ready. Meanwhile clean and wash the spinach and cook it without adding any more water. While it is cooking make a soffritto of garlic and seasoned olive oil, with which the spinach is then cooked for a few minutes more. Finally, combine the seppie, the spinach, the ink from 3 or 4 of the sacs, and cook all together briefly.

*But in Tuscany the name calamari is often applied, confusingly, to seppie, so that the dish might be presented as Calamari con Spinaci.

13. Recipes from Greece

Our first holiday in Greece was taken from a capital city where good fish was scarce. So we determined to have a fish dinner on the night of our arrival in Athens. We chose to go to Turkolímeno, the yachting and fishing village near the Piraeus, and were at once filled with pleasure at the sight of the long row of fish restaurants each with its tables along the quayside and twinkling lights overhead. Here, after making the difficult choice between the restaurants, we met the Greek custom of going to the refrigerator and choosing the fish we would eat. For some reason there were hardly any other customers that evening, perhaps because it was late in the year and rather cool for eating out of doors. The restaurants abut on each other without division along the quayside, and we had the impression of being alone at a series of about a thousand tables, with five hundred yachts drawn up alongside and a hundred waiters stretching into the distance – ranging from the life-sized one whose shadow fell over our table to the little black and white blob in the furthest restaurant of all. Da Chirico should have been there to translate the strange perspectives on to canvas.

The Greeks do not have lots of different recipes for the different fish which they eat. Most Greeks will tell you that there are various main styles of cooking fish, most of which apply to most fish, and that this is the extent of their fish cookery. The collection of recipes which follows includes some of these very general ones, which are particularly useful, but also a few of more specific application.

Kakaviá

Greek fish soup (serves four)

There are Greeks who maintain that the bouillabaisse of Marseille is of Greek origin, and that Greek fish soup is the fundamental and oldest one in the Mediterranean. There is no one 'correct' recipe for kakaviá. It would be surprising if there were. I give one of the simplest versions, which can plausibly be regarded as a survival of something very ancient.

You will need 1 kilo of smallish fish, preferably what the Greeks call petrópsaro or rock fish (a general term, which includes for example the rascasse). Clean, gut and salt these. Next put in a large deep pan, with water to cover, ½ kilo onions and ½ kilo tomatoes, cut up, with chopped celery tops if you wish, ¼ litre olive oil, salt and pepper, and boil all this for 40 minutes. Then put in the fish and continue boiling for another 15 minutes or so (finishing up with the fish cooked but still intact). Remove the fish, placing them on slices of toast which are waiting in soup plates, and then pour the soup over, having first added some lemon juice to it.

Avgolémono Psarósoupa

Egg-and-lemon fish soup (serves eight)

This soup is a distinctive one, which incorporates the famous Greek sauce of egg and lemon.

Begin by making 2 litres of fish stock. Strain it, bring it to the boil and cook in it (for about 15 minutes) 100 grammes of rice, no more and possibly less. While this is cooking beat well 3 eggs, then beat into them the juice of a lemon, then mix in 2 good ladlefuls of hot broth borrowed from the rice-cooking operation. Stir well, then add the sauce to the broth and rice, bring gently back to simmering point, cover, keep hot a few minutes, and serve.

Athenaikí Mayonaísa

Athenian fish mayonnaise

This is a pleasant summer dish.

Begin by buying a large fish, of good quality and preferably of a species which can be deboned fairly easily after cooking. I suggest sea bass (No. 113), amberjack (No. 161) or grey mullet (Nos. 105–10), but the choice is wide and there is no reason why readers elsewhere should not substitute non-Mediterranean fish.

Cook the fish in a court-bouillon – or simply in water to which you have added carrots, celery and tomatoes, the usual Greek practice. Remove the fish, skin and debone it, and break up the flesh into little bits. Then mix the bits with mayonnaise, mould the result into a similitude of the fish as it was, coat the whole with mayonnaise and decorate it with something green (for example, olives, sliced cucumber, gherkins). Serve chilled.

Borthéto

A Corfiot recipe for stewing fish or octopus (serves four)

Major Forte, when Vice Consul in Kérkyra (Corfu), kindly provided this and the following recipe. He tells me that borthéto is a Corfiot word not found in the Greek dictionary and probably derived from the Venetian occupation of two hundred or more years ago.

1–1½ kilos rascasse (Nos. 216–18), or 750 grammes dogfish (Nos. 10, 11 or similar fish) or 750 grammes octopus (Nos. 579, 580)
½ kilo onions, sliced
1 wineglassful olive oil

1 kilo tomatoes or 2 tablespoonfuls tomato purée diluted with water
1 kilo potatoes, peeled and cut as for boiling
2 teaspoonfuls cayenne pepper
3 tablespoonfuls chopped parsley
salt to taste

The rascasses should be cleaned in the usual way, but leave the heads in place. The dogfish or the octopus would be bought ready cleaned, hence the smaller weights specified for them. If you use octopus make sure that it is well beaten and tender.

First brown the onion in the olive oil, in a large pan. Then add a generous half litre (or pint) of water, and the tomatoes (peeled and roughly chopped) or the tomato purée diluted, and bring the whole to the boil. Having done this add the fish (or octopus if you are using it) and potatoes and parsley and cayenne, with salt to taste, and more water to cover. Stew this, covered, over a medium flame for about 20 minutes (dogfish) or 30 minutes (rascasses) or 1 hour (octopus – but in this instance do not put the potatoes in until 20 minutes after the octopus), adding a little more water if necessary during the cooking, but finishing up with a thick red sauce in which the fish and potatoes are then served.

This is only one of a number of methods of producing more or less the same result; there are probably as many methods as there are housewives in Kérkyra. And the same applies to the next recipe.

Biánco

A Corfiot recipe for cooking small white fish (serves four)

Biánco is also a name of Venetian origin. This recipe is suitable for any fairly small white fish (up to, say, 9″ or 30 cm.), but the dish is most often prepared with grey mullet (Nos. 105, etc.), fish of the whiting and hake family (Nos. 76, 77, 78, 81, 83–6) or very small dogfish (Nos. 10, 11, etc.).

The ingredients are as follows:

1 kilo fish (uncleaned weight)	juice of one good-sized lemon
1 kilo potatoes, cut into cubes as for sauté potatoes	2 tablespoonfuls parsley, chopped
6 cloves garlic, peeled and finely chopped	
½ wineglassful olive oil	
salt and black pepper	

The method is simple. Take a large casserole or pan, lay the fish (cleaned) on the bottom of this, cover them with the potato cubes and the olive oil, also the garlic and salt and pepper to taste, and enough water to cover the potatoes. Put this on a low flame, cover, and cook it until all the water has evaporated, leaving only the oil. Then add the lemon juice, bring to the boil, sprinkle with parsley all over, take off the fire and serve direct from the casserole or pan.

Psitó Psári
Grilled fish

Greeks often grill fish, using charcoal, but not always basting the fish sufficiently while it is being grilled. And they may not serve the fish as soon as it is cooked, but leave it to stand for a while in a dressing of olive oil – with results which they approve but which others may find disappointing.

To achieve a grilled fish dish which is properly Greek and calculated to induce nostalgia in Hellenophiles, yet instantly acceptable to foreigners, I recommend the following procedure. Choose as your fish either barboúnia (red mullet, No. 148) or tsipoúra (daurade, No. 128) or a Greek favourite, marída (picarel, No. 146). Prepare and grill it over charcoal in the usual way (p. 256), taking care to brush it regularly on the grill with a mixture of four parts olive oil to one of lemon juice. Make ready a further dressing of olive oil and lemon juice in the same proportions, this time with plenty of chopped parsley added to it. Once the fish is ready serve it, with the dressing offered separately.

Psári Plakí

A Greek recipe, or rather range of recipes, for cooking fish on top of the stove in an agreeable Mediterranean mixture of tomato, onion, garlic, lemon, etc., with olives added if you wish and lots of possible variations

(serves six)

1½ to 1¾ kilos fish, maybe half a
   dozen smallish ones whole, or
   one or two larger ones cut up
   (the weight will only be 1 kilo
   if the fish is bought cleaned)
1 wineglassful olive oil
3 onions, chopped
2 cloves garlic, chopped

4 large tomatoes, roughly chopped
¼ kilo fresh spinach (optional)
parsley, chopped
dill, chopped (or mint if you like)
1 wineglassful white wine
salt and pepper
juice of 1 lemon

First heat the olive oil in a large frying pan, and let the chopped onion and garlic take colour. Add next the tomatoes and optional spinach, the parsley and dill, the wine and the same amount of water (but judging the amount of liquid so that when you add the fish later it will be nearly covered, and bearing in mind that if you have put in spinach you will need less additional liquid). Season and cook this for 10 or 15 minutes until all is soft.

Meanwhile clean the fish, and cut them into manageable pieces if necessary, so that you can arrange them in a well-oiled pan with some of the lemon juice poured over them.

When the tomato mixture is ready pour it all over the fish, cover, and cook gently on top of the stove for about half an hour. Stoned olives may be added when the cooking is almost completed, and a further sprinkle of lemon juice. When the fish is ready it can be taken out and kept aside while the sauce is reduced before being poured back over the fish.

It is hard to go wrong with this recipe, so long as you give the fish enough time to cook. It would be madness to fuss over the exact quantities of the ingredients – or even over the choice of ingredients, although I suppose that tomatoes at least are essential. In this climate of relaxation and flexibility the reader will not be surprised to hear that the dish may be served either hot or cold or (in Greek fashion) luke-warm.

Psári Spetsiótiko

Fish baked in the manner of the islanders of Spétsai   (serves four)

Spétsai is an island in the Cyclades, not far from Athens. The recipe which follows is one of the comparatively few Greek fish dishes which has a title showing whence it comes.

1 whole fish weighing about 1 kilo, e.g. a sea bass (No. 113), denté (No. 125), bluefish (No. 154); or a pair of fish weighing $\frac{1}{2}$ kilo each, e.g. mackerel, or 4 fish steaks of up to 200 grammes each
1$\frac{1}{2}$ wineglassfuls olive oil

2–3 large tomatoes or 1 tablespoonful tomato purée
1 clove garlic, mashed
chopped parsley
salt and pepper
a handful of breadcrumbs
$\frac{1}{2}$ wineglassful white wine (optional)

Wash and clean the fish as usual. Make the sauce by mixing together the olive oil, tomatoes (peeled and chopped) or tomato purée, parsley and garlic, adding salt and pepper.

Oil a baking dish and lay the fish in it, surrounded and covered by sauce. Put half of the breadcrumbs on top of the fish, then spoon sauce over this, add the remaining breadcrumbs, and then more sauce and more parsley.

Cook in a medium oven for up to an hour (depending on the size of the fish), basting the fish from time to time with the sauce, and watching carefully to see whether the sauce is reducing too much and the fish tending to become dry. Should this happen, add a little water or white wine. But there should not be a great quantity of sauce when the cooking is finished. The dish may be eaten hot or cold. It should be served with lemon wedges, or sprinkled with lemon juice just before coming to the table.

Barboúnia Stó Hartí

Red mullet en papillote

Red mullet are usually fried or grilled in Greece. The smaller ones would be fried, and the bigger ones grilled. The Greek cook would in either event let them sit in a colander, sprinkled with salt and pepper and lemon juice, for 20 minutes or so before cooking them.

But the Greeks also use a method which is popular in many other Mediterranean countries – baking them in cooking parchment (or aluminium foil, not so well known there but probably the best material for the purpose). A piece of parchment or foil is cut for each fish, big enough to enfold it completely. The fish are then rubbed with olive oil. A mixture of equal parts of olive oil and lemon juice is prepared separately, seasoned with salt and pepper, and aromatized with marjoram (or thyme). Each fish is placed on a piece of parchment. Some of the olive oil and lemon juice mixture is spooned over it. A couple of slices of lemon are placed on top. Then the parchment is folded over and the edges secured (or, if foil is used, simply crimped together). The packages are placed in a baking dish, brushed with olive oil and baked in a moderate oven for half an hour.

Mayático Skorthaliá
Amberjack with garlic sauce

Amberjack is a good fish, and one familiar to Greeks although hard to find in some parts of the Mediterranean. My colleague John Little, when in Salonika, sent me details of two ways in which this fish is prepared there. In both the fish is first sliced and fried. In one the accompaniment is garlic sauce, in the other mayonnaise. The latter may be thought the better for a fish of good quality; indeed the former is most often used with salt cod. But it is the garlic sauce which I choose to give here – as something unusual and very Greek.

The ingredients required for skorthaliá are:

1 handful almonds or walnuts	up to 1½ wineglassfuls olive oil
3 or 4 or more cloves of garlic	a 1 lb. loaf of white bread
salt	wine vinegar

Blanch the nuts, peel them, and blend them in an electric blender with the garlic and 1 wineglassful or so (the almonds need more than the walnuts) of olive oil. Put the result in a wooden mortar and pound it with a little salt until it is of a creamy consistency.

Slice the crumb of the loaf and soak it in a very little water for a few minutes. Then squeeze well to drain, and knead by hand until soft.

Pound the softened bread with the almond and garlic mixture, and add drop by drop some more olive oil, pounding continuously until the mixture begins to shine, i.e. up to the point when the oil becomes just visible. Stop at that point, and add wine vinegar to taste. Serve the sauce with the hot fried slices of amberjack.

Garidopílafo

A Greek dish of prawns and rice (serves six)

Mrs Vedova of Salonika has given me careful directions for preparing this. She has made the dish with various types of rice, and thinks that it is best with a long-grain Patna rice, preferably the sort which has been parboiled (see p. 264). The ingredients are:

1 kilo prawns (Nos. 504, etc.)	1 tablespoonful tomato purée
12 oz. rice (350 grammes)	1 tablespoonful dry red wine
½ wineglassful olive oil	1 bay leaf
1 onion, or 2 smallish ones	pepper

Chop the onion and fry it in the olive oil until it is brown. Add the tomato purée, wine, bay leaf and season with pepper. Keep the mixture over the heat for a few minutes more, stirring.

Meanwhile the prawns are boiled in plenty of salt water until they are cooked and 'firm'. Peel them, discarding the debris into the cooking water, and put them aside. Strain the water, and then measure off $2\frac{1}{2}$ pints of it. Put this in a deep casserole and bring it to the boil. Add the rice, and the sauce which you have already prepared; stir a little, and then leave to continue cooking without any further stirring until all the water has been absorbed. If you want to test whether the rice is ready, stick a spoon into it vertically. If it stays upright the rice is ready.

Serve the rice with the prawns arrayed on top. Many people would offer grated Parmesan with the dish, but the Vedova family do not advocate this.

Soupiá Yachní

Cuttlefish cooked with their ink (serves six)

1 kilo fairly small cuttlefish	2 tablespoonfuls pine-nut kernels
2 onions	(optional)
2 wineglassfuls olive oil	parsley
2 wineglassfuls white wine	salt and pepper

Remove the guts, eyes and beaks from the cuttlefish, but keep several of their ink sacs. Wash them. Cut them up into convenient pieces.

Slice the onions. Heat the olive oil in a pan and let the onion take colour in this, then add the cuttlefish and let them take colour too. Add next the wine, and an equal quantity of water, the contents of two or three of the ink sacs, chopped parsley, salt and pepper and the pine-nut kernels if you are using them. Cover, bring to the boil and then keep boiling gently on a moderate flame until the wine and water have gone.

Ochtapódi Krassáto

Octopus cooked in red wine (serves six)

The Greeks are very keen on octopus. Here is one way in which they prepare it, given according to the old family recipe of an expert Athenian cook, Mrs Dimítri Gófas.

1 octopus (No. 579 or No. 580) of 1 kilo
½ kilo onions, finely chopped
¾ wineglassful olive oil
½ wineglassful red-wine vinegar
3 wineglassfuls dry red wine
½ kilo tomatoes, peeled and finely chopped

1 medium-sized sprig rosemary
1 bay leaf
1 teaspoonful black pepper
1 pinch each of nutmeg and cinnamon
2 cloves
1 tablespoonful tomato paste

Have the octopus cleaned; put it in a pan by itself over a medium flame. It will turn red. Take it out and chop it up. Meanwhile set the olive oil to heat.

Let the pieces of octopus brown slightly in the hot olive oil. Add the chopped onion and let it turn golden. At this point add all the remaining ingredients. Stir and cover. Simmer until the octopus is cooked, which will take between 2 and 3 hours.

Remove the pieces of octopus from the sauce, pass the sauce through a sieve, and pour it back over the octopus.

Kalamária Yemistá

Stuffed squid (serves six)

1½ kilos squid (No. 573) of medium size
salt and pepper
½ wineglassful olive oil
1 wineglassful tomato juice
1 wineglassful olive oil
2 large onions, chopped fine

150–175 grammes rice
3 tablespoonfuls parsley, chopped
2 tablespoonfuls mint (or dill), chopped
1 tablespoonful pine-nut kernels
1 wineglassful red wine

The squid must be cleaned (take care to remove the ink sacs*) and washed. The tentacles should be cut off, chopped up, and put aside to be used in the stuffing. The bodies should be seasoned and left to sit in the mixture of olive oil and tomato juice.

Heat the wineglassful of olive oil and lightly brown the onion in this. Add the chopped tentacles and let them take colour too, then the rice, parsley, mint (or dill) and pine-nut kernels. Cook all this gently for a few minutes. Set a kettle to boil. Remove the squid from their bath and stuff them with the mixture. They should not be filled completely, since the rice will need room to swell. Pour wine into each until you have used up the wineglassful. Sew up the tops or secure them with toothpicks, and place the stuffed squid upright and closely packed in a deep baking dish. Pour over them the mixture of olive oil and tomato juice in which they had been sitting previously, and enough boiling water to cover. Bake in a medium oven for an hour to an hour and a half, until the squid are tender. By then the sauce should be quite thick. Serve warm or cold.

Taramosaláta

The dried roe of the grey mullet, which is called avgotáracho, is preserved in wax in Greece as in other Mediterranean countries (see p. 72), and I understand that it was at one time used for making Taramosaláta. On the strength of this understanding (which it would be unkind to disprove) I can count the dish as an indigenous Mediterranean one, although nowadays the Greeks always make it with imported smoked cod roe instead, as avgotáracho has become an expensive delicacy. Do not hesitate to follow their example.

I have not said for how many people the quantities in the recipe below suffice. When I am around any quantity serves one. Why not make a *lot*? (it keeps).

½ kilo smoked cod roe
350 grammes cream cheese
3 tablespoonfuls olive oil

3 tablespoonfuls finely chopped
    fresh chives
3 tablespoonfuls lemon juice

Mix these ingredients together, putting in the lemon juice last, and chill.

I should not leave the impression that this is the only recipe. Some would use bread (soaked, squeezed dry and pounded) instead of the cream cheese. Others would not put in the chives.

*The ink can be fried in hot olive oil and served on little pieces of brown bread as an appetizer.

14. Recipes from Turkey

Turkey is surrounded by a remarkably interesting and varied collection of waters. The southern coast looks down across the eastern basin of the Mediterranean. The western coast bounds the island-dotted Aegean Sea. At the north-western corner lies the Marmara, entered by the Dardanelles from the Aegean and communicating through the Bosphorus with the Black Sea to the north. And a large part of the Black Sea coastline, stretching to Trabzon (Trebizond) and beyond, is Turkish. These varied waters yield rich crops of fish, and the Turks, whose cuisine is ranked by many among the finest in the world, do justice to it.

The best place to enjoy the fish is Istanbul, where the fish shops offer splendid displays and there are many excellent places for eating fish. The humblest is the cluster of boats by the Eminönü end of the Galata Bridge, from which passers-by are served with freshly fried pieces of çingene palamudu (literally, gypsy bonito) by the eager vendors, rocking in their small craft and reaching up with packages containing the hot and succulent morsels.

The favourite fish in Turkey include the bonito (torik and palamut), the bluefish (lüfer), the turbot (kalkan) and the swordfish (kılıç). But perhaps pride of place should be given to the anchovy (hamsi) which inspires remarkably intense feelings. These have found expression in folk poems of a kind which I have not found elsewhere in the Mediterranean area. These are really Black Sea poems, recited by itinerant troubadours and constantly renewed and modified to match the idiom of each successive generation. Nazmi Akiman, himself a poet, has translated two for me, with stirring lines which give the hamsi a quasi-religious as well as a nutritional significance:

> To the men of Trabzon it's a hero.
> A basketful is enough to give blood to the feeble,
> All the people in the world hear its call.

Balık Çorbası
Turkish fish soup

Mr Hugh Whittall noted this recipe from the practice of Turkish fishermen, with whom he was spending some days at sea.

Use comber (No. 122), gurnard (Nos. 221, etc.), or rascasse (Nos. 216, etc.). Clean the fish, salt them lightly and cut them into slices. Do not discard the heads and tails. Cover with water, bring to the boil, add some olive oil and keep the mixture boiling for 15 minutes. Meanwhile fry some onion and tomato (and green pepper if you wish) until you have a pulpy mixture. When you have finished boiling the fish add to it the tomato and onion mixture, and then simmer the whole for a while, stirring slowly. If you wish you may add beaten-up eggs during this process, but very gradually so that the egg does not solidify. Finally, strain. Serve the surviving bits of fish separately or put them back in the soup.

Balık Köftesi
Turkish fish balls or croquettes   (serves six)

These may be made with bonito (No. 191), grey mullet (Nos. 105, etc.) or sea bass (No. 113). You will need:

nearly 2 kilos fish	2 tablespoonfuls pine-nut kernels ⎱ optional
lemon juice, black peppercorns, bay leaves and parsley (for a court-bouillon)	2 tablespoonfuls currants ⎰
	1 teaspoonful allspice
250 grammes crustless stale bread	salt and pepper
1 onion, grated	breadcrumbs (optional)
1 egg	vegetable oil (for frying)

Cook the fish in a court-bouillon. Let it cool. Lift it out, remove the skin and bones, and break up the flesh into small pieces.

Soak the bread in water for a few minutes, then squeeze it well. Combine it in a large bowl with the fish, the onion, the pine-nut kernels and the currants (if used), the egg, the allspice and seasoning. Mix and knead this well for a few minutes. Then work it into balls or long finger-shaped croquettes. Roll these in dry breadcrumbs if you wish. Fry them in hot vegetable oil and serve them hot.

(Recipe of Mrs Mefkûre Üstün)

Elmalı ve Soğanlı Balık

Fish baked with apple and onion (serves six)

This Turkish recipe, which has been supplied by Ali Tomak of Bulancak on the Turkish Black Sea coast, is especially interesting since the use of apple echoes certain Russian fish recipes from the other side of the Black Sea. Any fish with firm white flesh can be used. Mr Tomak recommends turbot.

1 kilo (cleaned weight) fish	**salt**
1 kilo cooking apples	**cayenne pepper**
2 fairly large onions, sliced	**sprig of parsley, chopped**
3 or 4 bay leaves	**2 wineglassfuls olive oil**

The fish should be in slices of not more than 1 inch thick. Cook these gently in boiling water for 2 minutes only.

Core, peel and slice the apples. Cover the bottom of a fireproof pot (a clay one would be used at Bulancak) with a layer of apple and onion slices, using up about half the quantity. Place the bay leaves on top of this, then the slices of fish, then the rest of the apple and onion slices. Sprinkle salt and cayenne pepper and parsley on top, and pour the olive oil over all (so that in trickling down it moistens everything which is in the pot). Cook, covered, over a low flame for 45 minutes or so. Do not add any water. The cooking can be done in a slow oven if you prefer, but it is better to stick to the traditional Turkish method and do it on a charcoal fire or on top of the stove.

When the dish is cooked allow it to cool and serve it cold accompanied by cold cooked carrots and potatoes with yoghourt on them. (This is the Turkish method, but others may prefer to eat both the fish dish and the vegetables hot.)

Four Turkish Ways with Anchovy

Do not think that there are only four. There are many more. I even have a recipe for anchovy bread. But the examples below will serve to show what a wide range of recipes the Turks have devised for their beloved hamsi.

Hamsi Kızartması

Sauté anchovies

Clean and bone fresh anchovies, leaving the tails intact, and roll them in salted flour or corn meal. Fry them in hot oil and serve them hot, or as appetizers which can be held by the tail and eaten whole.

İçli Tava
Anchovy and rice (serves six)

A Turkish manual for professional fishermen, from which many facts about anchovies may be gleaned, offers the opinion that this is the most delectable as well as the best known of all the anchovy dishes.

1½ kilos fresh anchovy	hot water
salt	2 tablespoonfuls currants
400 grammes (1½ cups) rice	1 teaspoonful allspice
125 grammes butter	1 teaspoonful cinnamon
2 medium onions, chopped	1 teaspoonful sugar
2 tablespoonfuls pine-nut kernels	salt and pepper
a little more butter, melted	

Clean, debone and salt the anchovy. Leave it in a cool place. Soak the rice for an hour in warm water to which you have added several teaspoonfuls of salt. Wash it several times until the water comes out clear, then strain. (These instructions for preparing the rice will not apply if you are using packaged rice which needs no treatment before use – see p. 264.)

Heat the 125 grammes of butter in a pan, add the onion and pine-nut kernels, and let the onion brown slightly. Next add the rice, and continue cooking (and stirring) for 10 minutes. Add the hot water in whatever proportion you normally employ for the kind of rice which you are using. Add with it the remaining ingredients from the right-hand column above. Raise the heat. After a few minutes reduce it to a medium heat and progressively to a low heat as the water is absorbed, until the rice is ready.

Select a flameproof dish which is suitable for taking to table, has a cover and is fairly broad. Grease or oil it. Arrange half the anchovy in a single layer in this. Put all the rice mixture on top, Then add a second layer of the fish. Pour a little melted butter over all, cover and cook over a medium heat for 10 to 15 minutes until the fish is ready. Serve hot.

Hamsi Buğlaması
A cold anchovy dish (serves four)

1 kilo fresh anchovy	⅔ wineglassful olive oil
juice of 1 lemon	2 wineglassfuls water
	salt
	½ bunch dill, finely chopped
	½ bunch parsley, finely chopped

Clean, wash and pat dry the anchovy. Lay them out side by side in a shallow flameproof dish. Add the ingredients from the right-hand column above. Cover the dish (using foil if it has no fitted cover) and cook over a moderate heat for 7 or 8 minutes. Remove from the heat, add the lemon juice shortly afterwards, and serve cold.

Hamsi Kayganası
Anchovy omelette

This dish is prepared by adding small chunks of fresh anchovy flesh, with a little flour and some chopped parsley, to the usual egg mixture. The omelette is to be of the kind which you first cook on one side and then turn over and cook on the other.

Kefal Balığı Pilâkisi
Grey mullet with vegetables   (serves six)

For this recipe you will need 1½–1¾ kilos (uncleaned weight) of grey mullet (Nos. 105, etc.), which should be cleaned and cut into thick sections or slices. (Alternatively you can use bonito, or fairly small mackerel, gutted but otherwise whole.)

The other ingredients are:

1 wineglassful olive oil
2 wineglassfuls water
10 shallots
4 small potatoes, peeled and quartered
2 small celery roots, peeled and cut up

3 carrots, peeled and halved lengthways
1 clove garlic
salt
1 lemon, sliced
lots of parsley, chopped

Begin by putting the oil, water, vegetables, garlic and salt into a big pan and cooking them for half an hour, or until the vegetables are becoming tender. Then add the fish and the sliced lemon, and cook for another quarter of an hour. Remove from the fire, add the parsley, and allow to become cold before serving.

Kılıç Domatesli
Swordfish with tomatoes   (serves six)

Buy 1 kilo of steaks or slices of swordfish (No. 199). Wash and dry them, and put them aside.

Peel, seed and chop 4 large tomatoes. Heat $\frac{1}{2}$ wineglassful of olive oil in a deep pan, add the tomatoes and 2 teaspoonfuls of salt, and cook for 5 or 6 minutes, stirring frequently. This produces a kind of tomato sauce, of which half should be spread over the bottom of a shallow baking dish. Arrange the pieces of fish on this bed and pour the rest of the sauce over them. Add $\frac{1}{2}$ wineglassful of water (or fish stock). Cook in the oven, uncovered, for 40 minutes; or on a charcoal fire, covered, for 25 minutes.

Kılıç Şişte

Swordfish en brochette   (serves six)

This Turkish speciality can easily be prepared in North America as well as in the Mediterranean, and it can be adapted for use in Britain, where swordfish is not usually obtainable, by substituting other fish of sufficiently firm flesh (such as halibut).

1 kilo swordfish (No. 199)	*for the marinade:*
slices of lemon	2 tablespoonfuls lemon juice
slices of tomato	2 tablespoonfuls olive oil
	1 tablespoonful onion juice
for the dressing:	(optional)
juice of 1 lemon	1$\frac{1}{2}$ teaspoonfuls paprika
2 or 3 teaspoonfuls olive oil	12 bay leaves
1 or 2 sprigs parsley, chopped	2 teaspoonfuls salt

Dice the swordfish into pieces about 1″ by 1$\frac{1}{2}$″ by 2″. (Do not worry about the exact size. The important thing is to make the pieces of more or less uniform size.) Mix the marinade indicated above, and leave the pieces of swordfish in it for 4 to 6 hours (or more if it suits you).

Remove the pieces of fish and put them on skewers, with the long side of each piece parallel to the skewer. Insert slices of lemon and tomato between them. Then grill them on both sides over a charcoal fire, brushing them frequently with the left-over marinade. This should take about 10 minutes or a little longer. Serve hot, accompanied by the simple dressing indicated above.

Gurnard with Almond Sauce

                                                                (serves four)

Excellent fresh nuts of many kinds are to be found in Turkey: from the hazel nuts of the Black Sea coast to the walnuts and almonds of Anatolia, the pistachios of the east and the pine kernels of the Bosphorus. Milk and butter are scarce, so nuts are often ground to a cream to take their place, as in this recipe for an almond sauce for fish. It was given to friends of mine by Mine Birgi, who often serves it at her home in Ankara on the hill where Ataturk once lived. She finds that the sauce goes very well with sea bass, as indeed it does; but it is suited to many fish, and I like to serve it with a good gurnard. The recipe can be followed successfully in Britain or North America, although the sauce is best when made from fresh almonds in a country like Turkey where they are grown.

Select a large gurnard, preferably No. 221, and cook it in a court-bouillon (p. 258). While it is cooking, or (if you wish to serve it cold) while it is cooling in the court-bouillon, prepare the sauce as follows. Pound in a mortar, or blend very thoroughly in an electric blender, a cupful of freshly blanched almonds with a slice of white bread (from which the crust has been removed) and enough cold water to produce a creamy white paste. Add a wineglassful of olive oil, mixing all the time, and then lemon juice, and seasoning to taste. You will probably find that the juice of half a lemon is about the right quantity, but be careful not to add too much – the sauce should have the consistency of thick cream. Serve it cold with the fish, which may be cold too, or hot.

White fish, white sauce, and perhaps a white plate too? Hot off-white potatoes can be added to achieve an extraordinarily subtle colour scheme. But conventional ideas require more contrast. This can be achieved by garnishing the fish liberally with thin lemon slices, sprinkling chopped green coriander over the sauce and dusting the potatoes with just enough paprika to colour them.

Palamut Papaz Yahnisi

Bonito for eating cold   (serves six)

Clean a bonito (No. 191) and cut from it either 6 large steaks or 12 smaller ones. These should be whole sections of the fish cut crossways. Salt them lightly and put them aside.

Chop 5 medium onions into crescents. Chop 4 cloves of garlic. Slice 2 carrots into rounds. Fry all this gently for 15 minutes in ¾ wineglassful of olive oil.

Once the onion is browned add ½ wineglassful more of olive oil, 1½ wineglassfuls water (or fish stock), 4 tablespoonfuls of previously prepared tomato sauce, 1 teaspoonful of red pepper (cayenne if you want a hot dish, paprika if you prefer a milder taste) and 2 teaspoonfuls of salt. Continue cooking for another 15 minutes.

Select a pan which will accommodate the fish steaks side by side. Spread half your sauce over the bottom, place the fish steaks on this bed and pour the other half of the sauce over them. Add a wineglassful of white wine. Cover your pan and cook on top of the stove for 25 minutes or so. Serve cold, dressed with a little lemon juice.

This recipe can also be used for mackerel.

Uskumru Dolması
Stuffed mackerel   (serves six)

This is a speciality of Istanbul. Learning how to prepare the mackerel for being stuffed may require some practice, but the result is worth some effort and the stuffing itself is easy.

1½–1¾ kilos mackerel (No. 189)	*for the stuffing:*
flour	6–8 onions, chopped
3 or 4 eggs, beaten	4 tablespoonfuls pine-nut kernels
2 wineglassfuls olive oil	4 tablespoonfuls currants
breadcrumbs or crushed	1 tablespoonful ground walnut
(unsweetened) biscuit	½ teaspoonful cinnamon
2 wineglassfuls olive oil	½ teaspoonful allspice
	salt and pepper
	2 sprigs dill, chopped
	2 sprigs parsley, chopped

The mackerel should be of a good size. The first step is to gut them (through the gills, without opening the belly) and wash them. Then roll each fish backward and forward on a board, to loosen the flesh inside the skin. Without breaking the skin, snap the backbone just short of the tail, and again close to the head. Take hold of the backbone at the head end and work it up and down a little before drawing it out. Put aside any flesh which comes out with it. Squeeze the fish carefully between thumb and forefinger, moving your hand along from tail to head, in order to loosen the flesh a little more. Take out all the loose flesh.

Now make the stuffing. Heat the olive oil in a pan and let the chopped onion brown slightly in this. Add the pine-nut kernels, currants, walnuts, cinnamon, allspice, salt and pepper and the mackerel flesh, chopped, and cook for another 5 minutes or so. Then add the dill and parsley. Stuff the mixture gently into the fish from the neck openings.

Finally you must roll the stuffed fish successively in flour, in the beaten egg and in breadcrumbs or crushed biscuit, after which you fry it on both sides in hot olive oil. Serve cold, sliced.

Midye Tavası Biralı

Mussels with beer, served with a tarator sauce   (serves four)

Clean 40 large mussels (No. 545) as usual and open them by heating them in a saucepan. Once they are open take them out of their shells and let them drain on a towel.

Mix $1\frac{1}{2}$ cups ($\frac{1}{4}$ litre) beer with 250 grammes flour and a little salt in a bowl. Fold in 3 beaten egg whites, to produce a fairly thick mixture. Roll the mussels in flour, then dip them in the beer mixture and fry them in hot oil.

Mrs Mefkûre Üstün recommends serving the mussels with a tarator sauce. (Note that the ingredients do not include sesame oil paste, as in the Lebanese version on p. 391, but olive oil, which is usual in Turkey and gives a lighter result.)

You need 100 grammes of walnuts or hazelnuts (or a mixture of the two or a mixture of one of them with pine-nut kernels), 2 slices of crustless stale bread, $\frac{1}{2}$ cup olive oil, $\frac{1}{3}$ cup vinegar, 3 cloves of garlic and salt. Soak the bread in water, then squeeze it well. Blend all the ingredients in a blender (or put the bread, nuts and garlic through a grinder, add the other ingredients and mix).

15. Recipes from Tunisia, Algeria and Morocco

Tunisia's northern coastline is in the western basin of the Mediterranean, while the eastern shores, from Cap Bon down to the Gulf of Gabes, look across the Eastern basin and are lapped by slightly warmer waters. Between Cap Bon and Sicily a generous stretch of continental shelf provides good trawling grounds. The result is that Tunisians enjoy a variety and abundance of fish not surpassed anywhere else in the Mediterranean.

La Goulette, which takes its name from being the throat of the ship canal which connects Tunis itself with the sea, is the site of a group of fish restaurants, which extend their tables far out over the pavements and the square during the summer. What pleasure it was to sup there, starting with a chakchouka and going on to eat a grilled daurade or grey mullet selected from the glass-fronted cabinet in front of the restaurant, with family parties of Tunisians all round, the men in their cool white djebbahs, jasmine-sellers brushing past one's elbow, the legion of La Goulette cats brushing past one's ankles, and primitive strings of coloured lamps switched on overhead as dusk fell. Here was no nonsense of complicated menus – just marvellously good fish charcoal grilled and served with plenty of chopped parsley and lemon. I hope it is still the same.

But Tunisians have other ways of preparing fish – some of which are in any case not suited to the grill. The recipes are to be found by patient research, in homes rather than restaurants. The foreigner engaged on a quest of this sort is fortunate, for he will find all doors opened to him, and everyone, from cabinet ministers to the poorest fishermen, eager to help. But time is necessary. These matters are not to be hurried. I recall paying three visits of several hours each to a certain house where lived a venerable Tunisian who had once cooked for the Bey of Tunis. The first visit was taken up with the courtesies of meeting his family and explaining my business. The second involved taking tea with the venerable cook himself. At the third he imparted to me a recipe.

Marka (or Mreika)

Sfax fish soup (serves six)

olive oil	½ kilo tomatoes
1 large onion, chopped	2 hot green peppers
1 teaspoonful cayenne (piment rouge piquant)	salt
	1 kilo pataclés (No. 137)
1 teaspoonful cumin (kamoun)	4 small rascasses (Nos. 216, etc.)
1 clove garlic, crushed	1 piece mérou (No. 116) weighing 250 grammes

Take a roomy cooking pot and heat a small amount of olive oil in it. Cook the chopped onion in this until it turns golden. Then add the cayenne, followed by the cumin and garlic mixed together. Be careful not to burn.

Meanwhile sieve the tomatoes and take the resultant pulpy juice, adding it little by little (say, in 4 or 5 helpings) to the mixture in the pot which you then allow to simmer for 15 minutes. While this is going on take a couple of hot green peppers, remove their stalks and make slits in their sides, into which you introduce some salt before adding them to the mixture at the end of the simmering period.

Now add, gradually, about 1½ litres of water. Just before this boils add the fish (cleaned but not beheaded), let the whole cook over a low flame for about half an hour, and at the end add a dash of black pepper. You may now strain, discarding fish and peppers, and serve. If you wish, however, and if you have been careful not to cook the fish too hard or too long, so that it has not disintegrated, you may serve the fish too.

(Recipe of M. Hedi Gafsi)

Ramadan soup

(serves two)

This is another Tunisian fish soup, popular during Ramadan, or indeed at any other time.

Chop 2 medium onions and fry them lightly in olive oil. Add a teaspoonful of powdered red pepper and 50 grammes of tomato purée. Simmer for 5 minutes, then add 2 pints of boiling water and stir. Next, add the fish – 750 grammes of 'bouillabaisse' fish, cleaned – and cook it for 20 minutes. (In any Mediterranean fish market you will find a heap of mixed small fish being sold for soup-making. In Tunisia such a heap is labelled 'bouillabaisse' although not many Tunisians use the fish for that particular dish.)

Then take the fish out and pick it over to remove all bones, etc., after which you put the flesh of the fish back in, together with 150 grammes of pearl barley (orge perle, shorba sha'ir), salt and pepper. Allow to simmer for half an hour or until the barley is well cooked. When you serve the soup add some lemon juice.

(Contributed by Mme Huerman, Kairouan)

Fish Couscous

(serves eight)

Baharini Amor, our cook when we lived in Tunisia, came from the inland village of Sloughia, but none the less relished seafood as much as we did. Here is his recipe for fish couscous, which I preface with the explanation that couscous is granulated flour, now obtainable in many speciality food shops. It was invented in the Arab world in the fifteenth century, and has for long been a principal dish of the Maghreb countries; it is also found in such places as Sicily and the South of France.

The ingredients are:

8 steaks of mérou (No. 116), grey mullet (Nos. 105, etc.), pagre (No. 129), ombrine (No. 153) or similar fish, weighing rather more than 1 kilo in all

2 cups couscous

150 grammes chick peas (soaked in water overnight)

carrots
potatoes
turnips
onions
cabbage
} about 1½ kilos in all: this is a typical combination of vegetables but it can be varied

2 wineglassfuls olive oil
100 grammes tomato purée
salt and black pepper
a handful of raisins
a little cinnamon powder

There are two cooking operations, corresponding to the two parts of the cooking utensil which must be used. This is a couscoussier, a sort of very large double boiler of which the upper part has a perforated bottom. The bottom half, which is used for cooking the vegetables and fish, is known as the tajinat or marmite. The upper half, in which the couscous is cooked by the steam from below, is the keskes.

The instructions will be clearer if I assume that you are cooking the dish for a 12.45 lunch, and give times for the various operations.

At 10.00 drain the chick peas which have been soaking and set them to cook in gently boiling water. At 11.00 heat the olive oil in the marmite, then drain the chick peas again and add them. At 11.15 add the tomato purée and 1½ litres of hot water. At 11.30 add the carrots and onions, at 11.45 the potatoes and turnips and at 11.50 the cabbage. All these vegetables should be whole or halved, except for the cabbage which should be cut into manageable wedges. At 12.00 add the fish and season with salt and pepper.

Also at 12.00, moisten the couscous with a little cold water and put it in the keskes on top of the marmite. (The fit must be very close; if it isn't put a clean cloth over the marmite and then jam the keskes down on that.) As soon as steam begins to issue remove the keskes, transfer the couscous to a bowl and work it until the grains are separated. Then replace it in the keskes, and the keskes on the marmite. This time you carry on cooking for another 10 minutes after steam has begun to emerge. Then remove the keskes. Take a ladleful of sauce from the marmite and mix it in with the couscous, together with the raisins and a light sprinkling of cinnamon. It should now be about 12.30.

The final step is to arrange the couscous in a couscous dish, place the fish and vegetables on top of it and put the sauce in a sauceboat. You may, if you wish, divide the sauce into two parts, one mild and one (to which harissa – see p. 263 – is added) hot.

The best sort of couscous dish is to be ordered from Nabeul on Cap Bon, with matching plates. Both serving dish and plates are circular, with low pedestal bases, and slope down gently from rim to centre at an angle of about 10°. The food is piled up on them in convex fashion to match the concavity of the dishes.

Kousha

Ragoût of saupe, as prepared at Sfax   (serves six)

2 kilos saupe (No. 142)	4 handfuls of chick peas soaked
1 teaspoonful red pepper, ground	overnight and partly precooked
3 teaspoonfuls black pepper,	2 wineglassfuls olive oil
ground	1 kilo potatoes, peeled and cut up
2 onions, cut up	200 grammes peeled, quartered,
1 gramme saffron	seeded tomatoes
1½ litres water	3 or 4 hot red peppers

Gut and wash the fish, and cut them in half crosswise. Put them in a casserole (tajin foukhar is the name of the vessel preferred in Tunisia), add all the other ingredients and boil gently until everything is cooked. The heads of the fish may be discarded before or after the cooking.

(Recipe from *Les Usages et Rites Alimentaires des Tunisiens* by M. E. Gobert)

Shermoula

(serves six)

This dish is a speciality of Bizerta, and is remarkably similar to a Roman dish described by Apicius – the main differences consisting in the introduction by Tunisians of the red pepper (unknown to the Romans) in the form of harissa; the substitution of onions for dates; of ordinary salt for garum (see p. 246); and the disappearance of silphium, a plant which is no longer available.

Monsieur Gobert has described this recipe in his book *Les Usages et Rites Alimentaires des Tunisiens*, and also in a separate paper published in the Journal of the Institut des Belles Lettres Arabes (1942, vol. 1, p. 52). I have followed the latter as it is the fuller but have indicated two ingredients mentioned in the former only, supposing that they should at least count as optional additions (I put them in myself when I made this dish, and did not regret doing so).

1 kilo of steaks cut from a large daurade (No. 128) or a pagre (No. 129)
for the preliminary dressing:
harissa
crushed cumin
salt
for frying the fish:
flour
olive oil

for the third stage:
2 onions, very thinly sliced
2 or 3 teaspoonfuls harissa
salt
1 glass wine vinegar
water
optional for third stage:
1 teaspoonful grated cinnamon
1 teaspoonful shoush el ouard (rose-petal powder)
1 teaspoonful black pepper
for the fourth stage:
1 cup honey
¼ kilo raisins

The ingredients of the preliminary dressing are mixed and rubbed over the fish, which is then left to absorb their flavour for at least two hours. Next, the slices of fish are floured and cooked in very hot olive oil; then taken out and put aside.

In the third stage, the thin slices of onion are cooked in the olive oil which has been left in the pan (you should put in as much onion as the oil will cover). When the onion turns yellow the harissa, salt, wine vinegar and water are added. The quantity of water should be sufficient to last until the cooking of the onions is completed, and a little longer. (Note: of the three optional ingredients which can go in at this stage, the first two can be bought ready mixed together from Tunisian grocers, who are, incidentally, called djerbians as they have mostly come from the island of Djerba.)

When the onions are cooked the honey and raisins are added to the mixture, which should continue to simmer until all the water has evaporated. At this point the slices of fish are placed in the sauce, the heat is turned up briefly so that the mixture bubbles (and achieves a further impregnation of the fish), and the dish is ready.

Shermoula keeps well. It is often eaten cold. Pilgrims to Mecca have taken it as part of their provisions for the journey.

Ange de Mer au Four
Baked angel shark (serves six)

six sections of angel shark (No. 26), about 1½" thick
salt and pepper
1 tablespoonful, or a little more, of butter

1 sweet green pepper
4 tomatoes
2 tablespoonfuls lemon juice
2 eggs
1 tablespoonful flour

Butter an oven dish and set out the seasoned pieces of fish in it, laying the remaining butter on top, together with the green pepper (seeded and cut into rings) and the tomatoes (sliced), with the lemon juice over all. Place in a preheated moderate oven for about 25 minutes.

Meanwhile beat well the eggs and flour. Pour this mixture over the dish and return it to the oven for another 15 minutes.

(Recipe of Baharini Amor)

Baliste, Sauce aux Olives
Trigger-fish with a Tunisian sauce (serves four to six)

Take a baliste (No. 246) of about 2 kilos and have it cleaned and skinned. Now take a dish which will accommodate it – a turbotière is recommended – and put a little water and olive oil in it, followed by plenty of sliced onion, followed by the fish. Add sliced tomatoes, salt and pepper. Cook until done, in a medium oven.

The sauce is a Tunisian one, for which you need the following ingredients:

1 white turnip	1 sweet green pepper
2 carrots	100 grammes mushrooms
1 stick of celery	2 sprigs parsley
1 onion	salt and pepper
1 big or 2 smaller potatoes	black and green olives (say, 4 of
1 tomato	each, or 6 if they are small)

Cook all the ingredients except the olives in a little water until everything is done, then put it all through a moulin-légumes. Reheat if necessary and add the pitted sliced olives. Serve separately with the fish.

(Recipe of Baharini Amor)

Boulettes de Merlan Pannées
Tunisian fish balls (serves two)

Remove the raw flesh of a fair-sized whiting, and put it in a bowl. Add chopped parsley and onion, and pepper and salt, and mix it all up. Then break 2 or 3 eggs into the mixture and stir it up more. Next form the mixture into balls about the size of goose eggs. Roll these in flour, then in beaten egg, then put them straight into a pan containing 2 fingers of hot oil, and partly fry them – not enough to cook them right through but only to crisp the outsides.

Lightly fry a clove of garlic in olive oil, and on this basis build up a tomato sauce, incorporating in it a little harissa (p. 263). After this has cooked for about 15 minutes add the boulettes, and a little water if necessary, so that the boulettes are just about covered. Continue cooking gently until they are done, after 15 to 25 minutes, and serve them in the sauce.

(Recipe of Zohra El Naoui)

Mérou à la Sfaxienne
(serves six)

6 steaks of merou (No. 116)	1 kilo tomatoes
weighing 1 kilo in all	200 grammes sweet green peppers
1 wineglassful olive oil	salt and pepper
2 cloves garlic	parsley
2 onions	

Heat the olive oil in a suitable ovenproof dish, and then cook the pieces of fish very lightly in the oil – just enough to stiffen them without browning them. Remove the fish and then lightly cook in the same oil the chopped garlic and onion, after which add the chopped flesh of the tomatoes (no seeds or excess moisture) and the chopped seeded peppers. Season well and cook these too.

When you judge this sauce to be ready, take most of it out, leaving just enough to make a bed for the pieces of fish, which you then put in. Pour back over the fish the sauce which you had taken out. Sprinkle chopped parsley on top, put in the oven for 10 minutes and serve.

(Contributed by M. Darricades, Sfax)

Mérou Cooked with Tunisian Pickles

(serves four)

1 very large steak, weighing 750 grammes, of mérou (No. 116)
flour
salt and pepper
1 wineglassful olive oil
1 cup in all of the pickles – limoun qaris (lemon) and mellah (mixed vegetables)

1½ tablespoonfuls tomato purée
a dozen tiny onions
1 tablespoonful capers
6 black olives and 6 green ones
2 fresh tomatoes

Take the mérou steak, remove any skin, and roll it in flour, dusting also with salt and pepper. Heat olive oil in a heavy pan, and put the fish in it to fry. Brown it on both sides and then take it out.

Now make a tomato sauce by adding hot water to 1½ tablespoonfuls of tomato purée. Add the pickles, cut up as necessary, together with the onions, capers and olives, and quarters of fresh tomato. Put all this in the cocotte, return the piece of fish and let the whole simmer until ready.

(Recipe given by Zohra El Naoui)

Stuffed Grey Mullet

(serves four)

Select a grey mullet weighing rather more than 1 kilo, open it down the back and cut through the backbone in two places, close to the tail and about an inch short of the head. Remove the severed backbone and then reach further down inside and draw out the gut.

Hard boil an egg and chop it up. Add chopped parsley and onion and some roughly grated gruyère. Mix this up and stuff the fish with it, then sew up the back and dust the fish with flour. Put the fish in a suitable piece of ovenware with 80 grammes of smen (Tunisian butter – the ordinary kind will do, but will not give the same flavour to the dish).

Cut raw peeled potatoes in half and roll them in a mixture of saffron (not much), black pepper and salt. Place these potato halves round the fish, add cold water to cover the potatoes, and place the dish in a preheated oven to cook until done (the time varies with the size of the fish, but allow plenty and be prepared to baste from time to time).

This recipe was given to me by Zohra El Naoui in Sidi bou Said, the enchanting village in white and blue which is perched on the headland beyond Carthage. She added for good measure that it is possible to apply the recipe to whiting, and there is an alternative stuffing which I give here although I prefer the first one. Wash 2 heads of fennel and cook them in water with salt. Chop them up very fine, add grated gruyère and 4 beaten eggs. Mix all this up and use it as the stuffing. I understand that those who follow this second procedure roll the stuffed fish in beaten egg after dusting it with flour, and that the potatoes become optional instead of compulsory.

Grey Mullet with Piquant Sauce

A standard Tunisian way of serving fish. This version was explained to me by M. Ben Abdesselem, chef of the Restaurant de la République at Zarzis, after I had enjoyed eating it at his table.

Heat some olive oil in a pot, then lightly cook in it some chopped onion, after which add a good spoonful of tomato purée and a teaspoonful of piment piquant. Cook for 5 minutes. Then add enough water to cover the fish, which you put in at the same time. M. Abdesselem recommends fairly small grey mullet, but any fish of a suitable size and firm flesh will do. Cook gently for 20 minutes or so, and serve the fish swimming in the liquid in which it was cooked.

Brik à l'Oeuf au Thon

I should like to have explained how to make this Tunisian speciality from the very beginning, since the manufacture of brik pastry is as interesting as it is difficult. But even in Tunisia it is increasingly the custom to buy it ready made rather than make it at home. So I will save about two full pages by saying simply that you will need for this dish two leaves of brik pastry for each person. These leaves are circular and very, very thin. They may be found nowadays in specialist shops in London as well as in Paris and Marseille, and I believe that they are available also in New York.

The leaves are about 25 cm. in diameter. Each is to be folded over twice so as to make an envelope shaped like a triangle with one side curved. In this envelope is placed a raw egg, some chopped parsley, a few capers and a little tinned tunny meat. The envelope is sealed along the edges and deep-fried to a golden brown; after which it must be eaten without allowing any of the (now cooked) egg to spill, which is not easy at first. To be honest I must add that the tunny fish is an optional extra, and that it is really stretching a point to include the recipe here; but the briks are so delicious that I would be willing to use any subterfuge to help spread knowledge and consumption of them.

Tunisian Salads with Tunny

Add a moderate amount of tinned tunny, in small pieces, to either of the following salads.

Salade Meshouiya   Grill over a charcoal fire 4 sweet peppers, 2 tomatoes, 2 cloves of garlic and 1 onion. Remove the blackened skin. Hard boil two eggs. Then pound in a mortar some salt, a teaspoonful of caraway (karouiya), the cloves of garlic, the peppers and tomatoes, and lastly the onion. Put the mixture on a platter and chop the hard-boiled eggs into it. Add lemon juice and olive oil to make the whole moist, and arrange black olives on top.

Salade Sfaxienne   Take cucumber, onions, bitter apples, sweet or hot peppers and tomatoes. Chop everything into small pieces, mix it up, salt it and sprinkle it with lemon juice and then with finely chopped mint and olive oil.

Clovisses à la Carthaginienne

When we lived in Tunisia we were taught how to deal with clovisses by Mme Ben Mostafa Zakaria, who lived in the shadow of the hill of Carthage. Hence the title of the recipe; and although very similar prescriptions might be given to the inquirer in a score of other Mediterranean ports I like to keep this particular version distinct in my mind by retaining the name.

Wash the clovisses. Heat some olive oil (not very much) in a pan big enough for the clovisses. Add a little garlic, the flesh of fresh tomatoes, chopped parsley, a sprinkling of black pepper, and the clovisses. When the clovisses are all open serve them with the cooking liquid – rather like a Zuppa di Vongole, as described on p. 320.

Daurade aux Citrons Confits
Daurade with preserved lemons (serves six)

The most common way of preserving lemons in north Africa – universally used in Tunisia, anyway – is in a solution of salt and water just strong enough to float an egg. The lemons are stored in this in sealed jars for a month before use. (They are quartered lengthwise before being put in, but not cut right through at the ends until taken out and used). However, I like the following alternative method for my present purpose, even though it is more costly. Cut $\frac{1}{2}$ kilo of big lemons into fairly thick slices. Place these in a colander, sprinkled with 2 or 3 tablespoonfuls of salt, and leave them for a day. Then place them compactly in layers in a jar and cover with olive oil, of which you will need up to $\frac{1}{2}$ litre. Make quite sure that the uppermost slices are not left poking out of the olive oil and that there is a safety margin to allow for the absorption of some oil by the lemons. Store for 3 or 4 weeks before use.

Irène and Lucienne Karsenty explain, in their book *La Cuisine Pied-Noir* (i.e. the cuisine evolved by the prolonged cohabitation in Algeria of French colonists and Algerians), how these citrons confits are used in cooking a daurade. You will need:

1 daurade (No. 128) of $1\frac{1}{2}$ kilos	1 teaspoonful coriander (powder,
16–20 slices of citron confit	or fresh and chopped)
$1\frac{1}{2}$ wineglassfuls olive oil from the	1 tablespoonful paprika
citron confit jar	salt and pepper

After scaling, gutting and washing the fish make some light incisions in it along the sides. Lay 12–15 slices of citron confit in the bottom of a gratin dish, and place the daurade on this bed. Season the fish and sprinkle the coriander and paprika over it. Then place the few remaining slices of citron confit on top and pour the olive oil over all. Put the dish in a very hot oven, but reduce the heat shortly afterwards and continue to cook, basting occasionally, for another 40 minutes or so.

This dish has a delicious and unusual taste. The recipe may be adapted for use with other fish which have firm flesh of good quality.

Mérou, Sauce Rouge
Mérou with a red sauce (serves six)

This Algerian recipe, compared with that for Mérou à la Sfaxienne on p. 377, shows more Spanish influence.

6 steaks of mérou (No. 116), weighing 1 kilo in all	salt and pepper
1½ wineglassfuls olive oil	1 tablespoonful coriander (preferably fresh and chopped)
½ kilo tomatoes	1 tablespoonful paprika ⎱ combined
6 cloves of garlic	½ wineglassful olive oil ⎰
1 small hot red pepper	

Pour the 1½ wineglassfuls olive oil into a casserole. Cover the bottom with a layer of slices of peeled and seeded tomato. Put the mérou steaks on this bed, with the garlic and the hot red pepper. Season; cover with the remaining tomato slices; season again, including the coriander; pour the paprika-laced olive oil over all. Cook over a vigorous flame for 5 minutes, then lower the heat, cover, and continue to cook gently for half an hour.

Shad Cooked with Stuffed Dates (a recipe from Fez)
(serves eight or more)

a very large shad (No. 55)	½ teaspoonful powdered ginger
1 lb. black dates from the Tafilalet (prunes can be used instead)	3 oz. butter or smen
	black pepper
	salt, a little
3 oz. chopped almonds	a quarter onion, chopped fine
3 oz. semolina	½ teaspoonful powdered cinnamon
1 tablespoonful sugar	

Gut the shad and wash it in salt water. Boil or steam the semolina and leave it to become cold. Wash and stone the dates.

Mix the semolina with the chopped almonds, the sugar, a little butter and a pinch each of pepper and ginger. Stuff the dates with this mixture.

Fill the fish with the stuffed dates, then sew up the belly carefully. Lay it in a fireproof dish with the rest of the butter, a soup ladle of water, plenty of pepper and a little salt, a pinch of ginger and the finely chopped onion. Cook in a slow oven until done (probably more than 3 hours). Then undo the belly, take out the dates, put them around the fish (still in the same dish), and put it all back in the oven to brown. When the water has evaporated, and the juice caramelized, when the skin is crisp and golden, the shad is ready to be given a final dusting of cinnamon and served.

(Recipe of Mme Guinaudeau, author of *Fez Seen through its Cooking*)

A Moroccan Marinade for Fish

This Moroccan recipe, which properly belongs to the city of Fez, has in the past been applied particularly to the shad. But nowadays it is used also for the other sea fish which have become available in the Fez market, and it is indeed a notably polyvalent recipe, guaranteed to turn almost any fish into an unmistakably Moroccan dish.

12 cloves garlic	1 tablespoonful powdered cumin
a handful of rock salt	seed
a bunch of coriander	a pinch of cayenne
1 tablespoonful paprika	2 lemons

If you are making this dish you are probably in North Africa and have one of those big heavy brass pestle and mortar sets which create such resonant and evocative music in Maghrebi kitchens. Squat, then, on the floor with your pestle and mortar and spend a happy time reducing the garlic, rock salt and coriander to a powder (the paprika, cumin seed and cayenne will be in that state already). Now put all the seasonings in the bottom of a suitable dish, and add the juice of 2 lemons. Let the pieces of fish stand in this marinade for a couple of hours.

What you do next is up to you, and may depend on what kind of fish you have been treating. But in Fez the next step would probably be to flour well the pieces of fish, deep-fry them in very hot oil and let them cool before eating them.

16. Recipes from elsewhere in the Mediterranean

Here, to round off the collection, are recipes from Yugoslavia, from the islands of Malta and Cyprus, and from the eastern shores of the Mediterranean.

I have worked in the United Arab Republic, and still remember with pleasure our fish shop at the end of Sharia Shagarett El Dur in Cairo and the seafood which I enjoyed on visits to Alexandria. But this was long ago, before my interest in fish had been fully aroused. And along the eastern seaboard of the Mediterranean I know only Beirut. I offer therefore only a few Lebanese and Egyptian recipes. In doing so I draw attention to the relaxed attitude of Lebanese cooks over the choice of fish.* Where a French recipe will enjoin the purchase of a specific fish, perhaps even to be caught in certain waters at a particular time of the year, a Lebanese recipe is likely to say merely 'Buy a fish of about 2 kilos . . .' These recipes are thus readily adaptable for use elsewhere, a factor which balances the slight difficulty which may be met in finding some of the Levantine ingredients. Note too the importance of rice, and that many of the dishes may be served either hot or cold.

Brudet
A Yugoslav fish stew (serves four)

This is a Yugoslav version of the Italian brodetto. Ilse Maijcen, my principal Dalmatian mentress, lays down that it should be eaten lukewarm.

Buy 1 kilo of suitable fish, such as rascasses (Nos. 216, etc.) and conger eel (No. 68). Clean them and cut them into sections or slices.

*The relaxed attitude applies also to fish names. It is strange that many Lebanese recipes mention bar (sea bass, No. 113) as a fish likely to be obtainable and suitable. In fact it is rare in the Lebanon. What is usually meant is one of the mérous. I am told that even French residents, to whom the correct names are perfectly familiar, acquiesce in this puzzling practice.

Slice a large onion and fry it in a wineglassful of olive oil until it is beginning to turn golden brown. Then add the pieces of fish and let them fry lightly before adding also a chopped clove of garlic, chopped parsley, 3 or 4 tomatoes, a teaspoonful of wine vinegar and seasoning. Let all this cook gently for 10 minutes. Then add water to cover and cook slowly for about 1½ hours, without stirring but giving the pan a shake from time to time.

By no means the finest dish of its kind, but notably easy to prepare. The shopping is easy too – no complicated collection of fish to assemble. I have found that the recipe works well with gurnard.

Rižot od Škampi
Risotto of Dublin Bay prawns
(serves four)

Dublin Bay prawns are plentiful in parts of the Adriatic, although not common elsewhere in the Mediterranean; so it is appropriate to include this recipe from the Dalmatian coast.

Buy 8 to 12 Dublin Bay prawns (No. 512). Cut off the tails, peel them and cut up the flesh into bite-sized pieces. Put these aside. Crush the heads and carapaces and other debris of the prawns and set all this to boil in lightly seasoned water in order to produce a little prawn broth.

Heat 4 tablespoonfuls of olive oil in a large pan, and add 1 or 2 chopped cloves of garlic and 2 chopped sprigs of parsley. After a couple of minutes add also the pieces of prawn tail and the chopped flesh of 2 tomatoes (or the equivalent of diluted tomato purée). Let all this cook over a medium flame for several minutes, then add about ¾ of a measuring cup of rice (no need to be exact), seasoning and a tablespoonful of wine vinegar. Turn up the heat. As the rice cooks, add to it, a little at a time, some of the prawn broth, and stir regularly. The rice will take about 15 minutes to cook.

Let the dish rest for a few minutes before serving it with a sprinkling of Parmesan cheese.

Skuše Marinirane
Pickled mackerel, Yugoslav style
(serves four)

Buy 1 kilo of mackerel (No. 189).
Combine the following ingredients and boil for half an hour:

¼ pint olive oil	2 bay leaves
½ pint water	3 or 4 cloves garlic
1 fairly large onion, sliced	1 teaspoonful sugar
½ pint wine vinegar	salt
lemon peel	a sprig of rosemary
peppercorns	

Clean and grill the mackerel. Pour the marinade (which must have been allowed to cool to room temperature) over the grilled fish and leave them in it overnight.

Tunj Kao Pašticada

Tunny in a Dalmatian sauce   (serves six)

For 1 kilo of fresh tunny (No. 192, etc.) put ¼ litre olive oil in the pot. Cut the tunny into slices, place them in the heated olive oil and fry them on both sides briefly. Then add 5 cloves of garlic, chopped; 4 cloves (the spice); salt and pepper; and ½ wineglassful of wine vinegar.

Continue cooking the fish gently for 1 hour, adding (but not all at once) a wineglassful of red wine and also some water if necessary, so as to produce a sauce of good consistency. If using wine you should also put in 2 lumps of sugar. But the dish will be even tastier (says Mrs Marjanović-Radica, whose recipe this is) if instead of the wine you use a smaller quantity of prošeka, a drink akin to sweet sherry. The sugar lumps should then be omitted.

Lampuki Pie

                                                          (serves five or six)

There are various recipes for this Maltese speciality, but the general principle is clear enough. You fry steaks of dolphin fish and incorporate them with vegetables in a pie. The main vegetable which I have chosen is cauliflower.

1 lampuka (No. 166) weighing 1½ kilos	chopped parsley
flour	8 olives, stoned and chopped
olive oil	6 cooking tomatoes
1 cauliflower	2 tablespoonfuls capers
2 onions	½ teaspoonful dried mint
olive oil	pastry

Cut and wash the fish. Cut off the head and tail (which can be used separately for a fish soup). Cut the body of the fish into thick steaks or slices. Dip these in seasoned flour and fry them lightly in olive oil, taking care not to overcook them.

Now make the sauce as follows. Set the cauliflower to boil. Chop the onions and fry them in olive oil until they are golden brown. Use a fairly large pan for this, since the next step is to add to the fried onions the flowerheads of the cauliflower, together with the parsley, olives, tomatoes, capers and mint. Let the mixture simmer for 10 minutes or so, then remove from the heat and allow to cool.

Make the pastry in your usual way or using red wine as the liquid and olive oil as the fat. Cover the bottom and sides of a baking dish with this. Remove any bones from the fried lampuka steaks and arrange these on the pastry bed. Pour over them the cold sauce. Cover the top with pastry and cook in a moderate oven until golden brown. This may take an hour or so.

Maltese Turtle Stew

(serves six)

Few readers will have the opportunity to try this fruity dish; but it is agreeable to think that if you do have a sea turtle to cook you will know what to do. The ingredients are:

1 kilo fresh sea turtle	1 wineglassful red wine
2 onions, chopped	½ cup chopped nuts
1 wineglassful olive oil	100 grammes large seedless
1 tablespoonful tomato purée	raisins
2 bay leaves	200 grammes olives, chopped
fresh mint leaves, chopped	2 apples, peeled and finely sliced
(or dried mint)	2 chestnuts, peeled and chopped
salt and pepper	1 tablespoonful capers

Scald the turtle meat, remove the skin and cut it into small pieces.

Heat the olive oil and fry the onions in it lightly until they turn translucent. Add the tomato purée (diluted with 1½ wineglassfuls water), the bay leaves, mint leaves and seasoning. Simmer for 5 minutes. Then add the ingredients from the right-hand column and continue cooking for 30 minutes, adding a little more water to cover if this is needed.

Finally put in the pieces of turtle meat and the red wine, cover tightly and cook at least another 30 minutes. Serve with croûtons of fried bread.

(After Marie' Vella, *Cooking the Maltese Way*)

Synagrída (Denté) Baked with Tomatoes

(serves six)

The Mediterranean abounds in recipes for baking fish with tomatoes. This is a simple and good one from Cyprus.

a daurade (No. 128) or similar
   fish weighing 1¼ kilos or a little
   more uncleaned
2 sprigs or so of parsley, chopped
   fine
1 onion, chopped fine
2 wineglassfuls olive oil

1 wineglassful white wine
salt, pepper
2 tablespoonfuls tomato purée,
   diluted with water
4 or 5 tomatoes, sliced

Clean, scale, rinse and wipe dry the fish. Place it in an oven dish and sprinkle over it the chopped parsley and onion. Pour in the olive oil and wine, and add the salt and pepper. Bake in a preheated moderate oven for 20 minutes.

Remove the dish from the oven, pour the diluted tomato purée over the fish and cover it with the sliced tomatoes, put it back in the oven and leave it for another 20 minutes.

Sayadieh

Fish, with rice cooked in an oniony fish broth   (serves six)

There are many versions, in several Middle Eastern countries, of this popular dish. Cooking the rice in the oniony fish broth is standard practice; but some recipes provide for the fish itself to be poached in this, while others stipulate fried fish. The choice may well depend on what kind of fish is available. My own preference is for frying the fish as in the recipe below, which is based on that of M. Albert Barakat of Beirut. Fillets of any good white fish, suitable for frying, may be used and the choice need not be restricted to Mediterranean species. I have found that haddock, for example, does very well.

for the fish and sauce:
1 kilo fish fillets and ½ kilo or
   more fish heads and trimmings
1½ wineglassfuls olive oil
2 or 3 onions, well chopped
2 teaspoonfuls lemon juice

for the rice and garnishing:
2 tablespoonfuls blanched almonds
2 tablespoonfuls pine-nut kernels
1½ cups uncooked long-grain rice
50 grammes butter
2 pinches cumin
seasoning

Lightly salt the pieces of fish and leave them in the refrigerator for an hour or so. Wash the rice and set it to soak in hot water, also for an hour. (I should mention here that this familiar injunction to wash rice before use is appropriate when you have rice from the sack, but that the kind of packaged rice which is now widely sold – see p. 264 – is ready for immediate use.)

Heat the olive oil in a large frying-pan. Put in the almonds and half a minute later the pine-nut kernels, and let them turn brown. Remove and reserve them. Dry the pieces of fish carefully and fry them in the same oil. (Coating them beforehand with flour into which you have mixed paprika will help to give them a good golden-brown colour.) Remove them and keep them warm.

Sauté the onions, still in the same oil, until they are just brown. Transfer them to a larger pot and add 4 cups of water or a little more, and the fish heads and trimmings. Bring all this to the boil and let it simmer, covered, for 20 to 30 minutes. Then strain it.

Measure out $2\frac{1}{2}$ cups of the strained broth. Add the cumin and seasoning to it. Melt 50 grammes of butter in a deep pot. Add the measured quantity of broth, bring it to the boil, covered, and then add the (drained) rice and bring it to the boil again. Cook briefly over a strong heat, until the liquid begins to be absorbed. Reduce the heat and simmer, still covered, until all the liquid is absorbed (about 15 minutes – if the liquid has disappeared before the rice is cooked you will have to add a little more). Stir gently and leave on the side of the fire for 5 minutes.

Meanwhile dispose the almonds and pine-nut kernels in the bottom of a greased mould. Put the rice in this and unmould it on to the centre of a serving platter. Arrange the pieces of fish round it. The dish may be served lukewarm, in Middle Eastern fashion, or cold; but I like it hot.

Sauce is not essential. But you should have a cup of broth left over. Add the lemon juice to this, reduce it a little, and serve it separately.

Samaki Harra
Fish with coriander and a hot walnut sauce   (serves six)

This recipe, like the two following ones, owes much to Aida Karaoglan's book, *A Gourmet's Delight*, and to advice from Mrs Helen Essely and Mrs Susan Hamsa. It calls for a whole fish weighing (uncleaned) about 2 kilos. I suggest pagre (No. 129) or another large member of the bream family. Stone bass or mérou (Nos. 115–20) could be used. The other ingredients are:

10 cloves garlic (less if you prefer)	1 cup walnuts
1 bunch fresh coriander or 1 teaspoonful dried	juice of 3 or 4 lemons
1½ wineglassfuls olive oil	pinch or two of cayenne pepper
	salt and black pepper

Clean the gutted and scaled fish, wash it and pat it dry. Rub it well with salt inside and out. Pound the coriander with the garlic and rub this mixture into the inside of the fish, then fasten the belly together again.

Place the fish on a large piece of aluminium foil, pour the olive oil over it, and draw up the foil to make a sealed envelope for the fish. Bake it for 30 minutes in an oven preheated to 350° F. (This will be about the right length of time, but the size and shape of the fish will affect cooking time to some extent.)

While the fish is baking use a blender to combine the walnuts and lemon juice, adding a little water if necessary to obtain a creamy consistency. Add the cayenne and seasoning. This sauce may be poured over the fish or served on the side.

Tajen Samak bi Tahini

Fish with a sesame-paste sauce   (serves six)

Sesame is by origin an African crop, but the paste and oil made from the seeds are widely used in the Middle East. Tahini is the word for the paste (although often translated as sesame oil, which is a liquid and quite different). Tahini may be bought in tins, but it is better in the jars which Cypriot grocers in London stock. It looks like greyish honey.

For this dish you will need:

1½ kilos (cleaned weight) good quality bream or mérou or other white fish yielding bone-free fillets	2 large onions, sliced
	450 grammes tahini
	juice of 2 lemons
1 wineglassful olive oil	1½ teaspoonfuls salt

Wash and dry the fish fillets. Rub a little lemon juice into them and sprinkle them with salt. Put them back in the refrigerator for a few hours, but take them out again half an hour before the cooking begins. Wash and dry them again, then rub them with a little olive oil and bake them in a preheated oven at 400° F for 15 to 20 minutes. Baste them with a little more olive oil and put them briefly under the grill to crisp the outsides.

Sauté the sliced onions in the remaining olive oil and spread them over the fillets in the baking dish. Lower the oven heat to 350° F.

Blend the tahini, lemon juice and salt with enough water to obtain a creamy consistency. Pour this sauce over the fish and bake it for a further 30 minutes or until the sauce thickens. Then serve it hot with rice cooked as follows:

1¾ cups uncooked rice	4 medium onions, sliced
¾ wineglassful olive oil	½ teaspoonful saffron (optional)
4 tablespoonfuls pine-nut kernels	2½ teaspoonfuls salt

Heat the oil in a skillet and brown in it successively the pine-nut kernels and the onions. Then put half the browned nuts and all the onion into a large pan with the rice and salt and (optional) saffron. Stir for 1 minute over a medium flame. Then add 3 cups of boiling water, increase the heat until the liquid is beginning to be absorbed, reduce the heat again and simmer until all the water is absorbed and the rice cooked. Serve moulded with the remaining nuts as garnish on top.

Samkeh Mechwiyeh and Tarator Sauce with Pine-nut Kernels

Baked fish with a Lebanese sauce (serves six)

This recipe will do honour to a fine mérou (Nos. 116, etc.) weighing (uncleaned) about 2 kilos. The fish should be cleaned, rubbed with salt and lemon juice, left in the refrigerator for a while, then rinsed and dried. It can be stuffed with a sliced tomato and a sliced lemon, but this is not essential.

Cover the bottom of a baking dish with olive oil, then with slices of lemon. Put the fish on this bed, sprinkle it with olive oil and cover it if you wish with more sliced tomato and lemon. Bake it in a preheated oven at 450° F for a total of 40 to 50 minutes, taking it out and turning it very carefully after 25 minutes.

Meanwhile prepare the sauce. The basic tarator sauce is made by blending the following ingredients and beating the result with a little water or fish stock:

1½ cups tahini (sesame paste)	3 cloves garlic, crushed
juice of 3 lemons	1 teaspoonful salt

But here we are making the special version, achieved by including in the blending process:

1 cup pine-nut kernels, pounded	1 crustless slice European-type bread

The result should have the consistency of thick cream. To me it looks like rather thin porridge.

The fish can be served hot or cold. If it is to be served cold you should remove all the cooked lemon and tomato and garnish it with fresh lemon and tomato slices, parsley and strips of red and green pepper. The sauce is in either event served apart.

Samak Kebab

An Egyptian fish kebab   (serves four)

Here is a recipe from Alexandria, giving an Egyptian prescription for roasting pieces of fish on skewers. It may be compared with the Turkish recipe on p. 367.

¾ kilo filleted sea bass (No. 113, known locally as qarous) or other fish
    with firm flesh
juice of 3 lemons ⎫
juice of 3 onions ⎪
4 bay leaves ⎬ combined to make a marinade
2 teaspoonfuls ground cumin ⎪
salt and pepper ⎭
400 grammes (about 8) fairly small tomatoes
a little olive oil and lots of chopped parsley

Cut the fish into cubes measuring ½ inch or a little more. Leave them in the marinade for half an hour.

Cut the tomatoes into quarters. Impale the cubes of fish alternately with the tomato wedges on thin stainless-steel skewers. Brush with olive oil and grill over charcoal. Serve on a bed of parsley.

The dish should be garnished with lemon wedges and accompanied by babaghanoush 'salad', which is made as follows. Bake in the oven, just as they are, 3 medium aubergines and 1 smallish onion for an hour or until they are soft. Cut them in half, cool them, scoop out the flesh and mash it up with 4 finely chopped cloves of garlic. Combine this mixture with 200 grammes of tahini (sesame paste, of which this quantity is rather more than ½ a cup), a tablespoonful of vinegar and the juice of 3 lemons, adding seasoning and a pinch of ground cumin and blending the whole well. Garnish with parsley and a few black olives.

Samak Yakhni
Fish baked with vegetables   (serves four)

This recipe, a favourite of the people of Alexandria, differs from the corresponding Lebanese dishes, for example in the suggestion that a yoghourt salad be served – the Lebanese believe on the contrary that fish and yoghourt are never to be combined. Sea bass is of course more expensive than eel, and it is eel which is used in the popular version of this dish.

¾ kilo (cleaned weight) of sea bass (No. 113, the Egyptian qarous) or eel
   (No. 66, the Egyptian hannasha) cut into 8 pieces

juice of 3 lemons ⎫
salt and pepper   ⎬ **combined to make a marinade**
2 teaspoonfuls ground cumin ⎭
1½ wineglassfuls olive oil
600 grammes onion
3 or 4 cloves garlic ⎫
a bunch of parsley   ⎬ **all finely chopped**
a small bunch of celery leaves ⎭
2 bay leaves
½ kilo tomatoes, chopped

Place the pieces of fish in the marinade and leave them for an hour. Those who are not too keen on cumin will do well to reduce the quantity used.

   Heat the olive oil in a large frying pan and let the onion, followed by the garlic, take colour in this. Add the chopped parsley and celery leaves. Then add the bay leaves, the tomatoes and seasoning. Cook for a further 30 minutes. The result is called yakhni.

   Transfer half the yakhni to an oven dish, place the fish on top, cover it with the rest of the yakhni and lay a sheet of oiled cooking paper over all. Cook in a moderate oven for 30 minutes or so.

Serve hot with a pilaff of rice, or lukewarm with a yoghourt 'salad' (that is to say, yoghourt into which you have gently beaten finely chopped cloves of garlic and parsley and mint leaves, with salt).

Bibliography

Part 1. Works to do with the subjects covered in the catalogues and notes of this book.

ALEEM, A. A., 'Marine Resources of the United Arab Republic', in *Studies and Reviews of the G.F.C.M. of the F.A.O.*, No. 43, Rome, 1969.

American Fisheries Society, *A List of Common and Scientific Names of Fishes from the United States and Canada*; 3rd edn, Washington, D.C., 1970.

DE ANGELIS, R., 'Mediterranean Brackish Water Lagoons and their Exploitation', in *Studies and Reviews of the G.F.C.M. of the F.A.O.*, No. 12, Rome, 1960.

BINI, G., *Atlante dei Pesci delle Coste Italiane*, Mondo Sommerso, Vols. I–VIII, Rome, 1960–70 (with exceptionally fine colour illustrations).

BONAPARTE, C., *Iconografia della Fauna Italica per le Quattro Classi degli Animali Vertebrati*, Vol. III: *Pesci*, Rome, 1832–41.

BURDON, T. W., *A Report on the Fishing Industry of Malta*, Malta Government Printing Office, 1956.

ÇAKIROĞLU, SAID B., *Karadeniz' de Balıkçılığımız* (a manual of Black Sea fisheries), Ankara, 1969.

DE CARAFFA, T., *Essai sur les Poissons des Côtes de la Corse*, Bastia, 1902.

DEVEDJAN, K., *Pêche et Pêcheries de Turquie*, Ottoman Public Debt Office, Constantinople, 1926.

DIEUZEIDE, R., NOVELLA, M., ROLAND, J., *Catalogue des Poissons des Côtes Algériennes*, Vols. I–III, Algiers, 1953–5.

EUZIÈRE, J., *Les Pêches d'Amateurs en Méditerranée*, Robaudy, Cannes, 1951 (an erudite amateur study with full information on Provençal names and some recipes too).

FABER, G. L., *The Fisheries of the Adriatic and the Fish Thereof*, London, Bernard Quaritch, 1883 (the author was Her Majesty's Consul at Fiume).

FAGE, L., 'Reflexions d'un Biologiste sur la Méditerranée', in 'Océanographie Méditerranéenne', *Journées d'Études du Laboratoire Arago*, Supplément No. 2 à Vie et Milieu, May 1951; Paris, Hermann et Cie., 1952.

FAO, *Catalogue of Names of Fish, Molluscs and Crustaceans of Commercial Importance in the Mediterranean*, edited for the G.F.C.M. of the F.A.O. by Professor Giorgio Bini, Milan, Vito Bianco Editore, 1965.

FODERA, V., 'The Sicilian Tuna Trap', in *Studies and Reviews of the G.F.C.M. of the F.A.O.*, No. 15, Rome, 1961.

GEORGE, C. J., ATHANASSIOU, V. A., BOULOS, I., 'The Fishes of the Coastal Waters of the Lebanon', in *Miscellaneous Papers in the Natural Sciences*, No. 4, American University of Beirut, 1964.

GOUSSET, J., TIXERANT, G., *Les Produits de la Pêche*, Informations Techniques des Services Vétérinaires, Issy-les-Moulineaux, undated (probably 1973).

JENKINS, J. TRAVIS, *The Fishes of the British Isles*, Warne, London, 2nd edn 1936.

JOUBIN, L., LE DANOIS, Eds., *Catalogue Illustré des Animaux Marins Comestibles des Côtes de France et des Mers Limitrophes*, Paris 1925.

LANFRANCO, G. G., *A Complete Guide to the Fishes of Malta*, Department of Information and Tourist Services, Malta, 1958.

LOUIS, P. A., *Les Îles Kerkena, Étude d'Ethnographie Tunisienne et de Géographie Humaine*, Vol. 1 : *Les Travaux*, Publications de l'Institut des Belles Lettres Arabes, Tunis, 1961.

LOZANO, F., *Nomenclatura Ictiologica – Nombres Científicos y Vulgares de los Peces Españoles*, Instituto Español de Oceanografia, Madrid, 1963.

LOZANO Y REY, L., *Los Principales Peces Marinos y Fluviales de España*, 3rd edn revised by Fernando Lozano Cabo, Madrid, 1964.

LUTHER, W., FIEDLER, K., *Die Unterwasserfauna der Mittelmeerküsten*, Paul Parey, Hamburg and Berlin, 1961.

O.E.C.D., *Multilingual Dictionary of Fish and Fish Products*, Paris, 1968.

PALOMBI, A., SANTARELLI, M., *Gli Animali Commestibili dei Mari d'Italia*, Milan, 2nd edn, 1961.

SLASTENENKO, E. P., *Karadeiz Havzas Balıklar* (the fishes of the Black Sea basin), Istanbul, 1955–6.

ŠOLJAN, T., *Fishes of the Adriatic*, Vol. 1 of *Fauna and Flora of the Adriatic*, Nolit Publishing House, Belgrade, for the Department of the Interior and the National Science Foundation, Washington, D.C., 1963.

VARAGNOLO, S., 'Fishery of the Green Crab and Soft Crab Cultivation in the Lagoon of Venice', in *Studies and Reviews of the G.F.C.M. of the F.A.O.*, No. 37, Rome, 1968.

WHEELER, A., *The Fishes of the British Isles and North-West Europe*, Macmillan, London, 1969 (an authoritative and comprehensive survey, beautifully illustrated by Valerie du Heaume and covering freshwater as well as sea fish).

Part 2. Works to do with Mediterranean fish in classical times.

APICIUS, *De Re Coquinaria*, edited by Jacques André under the title *l'Art Culinaire*, Paris, 1965.

De Re Coquinaria, edited by Barbara Flower and Elisabeth Rosenbaum under the title *The Roman Cookery Book*, Harrap, London, 1958 (of special interest as the authors experimented with many of the recipes).

ARISTOTLE, *Collected Works*, Vol. IV, *Historia Animalium*, translated by d'Arcy Wentworth Thompson, Clarendon Press, Oxford, 1910 (and reprinted).

BADHAM, REV. C. D., *Prose Halieutics* or *Ancient and Modern Fish Tattle*, Parker, London, 1854.

COTTE, M. J., *Poissons et Animaux Aquatiques au Temps de Pline – Commentairse sur le Livre IX de l'Histoire Naturelle de Pline*, Paris, 1945.

DEONNA, W., RENARD, M., *Croyances et Superstitions de Table dans le Rome Antique*, Brussels, 1961.

JUVENAL, Satires, in *Juvenal and Persius*, with a translation by G. G. Ramsay, Loeb Classical Library, Heinemann, London, and Harvard University Press, revised edn, 1940.

LACROIX, M. L., *La Faune Marine Dans la Décoration des Plats à Poissons – Étude sur la Céramique Grecque d'Italie Méridionale*, Verviers, 1937.

OPPIAN, *The Halieutica*, in *Oppian, Colluthus, Tryphiodorus*, with a translation by A. W. Mair, Loeb Classical Library, Heinemann, London, and Harvard University Press, 1953.

OVID, *The Halieutica Ascribed to Ovid*, edited by J. A. Richmond, Athlone Press, 1962.

PLINY, *Natural History*, in ten volumes, especially Vol. III (Books VIII–XI, with a translation by H. Rackham) and Vol. VIII (Books XXVIII–XXXII, with a translation by W. H. S. Jones), Loeb Classical Library, Heinemann, London, and Harvard University Press, 1967.

RADCLIFFE, W., *Fishing from Earliest Times*, 2nd edn, John Murray, London, 1926.

SAINT DENIS, E. DE, *Le Vocabulaire des Animaux Marins en Latin Classique*, Paris, 1947.

THOMPSON, D'ARCY WENTWORTH, *A Glossary of Greek Fishes*, Oxford University Press, 1947.

Part 3. Works to do with cookery.

BERNAUDEAU, A., *La Cuisine Tunisienne d'Oummi Taïbat*, Tunis, 1937.

BONI, A., *Il Piccolo Talismano della Felicità*, Rome, 1967 (the abridged version of the classic Italian cookery book).

BONI, A., *Italian Regional Cooking*, translation by Maria Langdale and Ursula Whyte, London, 1969.

BRUN, M., *Groumandugi: Réflexions et Souvenirs d'un Gourmand Provençal*, Marseille, 1949.

CAMINITI, M., PASQUINI, L., QUONDAMATTEO, G., *Mangiari di Romagna*, Milan, 2nd edn 1961.

CAROLA, *See under* FRANCESCONI

DAVID, E., *A Book of Mediterranean Food*, John Lehmann, 1950, and in the Penguin series, 1955.

DAVID, E., *French Provincial Cooking*, Michael Joseph, London, 1960, and in the Penguin series, 1964.

DAVID, E., *Italian Food*, Macdonald, London, 1954, and in the Penguin series, 1963.

DEIGHTON, L., *Où est le Garlic?*, Penguin, 1965 (an illustrated guide to French cooking).

ESCUDIER, J.-N., *La Véritable Cuisine Provençale et Niçoise*, Toulon, 1964.

FRANCESCONI, JEANNE CARÒLA, *La Cucina Napoletana*, Naples, 1965 (400 pages of recipes with Neapolitan glossary and colour charts of pasta in use at Naples).

GOBERT, E. G., 'Les Références Historiques des Nourritures Tunisiennes', in *Cahiers de Tunisie*, 4th series, 1955.

GOBERT, E. G., 'Usages et Rites Alimentaires des Tunisiens', in *Archives de l'Institut Pasteur de Tunis*, Tome XXIX, No. 4, December 1940.

GUINAUDEAU, MME Z., *Fes vu par sa Cuisine*, Maroc, 1958.

HOWE, R., *Greek Cooking*, André Deutsch, London, 1966.

KARAOGLAN, A., *A Gourmet's Delight*, Beirut, 1969 (an up-to-date guide to Lebanese cooking).

KARSENTY, I. and L., *Le Livre de la Cuisine Pied-noir*, Paris, 1969.

KURTI, N., *The Physicist in the Kitchen*, lecture to the Royal Institution of Great Britain on 14 March 1969.

LYON, N., *Le Guide Marabout du Poisson*, Verviers, 1967 (also available in an English adaptation).

MARJANOVIĆ-RADICA, D., *Dalmatinska Kuhinja* (Dalmatian cookery), Slobodna Dalmacija, Split, 6th edn, 1967.

MASEFIELD, G. B., WALLIS, M., NICHOLSON, B. E., *The Oxford Book of Food Plants*, Oxford University Press, 1969 (a beautifully illustrated book, essential for all students of cooking).

MÉDECIN, J., *La Cuisine du Comté de Nice*, Julliard, Paris, 1972.

DA MOSTO, R., *Il Veneto in Cucina*, Milan, 1969.

NENCIOLI, M., *Cacciucco* (*come si cucina il pesce*), Editoriale Olimpia undated.

PÉREZ, D., *Guía del Buen Comer Español*, Madrid, 1929.

RATTO, G. B. and G., *Cuciniera Genovese*, Pagano, 15th edn, Genoa, 1963.

RAYES, G. N., *l'Art Culinaire Libanais*, published in the Lebanon, 1957.

REBOUL, J.-B., *La Cuisinière Provençale*, Marseille, 1st edn 1895, 21st edn current in 1970.

ROBY, *Les Poissons de la Pêche à la Poêle*, Librairie Arthème Fayard, 1960.

RODEN, C., *A Book of Middle Eastern Food*, Nelson, London, 1968, and in the Penguin series, 1970.

DELLA SALDA, A. G., *Le Ricette Regionali Italiane*, La Cucina Italiana, 1967.

SERRA, V., *Tia Victoria's Spanish Kitchen*, London, 1963 (translated from a popular Spanish cookery book).

STANSBY, M. E., Proximate Composition of Fish, in *Fish in Nutrition*, ed. Heen and Kreuzer, Fishing News (Books), London, 1962.

70 Médecins de France, *Le Trésor de la Cuisine du Bassin Méditerranéen*,

revision by Prosper Montagné, Éditions de la Tournelle, circa 1930.

TSELEMENTÉS, N., *O Néos Tselementés Odigós Mageirikís kaí Zacharoplastikís* (the new Tselementes cookery and pastry guide), Athens, 1963 (also available in an American version).

VELLA, M., *Cooking the Maltese Way*, 2nd edn undated, Cordina's Emporium, Valletta.

VIDAL, C. A., *Cocina Selecta Mallorquina*, published locally by the author, 7th edn 1968.

YEĞEN, E. M., *Alaturka ve Alafranga Yemek Öğretimi*, Istanbul, 1967.

Index of Names of Fish, Crustaceans, Molluscs, etc. in the Catalogues

Index of Recipes

More about Penguins and Pelicans

The Philosopher in the Kitchen

Jean-Anthelme Brillat-Savarin

'Whoever says "truffles" utters a great word which
arouses erotic and gastronomic memories among the
skirted sex, and memories gastronomic and erotic
among the bearded sex.
'This dual distinction is due to the fact that the noble
tuber is not only considered delicious to the taste, but
is also believed to foster powers the exercise of which
is extremely pleasurable.'

'"Rejoice, my dear," I said one day to Madame
de V—; "a loom has just been shown to the Society
for Encouragement on which it will be possible to
manufacture superb lace for practically nothing."
'"Why," the lady replied, with an air of supreme
indifference, "if lace were cheap, do you think anybody
would want to wear such rubbish?"'

Jean-Anthelme Brillat-Savarin (1755–1826), Mayor of
Belley, cousin of Madame Récamier, Chevalier de
l'Empire, author of a history of duelling and of a
number of racy stories (unfortunately lost), whose
sister died in her hundredth year having just finished
a good meal and shouting loudly for her dessert, is
now best known for his *Physiologie du Goût*, here
brilliantly translated as *The Philosopher in the Kitchen*,
which was first published in December 1825. The work
has a timeless appeal – being wise, witty and anecdotal,
containing some of the best recipes for food and some
of the most satisfactory observations on life.

Penguin Cordon Bleu Cookery

Rosemary Hume and Muriel Downes

The term 'Cordon Bleu' has come to be accepted as the hallmark of culinary perfection – the very highest standard of European cooking with a French accent. This new Penguin cookery book, prepared by the co-principals of the English Cordon Bleu School, needs little other recommendation.

It is enough to say that it is written for people who like good food, with all that this means. The recipes for all kinds of dishes are clear and detailed, and the authors continually stress the importance of presentation – of colour, shape, and garnish. Equally they give the technical reasons for the methods they suggest, knowing that so much careless cooking is the result of an imperfect understanding.

With this handbook in the kitchen, and herself – at least, in one cunning series of recipes – in the sitting-room, no woman need be frightened of entertaining the most exacting *gourmets*.

Cooking with Wine

Robin McDouall

'I have written about cooking with wine because there are some people who think there is something mysterious about cooking with wine, something un-English . . . I have tried to show, in a series of mainly simple recipes, that there is nothing odder about using wine as an ingredient than butter, eggs, flour, or, getting rather more way-out, garlic or tarragon.'

Here, as ever, Robin McDouall is unfailingly expert and urbane, whether marinating or poaching. He'll persuade you to use that bottom inch of vin blanc to make Mushrooms in Wine Vinaigrette – and you'll soon be stocking a cellar for Coquilles Saint-Jacques au vin blanc and Poulet Sauté Bagatelle. And then there are Rognons Sautés au Madère, Fried Pork a Marinheira and, to follow, Apples Fort Belvedere (Cox's Orange Pippins in rum). You'll be surprised at the delicious number of ways you can disguise Calvados, sherry, Champagne, Kirsch, beer and cider.

Elizabeth David

Elizabeth David is well known for the infectious enthusiasm
with which she presents her recipes.

'She has the happy knack of giving just as much detail as the
average cook finds desirable; she presumes neither on our
knowledge nor on our ignorance' – Elizabeth Nicholas in
the *Sunday Times*

Mediterranean Food
A practical collection of recipes made by the author when
she lived in France, Italy, the Greek Islands and Egypt,
evoking all the colour of the Mediterranean but making use
of ingredients obtainable in England.

French Country Cooking
Some of the splendid regional variations in French cookery
are described in this book.

French Provincial Cooking
'It is difficult to think of any home that can do without
Elizabeth David's *French Provincial Cooking* . . . One could
cook for a lifetime on the book alone' – *Observer*

Italian Food
Exploding once and for all the myth that Italians live entirely
on minestrone, spaghetti and veal escalopes, this exciting book
demonstrates the enormous and colourful variety of Italy's
regional cooking.

Summer Cooking
A selection of summer dishes that are light (not necessarily
cold), easy to prepare and based on the food in season.

English Cooking Ancient and Modern 1
Spices, Salt and Aromatics in the English Kitchen
Elizabeth David presents English recipes which are notable
for their employment of spices, salt and aromatics. As usual,
she seasons instruction with information, explaining the
origins and uses of her ingredients.